Fast Track ADO.NET

Kevin Hoffman
Kouresh Ardestani
Donald Xie

Wrox Press Ltd. ®

Fast Track ADO.NET

Published by Wrox Press Ltd,
Arden House, 1102 Warwick Road, Acocks Green,
Birmingham, B27 6BH, UK
Printed in the USA
ISBN 1-86100-760-4

Trademark Acknowledgments

Credits

Authors
Kevin Hoffman
Kouresh Ardestani
Donald Xie

Technical Reviewers
Carl Burnham
Paul Churchill
Slavomir Furman
Norman Gragasin
Don Lee
Jon Reid

Commisioning Editor
Daniel Richardson

Lead Technical Editor
Helen Callaghan

Technical Editor
Catherine Alexander

Managing Editors
Louay Fatoohi
Laurent Lafon

Author Agent
Cilmara Lion

Project Manager
Claire Robinson

Production Coordinator
Neil Lote

Proof Reader
Chris Smith

Cover
Natalie O'Donnell

Index
Martin Brooks

About the Authors

Kevin Hoffman

I'm a Software Engineer and Architect working with .NET and Web Services in Houston, Texas. I started programming when my grandfather gave me a Commodore VIC-20 that he'd managed to repair after my uncle found it in the trash. Since then, I've done everything from writing head-to-head DOS games for 2400-baud modems to building enterprise e-Commerce Web applications in ASP. Ever since I got my hands on the first beta of .NET I've been completely hooked on playing with my favorite new toy: C#. In my spare time between writing and working, I'm hopelessly addicted to computer role-playing games.

Kouresh Ardestani

Kouresh is a consultant, developer, and trainer focusing on .NET technologies in the enterprise. He has been working closely with ASP.NET and other .NET technologies since the preview release of the .NET runtime. Kouresh has a BSc in computer science, along with a degree in business management. He also has about a dozen IT certifications, including MCSD, MCSE, MCDBA, MCSA, and CISSP. When not working with computers, Kouresh enjoys reading, playing music, and watching nature shows. He can be reached at kpaars@yahoo.com.

Donald Xie

Donald specializes in developing business applications using Microsoft technologies. He started programming a long time ago and still loves the thrill. Away from work, Donald enjoys every minute with his beloved wife, Iris, and two beautiful girls, Belinda and Clare.

Table of Contents

Table of Contents

Table of Contents

Introduction

Welcome to *Fast Track ADO.NET*. ADO.NET is a core .NET technology, and the .NET Framework contains a rich data-access class library. This book will give you the information you need to understand ADO.NET, how to apply it, and when and where you should use it in your applications.

ADO.NET is the technology of choice for working with information in databases in .NET applications. In this book, we will provide you with the concise, high value, information that you need to understand ADO.NET and begin using it in a short, precisely targeted 'weekend' read.

We begin with an overview of ADO.NET, discussing its significance, its role in your business, and its relationship to the other .NET technologies. We then go on to present the key features of this technology, devoting a chapter to each of the major classes of ADO.NET, `DataSets`, `DataAdapters`, and `DataReaders`. We explain why each is important and show how they can be used effectively.

This book does not attempt to be comprehensive, and it will not teach basic techniques. To be able to deliver a concise and targeted guide to ADO.NET, we assume that you have grasped essential programming techniques, in this case, a basic knowledge of programming in C#, and experience using Visual Studio .NET, and that you can transfer these skills to a new technology.

Examples are carefully chosen to demonstrate the capabilities of ADO.NET and aid you in understanding the underlying concepts that you can apply when you begin to use this technology.

What Does This Book Cover?

This book covers those features of ADO.NET that you ll find yourself using time and again in your applications. We start by explaining how ADO.NET fits into the .NET platform and how it differs from previous versions of ADO. Then, we discuss the key parts of the ADO.NET class library and how it relates to other libraries in the .NET Framework:

- ❑ How we can store and manipulate data using `DataSets`

- ❑ The close relationship between ADO.NET and XML

- ❑ How we can gain quick, read-only, forward-only access using `DataReaders`

- ❑ How we can connect to a wide-range of data sources using `DataAdaptors`

- ❑ When and where you should use ADO.NET in your applications

- ❑ How Web Services can be used to transfer data in a distributed environment

Here is a quick breakdown of what you will find within the chapters of this book:

- ❑ **Chapter 1 – What is ADO.NET**: This chapter provides a roadmap for the book. It highlights and explains the core features of ADO.NET that all .NET programmers should learn. The architecture of ADO.NET is introduced and we discuss how it fits within the .NET platform.. The chapter concludes with a comparison of ADO.NET and ADO 2.*x* that details the major differences between the two.

- ❑ **Chapter 2 – The DataSet**: This chapter begins our detailed investigation of the most important types in the ADO.NET class library. We begin with the `DataSet`, which is a completely disconnected, in-memory data structure. This chapter takes you on an in-depth tour of the `DataSet`, including a discussion of the classes contained within a `DataSet`'s anatomy that provide support for relational data storage, data manipulation, and loading.

- ❑ **Chapter 3 – Strongly Typed DataSets**: This chapter, following on from Chapter 2, discusses a specialised version of the `DataSet`, the strongly typed `DataSet`. XML Schemas have an important role to play in strongly typed `DataSets` and this chapter explains how they are used.

- ❑ **Chapter 4 – XML and ADO.NET**: This chapter explores the various ways that .NET supports XML. ADO.NET makes extensive use of XML, so it's important that we understand how .NET supports the XML Document Object Model (DOM) and how the extensive support for XML is built into several of the core ADO.NET components – this includes support for XPath, XSL transformations, and treating an XML document as relational data.

- ❑ **Chapter 5 – DataReaders**: This chapter moves on to discuss how we can use a `DataReader` to perform forward-only, read-only access to data stores. We begin with a discussion of connecting to a data source via a .NET Data Provider, and how to perform data access and manipulation operations. We then go on to examine more advanced data retrieval techniques, such as for retrieving multiple or hierarchical result sets, and also binary data and schema information.

- ❑ **Chapter 6 – DataAdaptors**: This chapter looks at how we can load data from a data store into a `DataSet`, and then update the data store with changes made to the `DataSet`. We demonstrate the common techniques used to read and write data using `DataAdapters`. We finish with a discussion of how to manage concurrency issues.

❑ **Chapter 7 – ADO.NET in the Enterprise**: This chapter explains *where* and *when* to use ADO.NET in your applications. We begin with a discussion of where ADO.NET fits in the enterprise and in classic n-tier architectures. After that, we take a look at data binding in Windows and with ASP.NET, and we discuss some of the benefits and drawbacks of data binding. We finish with a discussion of how to create a COM+ component and your own standardized data-access layer.

❑ **Chapter 8 – Web Services and ADO.NET**: This chapter looks at how we can use Web Services with ADO.NET. We begin by examining the Web Service standards and protocols, such as SOAP, WSDL, UDDI, and DISCO. We then move on to see how to create a Web Service, and how we can use this Web Service to transfer data in a distributed environment. The chapter finishes with a discussion of other important Web Services issues, including security and caching.

Who Is This Book For?

This book is for programmers who want to learn how to use ADO.NET in .NET applications. However, this book isn't for beginners and it's assumed that you have:

❑ Some knowledge of C# – we don't use any particularly advanced features of C# in this book, but you'll need to be comfortable with the basic syntax

❑ Experience using Visual Studio .NET and the command-line C# compiler

What You Need to Use This Book

The examples are designed to be run with Visual Studio .NET Professional or Standard Edition, running on Windows 2000 or Windows XP Professional Edition. However, the examples can also be run using the command-line compiler that ships with the .NET Framework SDK.

The examples also make extensive use of the Northwind sample database. This database ships with a number of products, including:

❑ SQL Server 2000

❑ .NET Framework SDK

❑ Visual Studio .NET MSDE (Standard Edition or higher)

❑ Microsoft Access 2000 and XP

The Northwind database is also available for download from msdn.microsoft.com.

The complete source code for all the samples is available for download from our web site, http://www.wrox.com/.

Style Conventions

We have used a number of different styles of text and layout in this book to help differentiate between the different kinds of information. Here are examples of the styles we used and an explanation of what they mean.

Code has several font styles. If it is a word that we are talking about in the text – for example, when discussing an `if...else` structure – it is in `this font`. If it is a block of code that can be typed as a program and run, then it is in a gray box:

```
Private Sub Button1_Click(ByVal sender As System.Object, _
  ByVal e As System.EventArgs) Handles Button1.Click
End Sub
```

Sometimes, you will see code in a mixture of styles, like this:

```
Private Sub Button1_Click(ByVal sender As System.Object, _
  ByVal e As System.EventArgs) Handles Button1.Click

    MsgBox(TextBox1.Text)

End Sub
```

In cases like this, the code with a white background is code that we are already familiar with. The line highlighted in gray is a new addition to the code since we last looked at it. Code with a white background is also used for chunks of code which demonstrate a principle, but which cannot be typed in and run on their own.

Advice, hints, and background information come in this type of font.

> **Important pieces of information come in boxes like this.**

Important Words are in a bold type font.

Words that appear on the screen, or in menus like the File or Window menus, are in a similar font to the one you would see on a Windows desktop.

Keys that you press on the keyboard like *Ctrl* and *Enter* are in italics.

Commands that you need to type in on the command line are shown with a > for the prompt, and the input in **bold**, like this:

```
>something to type on the command line
```

Customer Support and Feedback

We always value hearing from our readers, and we want to know what you think about this book; what you liked, what you didn't like, and what you think we can do better next time. You can send us your comments, either by returning the reply card in the back of the book, or by e-mail to feedback@wrox.com. Please be sure to mention the book ISBN and the title in your message.

Source Code and Updates

As you work through the examples in this book, you may decide that you prefer to type in all the code by hand. Many readers prefer this because it is a good way to get familiar with the coding techniques that are being used. However, whether you want to type the code in or not, we have made all the source code for this book available at the Wrox.com web site.

When you log on to the Wrox.com site at http://www.wrox.com/, simply locate the title through our Search facility or by using one of the title lists. Then click on the Download Code link on the book's detail page and you can obtain all the source code.

The files that are available for download from our site have been archived using WinZip. When you have saved the attachments to a folder on your hard drive, you need to extract the files using a de-compression program such as WinZip or PKUnzip. When you extract the files, the code is usually extracted into chapter folders. When you start the extraction process, ensure your software (WinZip, PKUnzip, and so on) has Use folder names under Extract to: (or the equivalent) checked.

Even if you like to type in the code, you can use our source files to check the results you should be getting – they should be your first stop if you think you might have typed in an error. If you don't like typing, then downloading the source code from our web site is a must! Either way, it will help you with updates and debugging.

Errata

We have made every effort to make sure that there are no errors in the text or in the code. However, no one is perfect and mistakes do occur. If you find an error in this book, like a spelling mistake or a faulty piece of code, we would be very grateful for feedback. By sending in errata, you may save another reader hours of frustration, and of course, you will be helping us provide even higher quality information. Simply e-mail the information to support@wrox.com, your information will be checked and if correct, posted to the errata page for that title, or used in subsequent editions of the book.

To find errata on the web site, log on to http://www.wrox.com/, and simply locate the title through our Search facility or title list. Then, on the book details page, click on the Book Errata link. On this page you will be able to view all the errata that have been submitted and checked through by editorial. You will also be able to click the Submit Errata link to notify us of any errata that you may have found.

Technical Support

If you wish to directly query a problem in the book then e-mail support@wrox.com. A typical e-mail should include the following things:

- ❑ The **book name**, **last four digits of the ISBN** (7604 for this book), and **page number** of the problem in the Subject field.

- ❑ Your **name**, **contact information**, and the **problem** in the body of the message.

We *won't* send you junk mail. We need the details to save your time and ours. When you send an e-mail message, it will go through the following chain of support:

1. **Customer Support** – Your message is delivered to one of our customer support staff, who are the first people to read it. They have files on most frequently asked questions and will answer anything general about the book or the web site immediately.

2. **Editorial** – Deeper queries are forwarded to the technical editor responsible for that book. They have experience with the programming language or particular product, and are able to answer detailed technical questions on the subject. Once an issue has been resolved, the editor can post any errata to the web site.

3. **The Authors** – Finally, in the unlikely event that the editor cannot answer your problem, they will forward the request to the author. We do try to protect the author from any distractions to their writing, however, we are quite happy to forward specific requests to them. All Wrox authors help with the support on their books. They will mail the customer and the editor with their response, and again all readers should benefit.

> Note that the Wrox support process can only offer support to issues that are directly pertinent to the content of our published title. Support for questions that fall outside the scope of normal book support is provided via the community lists of our http://p2p.wrox.com/ forum.

p2p.wrox.com

For author and peer discussion, join the **P2P mailing lists**. Our unique system provides **programmer to programmer**™ contact on mailing lists, forums, and newsgroups, all *in addition* to our one-to-one e-mail support system. Be confident that your query is being examined by the many Wrox authors, and other industry experts, who are present on our mailing lists. At p2p.wrox.com you will find a number of different lists that will help you, not only while you read this book, but also as you develop your own applications.

To subscribe to a mailing list just follow this these steps:

1. Go to http://p2p.wrox.com/ and choose the appropriate category from the left menu bar.

2. Click on the mailing list you wish to join.

3. Follow the instructions to subscribe and fill in your e-mail address and password.

4. Reply to the confirmation e-mail you receive.

5. Use the subscription manager to join more lists and set your mail preferences.

1

What is ADO.NET?

ADO.NET is the successor to Microsoft's widely used object-oriented data access library, ActiveX® Data Objects (ADO). It is a common misconception to assume that ADO.NET is simply "ADO running on .NET". The truth is that this library has undergone a tremendous amount of re-working based on feedback from developers and managers alike. ADO.NET provides many enhancements, such as platform-independent/interoperable, scalable, high-performance data access.

In this chapter we will cover:

- ❏   Where ADO.NET fits within .NET
- ❏   The parts of the **.NET Framework Class Library** that are considered part of ADO.NET
- ❏   The different classes and namespaces that make up ADO.NET
- ❏   How we can access data using a **.NET data provider**
- ❏   The classes – `Connection`, `Command`, `DataAdaptor`, and `DataReader` – that make up a .NET data provider
- ❏   How a `DataSet` represents a relational database
- ❏   How we can store and manipulate data using a `DataSet`, a typed `DataSet`, and a `DataReader`
- ❏   How ADO.NET relates to ADO 2.*x*
- ❏   How we can use ADO 2.*x* from within our .NET applications

This chapter will serve as an introduction to the material covered in the rest of this book. This book is going to take you on a quick and practical tour of some of the most important aspects of ADO.NET and its components. We'll take a look at a roadmap of that tour in this chapter to let you know what it is you'll be learning in this book, and why this book is a valuable reference to be put on your bookshelf in your home or your office.

Where ADO.NET Fits into .NET

ADO.NET is a library of classes, interfaces, enumerations, and other tools that provide a structured, powerful, efficient toolkit for data access. As you know, the .NET Framework is an enormous, widespread framework that provides an entire environment that supports your applications. ADO.NET is a small section of that framework that provides your applications with data access abilities. ADO.NET contains all of the tools you need to run stored procedures, run SQL queries, perform data operations on **XML** (**Extensible Markup Language**), and much more. An added benefit of the rigid, object-oriented structure of ADO.NET is that if you are familiar with the standard ADO.NET, then your skills can be reused when a new data source provider is made available for ADO.NET, since they must all conform to a certain set of rules, which we'll talk about later.

Anatomy of ADO.NET

This book is a guided tour through the various components of the ADO.NET data access library. The following section will provide an overview of each of the various components that we will be discussing throughout this book.

Traditionally, programmers are used to a connection-based model, where the connection is fairly long-lived or remains instantiated for an extended period of time, for querying and updating their data. They obtain and configure a connection, perform some work live, and then close the connection. Gradually people have been realizing the various drawbacks to this type of architecture. If you're familiar with ADO 2.x then you know that the ADO RecordSet can operate in a disconnected fashion, but its disconnected functionality was added later in its life and feels difficult and inelegant to use.

As today's data processing becomes more and more complex and conforms more to multi-tier architectures, programmers are more often looking for multi-tier data access paradigms. ADO.NET fills this gap with a robust, object-oriented model that provides for and encourages disconnected data manipulation.

There are two core components (not in the COM sense of a component) to the ADO.NET library: the DataSet and the **.NET data provider**. As we'll see, the DataSet is a disconnected in-memory data store and the .NET data provider is a specific suite of components supplied to access a particular type of data source, such as an OLE DB data source, or a SQL Server database.

One of the biggest advantages of ADO.NET is its own structure. The functionality within ADO.NET is matched directly to the needs you might have for data access. The tools themselves don't perform so many functions that they don't excel at any of them (a symptom of ADO 2.x). For example, the tools you would use to obtain fast, forward-only, read-only data access are not the same tools you would use for performing batch updates of large amounts of dynamic data. Microsoft recognized that there are very specific data needs (fast reading, updating, manipulation, offline storage) and created specialized pieces of the architecture to meet those individual needs, rather than piling all of the functionality into a few classes.

The following diagram illustrates the basic architecture of ADO.NET, its two core components, and some of its supporting components:

```
┌─────────────────────────────────────────────────────────────────────────────┐
│                          ADO.NET Architecture                                  │
│  ┌──────────────────────────────────────────┐   ┌──────────────────────────┐ │
│  │ .NET Data Provider                         │   │ DataSet                   │ │
│  │                                            │   │                           │ │
│  │ ┌──────────────┐  ┌──────────────────────┐│   │ ┌───────────────────────┐│ │
│  │ │ xxConnection  │  │ xxDataAdapter         ││   │ │ DataTableCollection   ││ │
│  │ └──────────────┘  │  ┌──────────────────┐ ││   │ │                       ││ │
│  │                   │  │ InsertCommand     │ ││   │ │  ┌─────────────────┐  ││ │
│  │                   │  └──────────────────┘ ││   │ │  │   DataTable     │  ││ │
│  │ ┌──────────────┐  │  ┌──────────────────┐ ││   │ │  └─────────────────┘  ││ │
│  │ │ xxCommand     │  │ UpdateCommand     │ ││   │ └───────────────────────┘│ │
│  │ └──────────────┘  │  └──────────────────┘ ││   │                           │ │
│  │                   │  ┌──────────────────┐ ││   │ ┌───────────────────────┐│ │
│  │                   │  │ DeleteCommand     │ ││   │ │ DataRelationCollection││ │
│  │ ┌──────────────┐  │  └──────────────────┘ ││   │ └───────────────────────┘│ │
│  │ │ xxDataReader  │  │  ┌──────────────────┐ ││   │                           │ │
│  │ └──────────────┘  │  │ SelectCommand     │ ││   └──────────────────────────┘ │
│  │                   │  └──────────────────┘ ││                                  │
│  │                   └──────────────────────┘│                                  │
│  └──────────────────────────────────────────┘                                  │
│                      ▲                                        ▲                  │
│                      ▼                                        ▼                  │
│                 ┌─────────┐                         ┌──────────────────┐         │
│                 │ Database│                         │ XML Data Store/File│        │
│                 └─────────┘                         └──────────────────┘         │
└─────────────────────────────────────────────────────────────────────────────┘
```

The .NET Data Provider

The .NET data provider is appropriately named. It is, at its core, a provider of data. To be more specific, it is the job of the .NET data provider to provide a way in which data operations can be performed against a specific type of data source. In the days before ODBC, if you wanted to access data sources such as a relational database, or a flat-file database type such as Paradox, you needed to use the vendor's API for accessing that information, or write your own access code if you knew the file format or how to communicate with the server.

This kind of programming became tedious, time-consuming, expensive, and incredibly error-prone. The problem was that there was no standardization between providers of data. This is when ODBC arrived to standardize the method calls made to a data source, regardless of the data source (with a few exceptions, namely that ODBC only works against tabular data and not XML or other sources). This was accomplished with ODBC *Drivers* that acted as adaptors between the ODBC API and the actual underlying data source.

Now, there is the .NET data provider. This data provider is a suite of object-oriented classes that provide access to a particular type of data source such as an OLE DB data source, an ODBC Data Source, or a SQL Server database. In order to standardize things and make sure that the same object model is used regardless of the data source to which the provider facilitates access, certain rules were put in place. These rules take the form of **interfaces** that all .NET data providers must conform to.

Interfaces in the .NET Framework are a specialized form of class that define the methods and properties that all classes implementing that interface must implement. In order for a vendor to create a legitimate data provider, they must create classes that conform to the required interfaces. Because *all* vendors of data providers for ADO.NET *must* conform to a certain lowest common denominator, developers have some reasonable amount of assurance that they will be able to figure out how to use any provider's features without too much of a learning curve. Also, it is possible to create data access layers that are entirely (or mostly) provider-independent, because all of the providers contain classes that implement standard ADO.NET interfaces.

The architecture you see above is applicable to all .NET data providers. They all must have virtually the same architecture (they can have more than is required, but not less) or they cannot be considered a valid .NET data provider. The following is a list of the classes commonly found in a .NET data provider:

- ❑   Connection
- ❑   Command
- ❑   DataAdapter
- ❑   DataReader

One thing that you might find interesting, and should take note of, is that no .NET data provider is required to provide *any* data access beyond the ability to execute commands and retrieve *read-only*, *forward-only* result sets. What this means is that any other way of communicating with a database beyond retrieval of records and executing commands is something that is going to be specific to a particular provider, and not defined by one of the standard ADO.NET interfaces. This is a vast departure from the classic ADO 2.*x* policy, where the cursors are editable and can move back and forth by default.

Connection

A database Connection class is a class that exposes an object-oriented encapsulation of a live database connection. It contains methods to open and close the connection as well as properties that describe the current state of the connection. It also is required to implement the standard ADO.NET interface IDbConnection.

The standard naming convention with .NET data providers is to prefix the class name with a provider identifier. So, the OLE DB provider for .NET provides a class called OleDbConnection. This class is an encapsulation of a live database connection, specially designed and implemented for OLE DB data sources.

Any Connection class in a .NET data provider is also required to implement a method called CreateCommand. This method creates a new instance of a Command object appropriate for the particular provider, initialized to the currently active connection. What this means is that if you invoke the CreateCommand method on a SqlConnection, you will receive an instance of a SqlCommand class, whereas if you perform the same method call on an OleDbConnection, you will receive an instance of the OleDbCommand class.

Command

A database `Command` class is an encapsulation of a database command. This command can be either an in-line SQL statement or it can be a stored procedure (or Query in MS Access). As with other classes in a .NET data provider, it is typically created with a provider-specific prefix, such as `OleDb` or `Sql`. Therefore, the `Command` class for the SQL Server client is called `SqlCommand`. All `Command` classes from any data provider must implement the `IDbCommand` interface.

All `Command`s in .NET data providers are required to implement properties that allow you to modify the text and type of the `Command`, as well as its parameters, the timeout, and the transaction (if supported). `Command`s are also required to implement a minimum set of methods that provide you with the ability to execute the `Command` and return the number of rows affected. You can also execute `Command`s that return `DataReader` instances and scalar quantities (whatever value is in the first column of the first row returned by the `Command`).

DataAdapter

I've always liked to think of the `DataAdapter` as a long extension cord. You find the wall outlet (data source) that you need, and you simply plug your `DataSet` into that data source using the `DataAdapter` class.

`DataAdapter`s are essentially containers for four pre-configured `Command` instances, the `SelectCommand`, the `InsertCommand`, the `DeleteCommand`, and the `UpdateCommand`. Once the `DataAdapter` has been "plugged in" to a `DataSet`, it can be used to propagate changes made to the `DataSet` to the underlying `DataSource` via those four `Command`s. The combination of **C**reate, **R**etrieve, **U**pdate, and **D**elete as the core functionality provided by any data store is typically referred to as **CRUD** functionality. The `DataAdapter` is a class that provides the database `Command` instances essential to supporting CRUD functionality.

All `DataAdapter`s implement the `IDataAdapter` interface.

DataReader

The `DataReader` provides high-speed, forward-only data access to data contained within a particular data source. By its very nature, the `DataReader` is an always-connected object. One major change from the classic ADO architecture is that there is no built-in, default way of accessing the data in random access and connected modes at the same time. ADO.NET has split the random access and sequential access functionality into different classes. This is to provide for the fastest possible way to retrieve and iterate through result sets from the data store.

Available Data Providers

At the time of the writing of this chapter, there are *five* major .NET data providers available. More are available but these are the most notable. Each of these data providers serves a specific purpose and provides managed access to a particular data source type. In addition to the ones listed here, a provider for the MySQL relational database has also been released in beta form. The following is a list of the available .NET data providers, and some details on when and why to use them:

Microsoft SQL Client

This is Microsoft's SQL Server .NET data provider. This provider uses SQL's fast, native TCP/IP interface to provide an incredibly fast, robust, reliable method of accessing SQL Server. If your underlying data source is SQL Server, and you *know* that it will not change, then there is absolutely no reason not to use this data provider.

You can find this provider in the `System.Data.SqlClient` namespace, in the `System.Data.dll` assembly. All of the provider classes in this provider are prefixed with `Sql`. This means that the core classes for this provider are: `SqlConnection`, `SqlDataReader`, `SqlDataAdapter`, and `SqlCommand`.

Microsoft OLE DB .NET Data Provider

This provider uses COM Interop to communicate with the underlying OLE DB data access system. If you do not have SQL Server, and your data source cannot be accessed any other way, then using the OLE DB provider will work for you. Keep in mind that this provider must use the COM Interop layer so there is some additional overhead in working with OLE DB from within the .NET Framework. The OLE DB .NET data provider should be used for communicating with Access Databases, or using the OLE DB provider for Microsoft Exchange, for instance.

Microsoft .NET Provider for Oracle

At the time of this writing, Microsoft's .NET Data Provider for Oracle is still in beta testing. It utilizes the fast **Oracle Call Interface (OCI)** that native Oracle clients utilize in order to communicate with the Oracle database. This provider contains additional support for more data types than the OLE DB, such as the Oracle REF CURSOR. If you are using an Oracle data source, then using either of the Oracle providers for .NET will be a much faster, more reliable alternative (assuming the provider has successfully gotten out of beta phase).

Oracle Data Provider (ODP) for .NET

This beta provider has just been released to the public as we go to press. It is Oracle's own .NET data provider. The documentation for the *beta* release of this provider is over 830 pages! In all fairness to Microsoft, if you plan on doing any kind of heavy-duty data access with Oracle from .NET, you should definitely keep this particular provider in mind when developing your data access architecture.

Microsoft .NET ODBC Provider

If your data source is not SQL Server, Oracle, MS Access, or any other data source accessible via an OLE DB driver, then your only alternative is to use the ODBC Provider for .NET. This provider is intended more as a backward-compatibility support measure and is not to be considered a high-performance provider by any stretch. There are several extra steps involved in making calls through the ODBC provider. First, COM Interop is used to access an ODBC COM wrapper, and then the call is forwarded through to the ODBC API, which is inherently slow in comparison to other current data providers. Again, use this provider only if it is your only alternative.

Creating Your Own .NET Data Provider

Microsoft set up the concept of a data provider to make is easily duplicated. What this means is that if you want to create your own data provider that fits tightly into the ADO.NET data access paradigm and works with `DataSets`, all of the tools you need to do so are available to you.

There is a set of interfaces available within ADO.NET that are implemented by the classes contained in a .NET data provider. Implementing these interfaces and following Microsoft's guidelines for creating a new data provider will allow you to create a provider wrapped around a specific data source that fits tightly into the ADO.NET data access paradigm.

You might occasionally run into a situation where you have a particular form of data that you want to allow a team of ADO.NET programmers to access, without requiring them to learn the specific API for the data source. For example, let's say that your company has been maintaining its timesheet information in binary files on a Unix mainframe for years because the original application was written in C on the mainframe.

You could actually expose a clean, object-oriented wrapper around that data by creating a .NET data provider for those binary files. The result would be that the timesheet application could make use of the `DataSet`, advanced features such as data binding, batch operations, and much more, just by writing a .NET data provider for the binary files.

The DataSet

The `DataSet` is an in-memory cache of relational data. As you'll see in the chapter dedicated to this class, it can contain tables, columns, rows of data, and even relations between various tables, in order to perform common relational data tasks such as establishing a parent-child relationship.

The main thing to remember about `DataSet` is that it is an entirely disconnected, data source-agnostic class. This means that the data contained within the `DataSet` is represented the same way whether it came from an XML document, came from a relational database, or was entered programmatically by a user interface. Being disconnected means that the `DataSet` is operating in an offline mode, all of the time.

When you make changes to information in a `DataSet`, you have to get the assistance of a `DataAdapter` to *plug* the `DataSet` into the database and transfer the updates to the data source. In general, when working with classic ADO 2.*x*, most people recommended that you use disconnected recordsets to increase performance, even though recordsets were connected by default. Now, the `DataSet` is designed to operate without a connection. This fact allows it to manipulate data regardless of where it came from. You can take data from XML, put it into a `DataSet`, allow a user to edit it, and then plug that data into a relational database, such as SQL or Oracle, without causing catastrophic problems.

Tables

Think of a table as a small spreadsheet. Data within a table is organized into rows and columns. The `DataSet` maintains its data the same way. It can contain multiple tables, each of which contains its own columns and rows. Tables in a `DataSet` are represented by instances of the `DataTable` class. You'll read more about the `DataTable` class later in the book. It essentially allows each table to have a name, relationships with other tables, and columns.

Columns

A column represents a column (or field) of data. It has its own name, data type, and other information about it (such as whether or not it is a primary key). The columns of a table define the data structure of that table. The `DataColumn` class represents columns within a `DataSet`, and within a `DataTable` instance. The `DataColumn` class allows you to configure the data type, name, key information, and much more.

Rows

A row is a unique section (or record) of data within a given table. A single row might indicate a single customer, an order, a car, or an entry in a customer's shopping cart. A row contains many fields of data that correspond to the columns within the table. Rows within a `DataSet` are represented by instances of the `DataRow` class, which exposes members for accessing and manipulating the data within the row, as well as members that allow you to obtain parent and child rows based on relationships in the `DataSet`.

Relations

A relation is a relationship between two tables. This relationship is defined in terms of the columns within the tables being related. In relational database terms, it is a foreign key definition between two tables. Essentially it defines a table that is considered the parent, and a table that is considered the child (or peers for many-to-many relationships). By invoking a relationship on a row, programmers can obtain an array of all child (or parent) rows of the current row. Relationships within a `DataSet` are an incredibly powerful and flexible feature. The `DataRelation` class represents them.

The Typed DataSet

The typed `DataSet` provides a collection-oriented approach to accessing tables, columns, rows, and relationships. It is actually a class that *inherits from* the standard `DataSet` class. In order to gain access to a particular item, you must know the item's name or **key** within the collection. If you type the name wrong then you will end up with a null reference instead of the item you were attempting to modify. Tracking down these errors can be complicated and tedious.

For example, given a `DataSet` of customers, you would obtain a Customer ID with the following statement:

```
string custId = custData.Tables["Customers"].Rows[0]["CustomerId"].Value;
```

In addition, many development teams often decide upon a common format for accessing and manipulating data.

The typed `DataSet` not only provides an object-oriented view of the relational data beneath, but it also provides IntelliSense information that aids in preventing needless typographical errors. Finally, the typed `DataSet` enforces certain rules about how it can access and manipulate the data within. So, the same data containing customers' IDs can be accessed with strongly typed members and compile-time enforced column access:

```
string custId = custData.Customers[0].CustomerId;
```

As you can see, a typed `DataSet` provides a more robust, specialized type of access to a known set of data. Typed `DataSet`s are often used when the schema (data structure) of the data is known at design time. When the data being manipulated is so dynamic that the structure isn't known at design time, then typed `DataSet`s are not as practical.

The DataReader

In contrast to the `DataSet`, the `DataReader` is a connected, forward-only cursor-style class. It is used for traversing result sets in a read-only fashion. Because the additional overhead incurred by requiring the ability to move around in random access (backwards and forwards or indexed) is not necessary, the `DataReader` is much faster for pure read operations than similar operations performed by filling a `DataSet`.

For example, an application that performs a search and returns a set of results would more than likely make use of the `DataReader` for performance reasons, rather than using the additional overhead of adapters and `DataSets`, since read/write and random access functionality isn't required for a search engine.

The DataAdapter

As we mentioned, the `DataSet` has no concept of the source of its data. It doesn't know whether the information contained within it came from an Oracle database, a SQL Server database, from Microsoft Access or even from an XML document. The `DataSet` doesn't contain any functionality for accessing any relational data sources. This is part of its design.

In order to accommodate this, a separate class, the `DataAdapter`, is used to *adapt* information from a particular data source to the relational data format for the `DataSet`. As we'll see in the chapter dedicated to the `DataAdapter`, the adapter is a powerful class that is not only responsible for *plugging in* the `DataSet` to a relational data source, but can also automatically change the data structure of the `DataSet` to reflect the data structure from the data source being queried.

Making it Work

Before we move on to a detailed comparison of ADO 2.*x* against the new ADO.NET, let's take a look at how ADO.NET works in a typical application. Don't worry if the code here doesn't seem to make all that much sense, as it will all be explained in more detail throughout the book. It should help you see how all the different classes fit together to make data access an efficient, object-oriented reality.

This sample project runs a SQL query on the SQL 2000 Northwind database and displays customer information to the console.

To test this application out, you can install the free 90-day trial of SQL Server that is available for download from Microsoft's MSDN site. However, since the download for this is rather hefty, you might prefer to work with the MSDE Desktop Engine, which installs a cut-down instance of SQL Server along with Visual Studio Professional or Standard C#.

> To install MSDE, after you have installed Visual Studio (Standard or Professional) go to `C:\Program Files\Microsoft Visual Studio .NET\Setup\MSDE` and run the `setup` application there. This should create an instance of MSDE on your PC called *PCname*`\NetSDK` (depending on what the name of your PC is). This creates the bare bones of the instance, but we're also going to need the Northwind database if you are going to use it for this book. So go to `C:\Program Files\Microsoft Visual Studio .NET\FrameworkSDK\Samples\Setup` and run the `ConfigSamples.exe` there. This will also set up various IIS services, and we will be using IIS later when we talk about ADO.NET and Web Services.

It is easily adaptable to work with MS Access as well. It might look a little complicated to you if you're new to ADO.NET, but all of the techniques used here will be explained throughout the book.

If you're following along, create a new Console Application in VS.NET and call it `CustomerAccess`. The following is the code listing for the main class (`Class1.cs`):

```csharp
using System;
using System.Data;
using System.Data.SqlClient;

namespace CustomerAccess
{
    /// <summary>
    /// Summary description for Class1.
    /// </summary>
    class Class1
    {
        /// <summary>
        /// The main entry point for the application.
        /// </summary>
        [STAThread]
        static void Main(string[] args)
        {
            //
            // TODO: Add code to start application here
            //
            SqlConnection conn =
             new SqlConnection("server=localhost; Initial Catalog=Northwind;
                 User Id=sa; Password=;");
            conn.Open();
            SqlCommand cmd = conn.CreateCommand();
            cmd.CommandText = "SELECT * FROM Customers";
            cmd.CommandType = CommandType.Text;
            SqlDataReader reader =
                cmd.ExecuteReader(CommandBehavior.CloseConnection);
            string output;
            while (reader.Read())
            {
                output = string.Format("Customer {0}: {1} works for {2}",
                    reader.GetString(0), reader.GetString(1), reader.GetString(2));
                Console.WriteLine(output);
            }
        }
    }
}
```

When we run this application from the command prompt we get the following output:

If your Northwind Database `Customer` table contains null values, then you may find that this program throws an exception. Make sure that the data is complete before running this example.

ADO vs. ADO.NET

It would be a mistake to assume that everyone learning about ADO.NET is learning about data access for the first time. The truth is, that many programmers are coming from development environments firmly entrenched in ADO 2.6 or earlier, as well as other data access platforms (such as JDBC). The following section will address some of the major differences and upgrades between the various ADO and ADO.NET components.

The first and most important thing to notice is that there are no one-to-one relationships between ADO objects and ADO.NET objects. ADO.NET takes an entirely different approach to data access. It separates the task of data *access* from data viewing and manipulation.

Data Type Comparison

In ADO 2.6, the various database types are represented by constants that have an 'ad' prefix. This is because data is almost entirely treated as variants until the developer finally accesses it. ADO.NET allows you to map data directly to intrinsic data types, allowing a much tighter (and more efficient) control of data access.

The following table compares data types between ADO 2.6 and .NET Framework basic data types. The information in this table can be found in the MSDN .NET Framework SDK documentation:

ADO 2.6 Data Type Constant	.NET Framework Intrinsic Type
adEmpty	Null
adBoolean	Int16
adTinyInt	Sbyte
adSmallInt	Int16
adInteger	Int32
adBigInt	Int64
adUnsignedTinyInt	Value is converted/promoted to Int16
adUnsignedSmallInt	Value is converted/promoted to Int32
adUnsignedInt	Value is converted/promoted to Int64
adUnsignedBigInt	Value is converted/promoted to Decimal
adSingle	Single
adDouble	Double
adCurrency	Decimal
adDecimal	Decimal
adNumeric	Decimal
adDate	DateTime
adDbDate	DateTime
adDBTime	DateTime
adDbTimeStamp	DateTime
adFileTime	DateTime
adError	ExternalException
adVariant	Object
adBinary	Array of Bytes (byte[])
adChar	String
adWChar	String
adBSTR	String
adUserDefined	This data type is not supported

Gone are the days of inserting a typo in the ADO 2.6 type constant. When setting up columns and parameters to stored procedures in ADO.NET, you can simply use intrinsic types rather than type constants.

Connections

Both ADO and ADO.NET rely on the use of a database connection to establish a live communications link with the database. We'll learn more about the use of ADO.NET connections throughout the rest of this book. Of all of the various ADO 2.6 objects, the connection is the one that retains the most similar functionality in ADO.NET.

Connections are used to create a live, active communications link with a data source of some kind. That data source can be to a text file, an ODBC data source, an OLE DB data source, or, in the case of .NET's native managed providers, a connection can be a live communications link to SQL Server or Oracle using their fastest, native communication protocols. For example, the current beta version of the Oracle managed provider establishes a communication link with the Oracle database using OCI (the Oracle Call Interface), the fastest and most efficient way to communicate with an Oracle database.

Recordsets

Ah, the recordset. ADO 2.6 programmers both love and hate this monstrous creation. In the early days of ADO, this was a very simple cursor-style implementation of data access. As more and more demand for more robust and various ways of accessing data arose, more and more functionality was squeezed into this poor, unsuspecting object.

By the time ADO 2.6 rolled around, the `RecordSet` was capable of storing multiple result sets, operating in both live and disconnected mode, operating on data contained in the newly introduced `Stream` object, as well as dealing with XML persistence.

What you'll find out as you read through this text is that the recordset doesn't exist in its old form in ADO.NET. Its ADO 2.6 form is bloated and contains so much potential functionality that it is a fairly poor performer at doing most of its tasks. ADO.NET alleviates this problem by separating out the forward-only functionality, the disconnected functionality, and the XML persistence infrastructure.

Forward-Only Data

As we said, the forward-only functionality previously available in the recordset through the use of an `adForwardOnly` type of cursor has been separated out into a class designed to do *nothing but* fast, forward-only, read-only access. This book has an entire chapter dedicated to the use of the `DataReader`, ADO.NET's high-speed, forward-only, read-only data access class.

Stored Procedures

Stored procedures are still an incredibly important part of any data-centric application that accesses an RDBMS server such as SQL Server or Oracle. They add a level of performance and scalability that most application developers can't turn down.

In ADO 2.6, stored procedures were accessed using a `Command` object. ADO.NET also has a `Command` object as well as some other tools that make using stored procedures easier, such as automatic `Command` builder tools that can read and interpret stored procedure parameters and metadata information at run time.

Using ADO in .NET

Lastly, it is possible to utilize the features of the classic ADO 2.*x* releases from within your .NET managed code. Typically this is done for backwards-compatibility purposes. If you can avoid using classic ADO in your managed code at all, you should do so. Utilizing classic ADO 2.*x* from within your managed code uses something called COM Interop, and incurs some performance overhead that occurs as a result of translating managed .NET calls to COM method invocations and results processing.

There should be very few times when this is necessary. If you persist a classic ADO 2.*x* RecordSet in XML format, the ADO.NET will actually be able to read it without too much trouble. The DataSet will not be identical, but it is enough to achieve some level of backwards-compatibility. However, if you have RecordSets persisted in ADO's **ADTG (Advanced Data Table-Gram)** binary format, you'll have to use ADO Interop to get that data in your managed application.

The following is the code for the main class for a Console Application we created called ADOInterOp. To create the project for this, we created a new (C#) Console Application. Then, we opened the **Add Reference** dialog. Rather than picking something from the Global Assembly Cache, we clicked the **COM** tab and chose the *Microsoft ActiveX Data Objects Type Library* version 2.7. This creates a COM Interop reference to a COM library.

Here's the code for Class1.cs, which was coded to produce the same output as the previous sample:

```
using System;

namespace ADOInterOp
{
  /// <summary>
  /// Summary description for Class1.
  /// </summary>
  class Class1
  {
    /// <summary>
    /// The main entry point for the application.
    /// </summary>
    [STAThread]
    static void Main(string[] args)
    {
      //
      // TODO: Add code to start application here
      //
      ADODB.Connection conn = new ADODB.Connection();
      conn.Open("Provider=SQLOLEDB.1;Persist Security Info=False;"+
          "User ID=sa;Initial Catalog=Northwind;Data Source=localhost;",
          "sa", "", 0);
      ADODB.Recordset rs = new ADODB.Recordset();
      rs.Open("SELECT * FROM Customers", conn,
          ADODB.CursorTypeEnum.adOpenForwardOnly,
          ADODB.LockTypeEnum.adLockReadOnly,0);
      string output;
      while (!rs.EOF)
      {
```

```
            output = string.Format( "Customer {0}: {1} works for {2}",
                rs.Fields[0].Value,
                rs.Fields[1].Value,
                rs.Fields[2].Value);
            Console.WriteLine(output);
            rs.MoveNext();
        }
        rs.Close();
        conn.Close();
    }
}
}
```

The above code should look pretty familiar to those of you who have experience using ADO 2.6 or 2.7. Here's a screenshot of the output we see when running the application from the command prompt:

As we can see, the output of the project is completely identical to the previous project. This time, however, we went through the OLE DB driver for SQL Server (rather than going directly to SQL via .NET), and we used COM Interop. Each method call to ADO 2.7 costs us a little bit of overhead in marshaling information back and forth between COM and the .NET runtime.

Summary

This brief chapter has been a quick introduction to the content you'll be seeing throughout this book. You should hopefully have some idea of what information we're going to present, and why, and how it might be useful to you or your organization.

In the next chapter, we will go on to look at the Dataset, the disconnected, in-memory data cache that is the staple of ADO.NET.

2

The DataSet

This book is all about learning ADO.NET. It is impossible to talk about ADO.NET without talking about the DataSet. To put it simply, the DataSet is a disconnected in-memory cache of data. Throughout this chapter we'll find that there is far more to the DataSet than that simple statement. It is capable of storing multiple related tables and large amounts of data and metadata in a format that is not bound or tied to any one particular data source.

So, to expand on our definition of the DataSet, it is a disconnected, in-memory cache of relational data stored in a generalized format that does not depend on any one data source or RDBMS platform. This makes it a significant upgrade over its predecessor, the **ADO Recordset**.

This chapter will take you on an in-depth tour of the DataSet, including a discussion of the various classes that comprise the DataSet anatomy, support for relational data, and how to actually go about using the DataSet for data loading, manipulation, and storage. Finally, we'll take a look at a sample application that ties together a lot of the functionality of the DataSet, and shows off some of its power in action.

The Anatomy of a DataSet

The DataSet is a complex structure that contains many different objects in an involved hierarchy. Before we start looking at the ins and outs of working with the DataSet, we'll take a look at the various components that make up the DataSet. The following illustration is a mapping of the hierarchy of the DataSet. It doesn't contain every single class, but rather shows the more important ones to keep the illustration clear and concise:

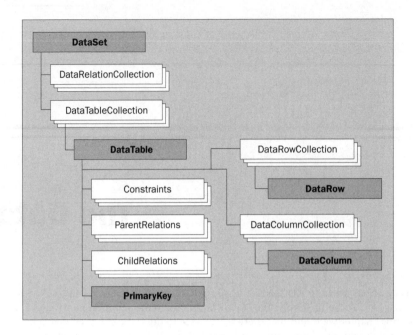

The DataSet

The DataSet class sits at the top of the hierarchy of classes under discussion, and we will look at its uses in depth in this chapter. For now, here is a quick reference table containing its properties and methods.

Property	Data Type	Description
CaseSensitive	Boolean	Gets or sets a value indicating whether the DataTable objects' string comparisons are case sensitive
Container (inherited from MarshalByValueComponent)	IContainer	Gets the component's container
DataSetName	String	Gets or sets the name of the current DataSet
DefaultViewManager	DataViewManager	Allows filtering, searching, and navigating a custom view of the data contained by the DataSet through using a custom DataViewManager
DesignMode (inherited from MarshalByValueComponent)	Boolean	Returns a value that describes whether the component is currently in design mode or not

Property	Data Type	Description
EnforceConstraints	Boolean	Gets or sets a value indicating whether constraint rules should be followed when attempting an update operation
Events (inherited from MarshalByValueComponent)	EventHandlerList	Gets the list of event handlers attached to the component
ExtendedProperties	PropertyCollection	Returns a collection of custom user information
HasErrors	Boolean	Returns a value indicating whether there are errors in the rows in any of the tables of this DataSet
Locale	CultureInfo	Gets or sets information about the locale used to compare strings within the table
Namespace	String	Gets or sets the DataSet namespace
Prefix	String	Gets or sets an XML prefix that acts as an alias for the namespace of the DataSet
Relations	DataRelationCollection	Allows navigation from parent tables to child tables by returning the collection of relations that link tables
Site	ISite	Gets or sets the DataSet's System.ComponentModel.ISite
Tables	DataTableCollection	Returns the collection of tables contained in the DataSet

Here are the methods for this class. The .NET documentation will describe them in more detail.

Methods	Description
AcceptChanges	Commits changes made to the DataSet since the last time AcceptChanges was called it or the DataSet was loaded.
Clear	Clears data by removing all rows in all of the tables of the DataSet.
Clone	Copies the DataSet's structure (DataTable schemas, relations, and constraints) but does not copy any data.
Copy	Copies both the structure and data of the DataSet.
Dispose (inherited from MarshalByValueComponent)	Releases resources used by MarshalByValueComponent.
Equals (inherited from Object)	Determines whether one Object instance is equal to another.
Finalize (inherited from Object)	This is used to free resources and clean up operations before the Object is reclaimed by garbage collection. It is expressed using destructor syntax.
GetChanges	Returns a copy of the DataSet containing changes made to it since it was last loaded, or since AcceptChanges was called.
GetHashCode (inherited from Object)	Hash function for a particular type, used for hashing algorithms and data structures similar to a hash table.
GetService (inherited from MarshalByValueComponent)	Returns the IServiceProvider implementer.
GetType (inherited from Object)	Returns the Type of the current instance.
GetXml	Returns the data stored in the DataSet as an XML representation.
GetXmlSchema	Returns an XSD schema for the XML representation of the data stored in the current DataSet.
HasChanges	Returns a value indicating whether the DataSet has changed (such as new, deleted, or modified rows).
InferXmlSchema	Infers the XML schema from a TextReader or file into the DataSet.
MemberwiseClone (inherited from Object)	Used to create a shallow copy of the Object.
Merge	Merges one DataSet with another DataSet.
OnPropertyChanging	Raises the OnPropertyChanging event.

Methods	Description
OnRemoveRelation	This method should be overriden by subclasses. It exists to restrict tables from being removed.
OnRemoveTable	Occurs when a DataTable is removed.
RaisePropertyChanging	Notifies that a DataSet property is about to be changed.
ReadXml	Reads XML schema and data into the DataSet.
ReadXmlSchema	Reads an XML schema into the DataSet.
RejectChanges	Undoes the changes made to the DataSet since it was created, or since the last time AcceptChanges was called.
Reset	Resets the DataSet to its original state. Subclasses should override Reset to restore a DataSet to its original state.
ShouldSerializeRelations	Returns a value that indicates whether the Relations property should be persisted.
ShouldSerializeTables	Returns a value that indicates whether the Tables property should be persisted.
ToString (inherited from Object)	Gets a String representing the current Object.
WriteXml	Writes XML data (and the schema if required) from the DataSet.
WriteXmlSchema	Writes the DataSet structure as an XML schema.

The DataTable

The DataTable sits somewhere near the top of the hierarchy of classes that make up the contents of the DataSet. It represents one table of in-memory data. There are a couple of different ways that you can create tables. DataTables can be created automatically when data is loaded into the DataSet, or you can create them programmatically by instantiating a new DataTable object and adding it to the Tables collection of the DataSet. We'll illustrate an example of manually creating a DataTable after we've discussed two more things that make up a table: The DataColumn and the DataRow.

Think of the DataTable as an object-oriented abstraction of a traditional database table. It is made up of columns and can contain multiple rows. Just like any other table, it can have a primary key composed of multiple columns, and it can be related to other tables.

The following is a quick reference guide that contains some of the most commonly used properties and methods of the `DataTable` class:

Property	Data Type	Description
ChildRelations	DataRelationCollection	The collection of `DataRelation` instances that indicate the child relations.
Columns	DataColumnCollection	The collection of `DataColumn` instances representing the columns for this table.
Constraints	ConstraintCollection	The collection of `Constraint` instances that indicate the rules being enforced on the table.
DataSet	DataSet	Each table contains a property that indicates the `DataSet` to which it belongs.
HasErrors	Boolean	Indicates whether there are errors in *any* of the rows in *any* of the tables in the `DataSet` to which this table belongs. These errors can be missing data, invalid data, or even broken foreign-key relationships.
Locale	CultureInfo	Sorting, comparisons and filtering can be specific to a certain culture (such as `en-us` or `en-gb`). Use this property to indicate the culture to which the data within the table belongs.
ParentRelations	DataRelationCollection	The collection of `DataRelation` instances that indicate the parent relations for the rows within the table.
PrimaryKey	DataColumn[]	Allows you to examine or modify the array that contains the list of all columns that make up the table's primary key.
Rows	DataRowCollection	The actual data belonging to the table, in the form of a collection of `DataRow` instances.
TableName	String	The name of the table itself. Used in conjunction with `DataAdapters` and other objects that perform operations on the table.

Method	Description
AcceptChanges	Commits all of the pending changes in the table. This doesn't actually save the changes to a database, only marks the rows as updated.
Clear	Empties all data in the table.
Clone	Creates an exact copy of the table, including its structural information (schema).
Copy	Creates a copy of both the structure (schema) *and* the data contained within it.
GetChanges	Obtains a copy of the DataTable that is limited to only those rows that are marked as having been modified since the table was created or since AcceptChanges() was called.
GetErrors	Returns an array of DataRow instances that are marked as containing errors.
ImportRow	Imports a DataRow instance into the table. The new row is given the default values for each column in the table's schema, and its state (added, updated, etc.) is preserved.
LoadDataRow	Based on supplied input, will find a row in the table and modify it. If the row isn't in the table, a new one is created with the values supplied.
NewRow	Creates a new row. The new row has the same schema information as the table. Note that this method does *not* automatically add the new row to the table's Rows collection.
RejectChanges	Rolls back/cancels changes made since the last load or since the last time AcceptChanges() was called.
Reset	This method resets the table to its original state.
Select	A method that returns an array of DataRow objects that match certain criteria. You specify the criteria in much the same way as you would in the WHERE clause of a SQL statement, for example CustomerID > 25. Also allows you to optionally sort the result of your select.

The DataColumn

The DataColumn is a class that represents the schema, or data structure, of a column within a DataTable. The DataColumn is the core of building the data structure for a table. The DataColumn determines the data type and size of the data that resides in that column. Through other properties you can determine whether the data in the column is read-only and whether or not the column allows null values. In addition, you can have the column automatically increment values based on an initial seed value and an optionally defined step value. This behavior is very similar to the AutoNumber column type in Microsoft Access database tables and the identity column in a table in a SQL Server database.

As we mentioned, the data contained in a `DataSet` is completely indifferent to the source of the data. Ideally, this means that you can use a `DataSet` object to work with data from Oracle, SQL, and any other provider without many problems. This also means that you can work with data that came from XML files or streams. Because the `DataSet` is not directly tied to any particular data source, and it is a disconnected cache of data, it can be passed around between components intact without any negative impact to its data, something the `Recordset` could never accomplish.

Unfortunately, the data types for the `DataColumn` might not always completely match the data types used in the source for your data. For this reason, the `DataColumn` provides ways in which you can determine how the data type of the column maps to the data type of the original data source.

The schema for a column within a table can be inferred by having data pushed into the table: it can either be created by a `DataAdapter` (which we'll discuss later), or you can manually configure the column yourself. There is also a great feature that allows you to create columns in your `DataTable` that are actually calculated with an expression, such as summary columns or Boolean columns based on comparing two other columns. Before we look at a sample that illustrates programmatically creating your own columns and tables, we'll take a look at a quick reference guide for the `DataColumn` class and then move on to a quick discussion of the `DataRow` class:

Property	Data Type	Description
AllowDBNull	Boolean	Flag that allows the use of nulls in the column.
AutoIncrement	Boolean	Allows new rows to be automatically given an incremental value each time a row is created, like an Access AutoNumber or SQL Identity column.
AutoIncrementSeed	Long	The number at which the automatic incrementing starts if the `AutoIncrement` flag is set to `true`.
AutoIncrementStep	Long	This number is added to the last used value for the auto-incrementing column. The default is 1.
Caption	String	The header caption for the column. This will be displayed by default when UI controls are bound to this table.
ColumnMapping	MappingType	This property determines how the column's data will be mapped to XML when the `DataSet` is written to an XML stream or file. It can be any of the following types: `Attribute`, `Element`, `Hidden`, `SimpleContent`.
ColumnName	String	Sets the name of the column. This name is the identifying key within the `DataColumnCollection` (the Columns property of the container table).
DataType	Type	Data type of the column. Can be any of the base .NET Framework data types.

Property	Data Type	Description
DefaultValue	Object	When new rows are created this value is inserted for this column by default.
MaxLength	Long	Maximum string length of the data in the column. If this value is left at -1, the DataTable will not enforce any length limit. This is a maximum, and not a fixed-length indicator. A 3-character string will use up 3 characters of length, regardless of the maximum.
Ordinal	Integer	Returns the numerical index (ordinal position) of the column within the table.
ReadOnly	Boolean	A Boolean flag indicating that the data within the column is read-only.
Table	DataTable	Just like all DataTable objects have a DataSet property that indicates their parent DataSet, all DataColumn objects have a Table property that indicates the table to which they belong.
Unique	Boolean	Indicates whether the values in the column must be unique in comparison to all other rows in the table. If this flag is true, then no duplicate values will be allowed in the table for this column.

The DataRow

If you've done any work with ADO or even relational databases in general, you should be familiar with the concept behind the DataRow. The DataRow represents a single row of data within a DataTable. The methods of the DataRow object are the way in which data is inserted, deleted, updated, or viewed within a table.

Unlike the ADO concept of a row of data, the DataRow class supports the notion of versioning. By versioning, we mean that there can be multiple versions of the same row within a given table. This allows you, as the programmer, to distinguish between the *original* version of the row and the *updated* version of the row. There is also the concept of a row **state**, which is represented by the RowState property. This can be any of the following: Added, Deleted, Detached, Modified, or Unchanged.

So, in addition to the standard functionality allowing you to query, insert, delete, and update data from within the row, you can also perform some pretty advanced tricks with row versioning and row states that makes the DataSet an extremely full-featured in-memory data cache. Because of these abilities, most people prefer to think of the DataSet as an in-memory *database* because the term 'cache' doesn't seem to do its features justice.

The following is a quick reference guide on some of the most commonly used properties and methods for the `DataRow` class:

Property	Data Type	Description
HasErrors	Boolean	This flag is true if there is an error on the row, such as a violation of a constraint, key, or column property.
Item	Object	Gets or sets data within a specific column. In C#, this is the default array indexer for a `DataRow` object.
ItemArray	Object[]	Array of objects indicating all of the values for the columns in the row.
RowError	String	Indicates a custom error message for the row itself. This can be set before an error occurs and queried after.
RowState	DataRowState	Gets the current state of the row, such as `Added`, `Deleted`, `Detached`, `Modified`, or `Unchanged`.
Table	DataTable	Just like all classes within the `DataSet` hierarchy, they all contain a reference to their parent container. As such, the `DataRow` contains a reference to the `DataTable` to which it belongs.

Method	Description
AcceptChanges	Marks all of the changed data in the row as current.
BeginEdit	Puts the current row into edit mode. In this mode, code can make changes to multiple rows within a table without triggering events and validation rules.
Delete	Deletes this row. The row actually remains part of the `DataTable` flagged as "Deleted" until an `AcceptChanges` method is called. After that, the row is discarded entirely.
CancelEdit	Cancels an edit operation and undoes all actions taken during the edit.
ClearErrors	Erases the list of all errors for the current row.
EndEdit	Completes an edit operation on the row.
GetChildRows	Returns an array of `DataRow` objects that contain all rows considered "child" rows of this row based on a given relationship supplied as an argument to the method.
GetColumnsInError	Returns an array of all columns that indicate they contain an error.
GetParentRow	Returns the `DataRow` instance of the "parent" row as per the `DataRelation` specified in the method call.
GetParentRows	Obtains the parent rows (array of `DataRow`) as indicated by the supplied parent-child relationship.

Method	Description
HasVersion	Boolean indicating whether or not a specific version of the row exists.
IsNull	Indicates whether or not the row itself is NULL/empty.
RejectChanges	Roll back/cancel all changes made to the row since the last load or since the last time AcceptChanges was called.
SetColumnError	Sets the description to be used when an error occurs with the column.
SetParentRow	Manually force the setting of an existing DataRow instance as the parent row.

Manual Data Example

Now that we've given you a brief introduction to the DataTable, DataColumn, and DataRow classes and presented you with some reference information on how to use those classes, let's take a look at an example that uses all three of these classes.

This next example is a console application that illustrates manually creating instances of the DataTable, DataColumn, and DataRow classes to define the data structure of a table within the DataSet, as well as actually place some data into that DataSet. If you're planning on creating the example as you read the book, go ahead and create a new C# **Console Application** now and call it ManualData. Our example is in a subfolder called FTrackADONET\Chapter02\ManualData to keep things organized.

One thing to keep in mind is that while Visual Studio .NET will always add a **reference** to System.Data in any new project that you create, it won't always add the using System.Data namespace declaration at the top of your new class.

I typically delete the created default class and write myself a new one, but you can feel free to simply rename the .cs (unless you want to follow along in VB.NET) file and the class itself. When you're ready, you should have a class called DataMain. Make sure you add the using System.Data; line just below the using System; line at the top of your class.

Now let's take a look at the source code to our DataMain class (DataMain.cs):

```
using System;
using System.Data;

namespace ManualData
{
    /// <summary>
    /// DataMain Class
    /// Demonstrates manually creating a DataTable, DataColumns, and DataRows
    /// </summary>
    class DataMain
    {
        /// <summary>
        /// The main entry point for the application.
        /// </summary>
        [STAThread]
```

```
static void Main(string[] args)
{
```

In these next couple of lines of code, we create a new empty `DataSet`, and then create a `DataTable` named `Quotes`, and a `DataColumn` named `Symbol`. Then, we indicate that the `Symbol` column is a string with a maximum length of 4, and another column, `Description`, is a string with a maximum length of 50.

```
DataSet ds = new DataSet();
DataTable quotes = new DataTable("Quotes");
DataColumn symbol = new DataColumn("Symbol");
symbol.DataType = typeof(string);
symbol.MaxLength = 4;
DataColumn description = new DataColumn("Description");
description.DataType = typeof(string);
description.MaxLength = 50;
```

One thing that can be misleading is that the act of simply instantiating new columns doesn't actually finish the job. We need to add the new columns to the `Columns` collection (`DataColumnCollection` type) of the table we're putting the columns in:

```
quotes.Columns.Add( symbol );
quotes.Columns.Add( description );
```

So now we have a `DataTable` with some well-defined columns. Again, this is only half the work. To do us any good, we need to put that table into a `DataSet`:

```
ds.Tables.Add( quotes );
```

Now that we have the data structure of our `DataSet` defined and we have our `DataTable` and `DataColumns` defined, we need to add some data to the table. This is done fairly easily by obtaining a new `DataRow` instance. Rather than simply creating a new instance of a `DataRow`, we'll use a handy method on the parent table called `NewRow()` that will create an instance of a new row with the appropriate schema. In C# we have the luxury of being able to use the default indexer property on the `DataRow` object that allows us to access the columns by name or ordinal index. In VB.NET, we would have to use the `Item` property to access each column by name or ordinal position.

```
// Now add some data to the table.
DataRow newQuote = quotes.NewRow();
newQuote["Symbol"] = "MSFT";
newQuote["Description"] = "Microsoft Corporation";
quotes.Rows.Add( newQuote );

// Now display it to make sure the data is in the table.
Console.WriteLine("Stock Quote");
Console.WriteLine("Symbol: {0}, Description: {1}",
    quotes.Rows[0]["Symbol"].ToString(),
    quotes.Rows[0]["Description"].ToString());
Console.ReadLine();
    }
  }
}
```

Our DataTable instance, quotes, is still valid and functional after we've added it to the DataTableCollection on our DataSet. So, in the code above, we use the indexer property on the Rows property (DataRowCollection type) to get access to the data. This method of accessing the data always returns data of type Object, so we use the ToString() method to make sure we have the appropriate data type.

The following is a screenshot of the output of the application. To get this we built the application using Visual Studio .NET and then opened a command prompt and executed the program from the debug directory:

Our little example was just the tip of the iceberg in demonstrating the power and flexibility of the DataSet. While we were able to create some columns and some data within a DataSet, there is much more that we can do.

Relational Data Model Support

In this next section of the chapter we're going to go over the DataSet's support for containing and manipulating data in a relational way. In a traditional relational database, you can define relationships between multiple tables, specifying how various columns in one table relate to columns in another table. This is done through the use of foreign and primary keys, as well as constraints. This next section will show you how to use constraints, keys, and relations within the context of a DataSet.

Constraints and Keys

Constraints are restrictions, or rules, that are enforced on the data within a DataTable in order to maintain the integrity of that data. These rules are automatic once we have defined them, and are applied to columns or related columns, whenever the associated data is altered somehow by being inserted, updated, or deleted. These constraints are only enforced when the EnforceConstraints property of the DataSet is set to true and, of course, only after we've created these constraints.

There are two different kinds of constraints available to you for the DataSet: the **unique constraint** and the **foreign key constraint**.

Unique Constraint

The UniqueConstraint class enforces uniqueness of data within a single row of data. It can be assigned to a single column or an array of columns. The data in a row for each column assigned to the UniqueConstraint must not match any data in that same column (or array of columns) for any other row in the parent table's DataRowCollection. Both this constraint and the foreign-key constraint are created automatically when a new relation is placed on the table. We'll talk more about DataRelations later.

The following little snippet of code illustrates the use of a unique constraint in code. Since it is just a couple of lines, this section of code isn't in the download section for this chapter:

```
DataTable stockQuotes = stockDataSet.Tables["StockQuotes"] ;
UniqueConstraint uc = new UniqueConstraint(new DataColumn[] {
    stockQuotes.Columns["Symbol"], stockQuotes.Columns["Description"]});
stockQuotes.Constraints.Add( uc );
```

The above little sample illustrated creating a `UniqueConstraint` on two columns, requiring that for each row, the combination of *both* the `Symbol` and the `Description` column must be unique.

Foreign Key Constraint

A foreign key constraint enforces rules about how updates and deletes to related tables are dealt with. We haven't covered actually creating related tables yet, but we'll get to that shortly. You have some control over how you want the `DataSet` to automatically manage propagating updates and deletes on related tables.

The `ForeignKeyConstraint` class has two properties that allow you to control this behavior: `DeleteRule` and `UpdateRule`. Both of these properties are of the data type enumeration `Rule`. The following is a list of the possible values of the `DeleteRule` and `UpdateRule` properties:

- ❑ `Cascade` – The delete or update operation is also performed on all related rows. This is the default value for both properties.

- ❑ `None` – No action is taken on any related rows.

- ❑ `SetDefault` – The values in the related rows will be set to their default values as indicated by the `DataColumn`'s `DefaultValue` property.

- ❑ `SetNull` – All values in the related rows will be set to `NULL`.

Let's take a look at a quick few lines of code to see what a foreign key constraint looks like in action:

```
DataTable custOrders = orderDataSet.Tables["Orders"];
DataTable custOrderDetail = orderDataSet.Tables["OrderDetails"];
DataColumn orderIdMaster = custOrders.Columns["OrderId"];
DataColumn orderIdChild = custOrderDetail.Columns["OrderId"];
ForeignKeyConstraint fkc = new ForeignKeyConstraint("OrdersFKC", orderIdMaster,
orderIdChild);
fkc.DeleteRule = Rule.Cascade;
fkc.UpdateRule = Rule.None;
```

In the sample above, we have the typical parent-child example of `Orders` and `OrderDetails`. We created a foreign-key constraint and set the rules such that deleting an order will remove all order detail rows, but modifying an order will not automatically update order details (since, theoretically, we shouldn't ever be modifying the `OrderId` column).

Primary Key

As most of us who've had some experience with relational databases know, the **primary key** of any table is the column (or collection of columns) that uniquely distinguishes one row in the table from all other rows in the table. Quite often, this primary key is a numeric identifier, possibly a number that increments each time a new row is created, such as an Identity column in SQL Server. Tables that contain Orders often work like this. However, other primary keys might be more complicated, consisting of something like an eight character user name, a site identifier, and a customer ID as a complex, three-column composite primary key.

When you define a primary key for a table that consists of only one column, the column automatically has the AllowDBNull property set to false, and the Unique property set to true. For multi-column primary keys, only the AllowDBNull property is set.

Setting a primary key on a table is as easy as specifying the column or list of columns that you would like to compose the primary key:

```
customerTable.PrimaryKey = new DataColumn[] { customerTable.Columns["CustomerID"]
};
```

or you could set the primary key this way:

```
DataColumn[] pkeyArray = new DataColumn[2];
pkeyArray[0] = customerTable.Columns["LoginId"];
pkeyArray[1] = customerTable.Columns["SiteId"];
customerTable.PrimaryKey = pkeyArray;
```

In the first one-line example, we define a single-column primary key (note that we still must use array syntax). In the second example, we create an array in a separate variable and then assign that variable to the PrimaryKey property of our table.

Relations

Now that we have covered the basic concepts behind constraints and keys, let's take a look at how to put constraints and keys to work for us in order to create DataRelations. DataRelation is a class that, as its name implies, represents a single relationship between two tables.

A relation is a special kind of combination of foreign key constraints. To relate one table to another, you simply create a new DataRelation and indicate which columns in one table are related to which columns in another. The following is a quick reference guide for the DataRelation class:

Property	Data Type	Description
ChildColumns	DataColumn[]	An array containing the columns that make up the key columns in the child table
ChildKeyConstraint	ForeignKeyConstraint	The foreign-key constraint for the child side of the relation

Table continued on following page

Property	Data Type	Description
ChildTable	DataTable	The table containing the child rows of the relation
DataSet	DataSet	The DataSet to which this relation belongs
Nested	Boolean	Indicates whether the child rows are nested within the parent rows in the DataSet
ParentColumns	DataColumn[]	An array containing the columns that make up the key columns in the parent table
ParentKeyConstraint	ForeignKeyConstraint	Gets the parent foreign-key constraint for this relation
ParentTable	DataTable	Gets the parent DataTable for this relation
RelationName	String	Gets/Sets the name used to retrieve this relation from the DataRelationCollection

Now that we have some familiarity with constraints and keys, and we've taken a look at the core information that belongs to a DataRelation class, let's take a look at this class in action. The classic example of a parent-child table relationship is in matching Orders with OrderItems. Our next example is going to show you how to traverse a master-detail table relationship using relation-based operations on DataRow objects.

For this project, we'll create a new C# **Console Application** called Relations. This is also available in the code download for this chapter, in the folder FTrackADONET/Chapter02/Relations. After renaming our main class to RelationsDemo and changing the filename to RelationsDemo.cs, the following is the source code listing:

```
using System;
using System.Data;

namespace Relations
{
  /// <summary>
  /// Summary description for RelationsDemo.
  /// </summary>
  class RelationsDemo
  {
    /// <summary>
    /// The main entry point for the application.
    /// </summary>
    [STAThread]
    static void Main(string[] args)
    {
```

```
// First thing we're going to do is create two tables
// and their columns.
DataSet orders = new DataSet();
DataTable orderMaster = new DataTable("Orders");
DataTable orderItems = new DataTable("OrderItems");
```

We've already seen how to create columns and define their data types, so this next section of a few lines of code should look pretty familiar:

```
// create orders-master columns.
DataColumn omOrderId = new DataColumn("OrderId", typeof(string));
DataColumn omCustomer = new DataColumn("Customer", typeof(string));
orderMaster.Columns.Add( omOrderId );
orderMaster.Columns.Add( omCustomer );
orderMaster.PrimaryKey = new DataColumn[] { omOrderId };

// create order-items columns.
DataColumn oiOrderId = new DataColumn("OrderId", typeof(string));
DataColumn oiAmount = new DataColumn("Amount", typeof(float));
DataColumn oiSKU = new DataColumn("Sku", typeof(string));
DataColumn oiDescription = new DataColumn("Description",
    typeof(string));
orderItems.Columns.Add( oiOrderId );
orderItems.Columns.Add( oiAmount );
orderItems.Columns.Add( oiSKU );
orderItems.Columns.Add( oiDescription );

// add our tables to the DataSet
orders.Tables.Add( orderMaster );
orders.Tables.Add( orderItems );

// now create a parent/child relationship
```

As with most operations involving creating new items within a DataSet, instantiation is only half of the operation. You have to instantiate the new item and also add it to the appropriate collection. In our case in the following two lines we're going to create a DataRelation and add it to the Relations collection of our DataSet.

```
DataRelation relOrderItems = new DataRelation("OrderItems", omOrderId,
    oiOrderId, false);
orders.Relations.Add( relOrderItems );
```

Next we use one of the more important methods in the DataRow object with regards to DataRelations: GetChildRows. GetChildRows obtains all rows that qualify as child rows of the current row based on the name of a relation. In our case, we're going to obtain all child rows via the OrderItems named relation. Because the GetChildRows method returns an array of DataRow objects, we can iterate through that array using the foreach keyword.

41

We've written a small helper function called `FillOrders` to populate the `Orders DataSet` with some dummy data.

```
        FillOrders( ref orders );
        float orderTotal;
        foreach(DataRow order in orderMaster.Rows)
        {
          orderTotal = 0;
          Console.WriteLine("Order ID: {0}, Customer: {1}",
              order["OrderId"].ToString(), order["Customer"].ToString());
          foreach (DataRow orderItem in order.GetChildRows("OrderItems"))
          {
            orderTotal += (float)orderItem["Amount"];
            Console.WriteLine("\t{0} purchased for ${1}",
                orderItem["SKU"].ToString(), (float)orderItem["Amount"]);
          }
          Console.WriteLine("Order Total: ${0}\n\n", orderTotal);
          Console.WriteLine("Press Enter to continue");
          Console.ReadLine();
        }
    }

    private static void FillOrders(ref DataSet ordersData)
    {
      DataTable orderMaster = ordersData.Tables["Orders"];
      DataTable orderItems = ordersData.Tables["OrderItems"];
      DataRow newOrder = orderMaster.NewRow();
      DataRow orderItem;

      newOrder["OrderId"] = "0001";
      newOrder["Customer"] = "Joan Doe";
        orderItem = orderItems.NewRow();
        orderItem["OrderId"] = "0001";
        orderItem["Amount"] = 12.45f;
        orderItem["SKU"] = "10101010";
        orderItem["Description"] = "Universal Fix-It All Product Device";
        orderItems.Rows.Add( orderItem );
        orderItem = orderItems.NewRow ();
        orderItem["OrderId"] = "0001";
        orderItem["Amount"] = 2.99f;
        orderItem["SKU"] = "11111111";
        orderItem["Description"] = "Somewhat less universal do-it-all
            Device";
      orderItems.Rows.Add( orderItem );
      orderMaster.Rows.Add( newOrder );
      newOrder = orderMaster.NewRow();
      newOrder["OrderId"] = "0002";
      newOrder["Customer"] = "John Smith";
      orderMaster.Rows.Add( newOrder );
        orderItem = orderItems.NewRow();
        orderItem["OrderId"] = "0002";
        orderItem["Amount"] = 12.45f;
        orderItem["SKU"] = "1010101010";
        orderItem["Description"] = "Universal Fix-It All Product Device";
```

```
            orderItems.Rows.Add( orderItem );

        ordersData.AcceptChanges();
    }
  }
}
```

After compiling this, we execute the program and get the following output:

The example above illustrates that in a single `DataSet`, we have two complete and separate tables with their own sets of data. Through a `DataRelation`, we can create a parent-child relationship and traverse the tables and data in the `DataSet` in a hierarchical fashion.

Communicating with the DataSet

So far throughout this chapter we've had a pretty good look at how to build the structure of a `DataSet`, and how to create keys, constraints, and relations among multiple tables within the `DataSet`. This next section of the chapter will take you through the various ways in which you can get data in and out of the `DataSet` and how to put that knowledge to practical use.

The DataAdapter

We can't have a discussion about the `DataSet` without mentioning one of the most common uses: communicating with a database. While it is true that the `DataSet` itself is a completely disconnected memory cache that has no preference for or knowledge of any RDBMS implementation, it is possible to *plug it in* to a database through a special class called the `DataAdapter`. The `DataAdapter` is a required piece of all data providers for .NET, and as such can be used to populate `DataSets` with information from non-relational data sources, or proprietary data sources that do not normally expose an OLE DB or ODBC connection.

There are some classes in ADO.NET, like the `DataSet`, that are data source implementation agnostic. However, classes like the `DataAdapter` are not. What that means is that there is a data adapter for each **data provider**. Much like the name implies, this class knows how to *adapt* the data from the RDBMS source to the format of the `DataSet` and vice versa. It knows how to take change information from the `DataSet` and perform the appropriate inserts, updates, and deletes in the associated database.

Think of the `DataAdapter` as a container that holds database commands. It is where objects that perform the SELECT, UPDATE, DELETE, and INSERT operations are housed. Picture it this way: on the left-hand side you have a `DataSet`. In the middle is the `DataAdapter`. Coming out of the adapter on the right-hand side are SELECT, UPDATE, DELETE, and INSERT operations, which interface directly to a database. Having the `DataAdapter` take a position of abstraction in the middle allows the `DataSet` to continue to manipulate and view data without regard to the source of the data itself. This allows the `DataAdapter` to retrieve information from a data source and place it in the `DataSet`, and it allows information contained in a `DataSet` to be carried across to the data store. The following diagram illustrates this principle graphically:

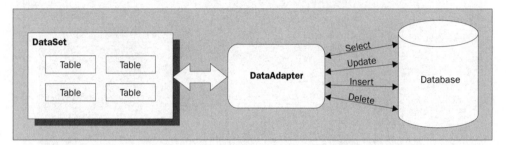

The `DataAdapter` class is an abstract base class that defines the basic set of functionality that all `DataAdapters` must provide. The following is a quick reference on the `DataAdapter` class:

Property	Data Type	Description
AcceptChangesDuringFill	Boolean	Gets or sets a value indicating whether the `AcceptChanges` method is called on a `DataRow` after it is added to the `DataTable` by this adapter
ContinueUpdateOnError	Boolean	Gets or sets a value indicating whether an exception will be thrown or the error will be flagged on the row and the update continue
MissingMappingAction	MissingMapping Action	Indicates the action to take when incoming data from the adapter does not have a matching table or column
MissingSchemaAction	MissingSchema Action	Determines the action to be taken when the `DataSet` schema does not match incoming data from the adapter
TableMappings	DataTableMapping Collection	Gets a collection indicating the master mapping between source tables in the data source and a `DataTable`

Method	Description
Fill	Adds or refreshes rows in the DataSet from the data source and creates a table if necessary
FillSchema	Updates or creates the data structure in the DataSet based on the data structure of the "live" data source
GetFillParameters	Gets the parameters set when executing a SELECT statement
Update	Calls the appropriate INSERT, UPDATE, or DELETE command for each row in the DataSet that has been inserted, updated, or deleted

The following is a short example of utilizing a DataAdapter. We use an adapter to pull data out of a Microsoft Access 2000 version of the Northwind database, which also ships with SQL Server. This file (Northwind2k.mdb) is included in the download section for this chapter. If you have Microsoft Office 2000, you can also find the Northwind database in (Program Files)\Microsoft Office\Office\Samples\Northwind.mdb.

To create this sample, we followed the same procedure we have been using throughout this chapter and created a simple C# **Console Application** and renamed the main class and the main class's source file. In this case we created a project called DataAdapter and called the main class AdapterDemo. The following the source code listing for that class:

```
using System;
using System.Data;
using System.Data.OleDb;
```

The first thing that you might notice in the line above is that we're now using another namespace. This namespace is for the OLE DB managed provider, a database driver library that ships with .NET. We'll cover managed providers in more detail later in the book. For now, it should be enough to think of the managed provider as an implementation of an ADO.NET standard set of data interface routines specific to the OLE DB drivers.

```
namespace DataAdapter
{
  /// <summary>
  /// Summary description for AdapterDemo.
  /// </summary>
  class AdapterDemo
  {
    /// <summary>
    /// The main entry point for the application.
    /// </summary>
    [STAThread]
    static void Main(string[] args)
    {
```

Here we're creating a live connection to an OLE DB database. In our case it happens to be the Northwind2k.mdb file, a file that contains the Northwind database that ships with SQL 2000. The connection constructor takes a traditional connection string as an argument. Then we open the connection.

45

```
OleDbConnection conn = new OleDbConnection(@"PROVIDER=
Microsoft.Jet.OLEDB.4.0;Data Source=..\..\..\Northwind2k.mdb");
    conn.Open();
```

Now we actually create the `DataAdapter`. We are actually creating an `OleDbDataAdapter`, which is a specialized implementation of the `DataAdapter` abstract base class designed specifically to work with OLE DB compatible databases. As we mentioned above, the `DataAdapter` is really a two-sided *conduit* or "bridge" between a `DataSet` and a data source. One side contains an interface to the `DataSet`. The other side contains a set of commands that interface with the database itself. By default, when you create an `OleDbDataAdapter`, the first argument to the constructor can be the SQL statement to be executed for the `SelectCommand`.

```
OleDbDataAdapter da = new OleDbDataAdapter("SELECT * FROM Customers",
    conn);
DataSet customers = new DataSet();
```

Now that we've initialized our `DataAdapter` with a SQL `SELECT` statement, the adapter is now capable of reading data from the database. Without additional commands configured, it can't perform actions like updating or deleting, but we don't need to do those for this example. In order to pull data from the database into our `DataSet`, we need to use the `Fill` method. The most common overloaded form of this method takes a `DataSet` and the name of a table as arguments. The data pulled from the database (via the `SELECT` statement we provided) will be stored in the `DataSet` in a table with the name we supply as an argument to `Fill`.

```
da.Fill( customers, "Customers" );
conn.Close();
da.Dispose();
```

Now that we have the data stored in our `DataSet`, we can continue with the live connection to the database actually closed. As we've stressed before, the `DataSet` on its own is a completely disconnected memory cache. The `DataAdapter` is only for short term bursts of "live" (connected) activity in order to transfer changed information to and from a data source.

```
DataTable custTable = customers.Tables["Customers"];
Console.WriteLine("Customers Found {0}", custTable.Rows.Count);
Console.Write("Customers Column Names: ");
foreach (DataColumn col in custTable.Columns)
{
    Console.Write("{0}  ", col.ColumnName);
}
Console.WriteLine();
foreach (DataRow customer in custTable.Rows)
{
    Console.WriteLine("{0}:{1}", customer["CustomerID"].ToString(),
        customer["ContactName"].ToString());
}
    }
}
```

When this application is compiled and executed, it produces the following output to the console prompt:

While there are many more things you can do with a DataAdapter, we'll only be covering this small section in this chapter. Throughout the book you will see more complex uses for the DataAdapter. Keep in mind that the DataAdapter is used for all four types of data access: INSERT, UPDATE, DELETE, and SELECT.

Loading from Disk

If you are familiar with ADO programming from back in the "good old days" you might be familiar with using Recordset persistence to save and load data to and from disk. In the early days of ADO, this was accomplished only with the ADTG (Advanced Data TableGram) format. This was a binary serialization of data contained within the Recordset, and could only be read and understood by a compatible version of ADO. This was fairly limiting and had few specialized uses until ADO supported the concept of XML-persisted Recordsets.

XML-persisted RecordSets were, as you can imagine, Recordsets that persisted to disk (or stream) in a standardized XML format that can even be read by ADO.NET DataSets today. This embracing of XML added quite a bit of flexibility to classic ADO programs and components.

The DataSet has this kind of support for XML, plus much, much more. We'll get more into how the DataSet (and much of the rest of ADO.NET) has embraced XML in the next chapter. For now, let's take a quick look at how the DataSet can receive data from an XML file and output its changes to an XML file.

To illustrate something like this, there is really no better way to get the point across than to simply show you. So we'll work up a small example that illustrates loading XML data into a DataSet, making some in-memory changes to the DataSet, and persisting that information back to disk. To follow along, create a C# Console Application called DiskData. We'll be using two methods in this sample: ReadXml and WriteXml. Both are methods of the DataSet class.

Here's the source XML file we'll be using
(FTrackADONET\Chapter02\DiskData\sourcedata.xml):

```xml
<?xml version="1.0"?>
<sourcedata>
  <channel number="9997" id="SNOW" description="The snow channel. No
      reception. Ever."/>
  <channel number="9998" id="WROX" description="The Wrox Network"/>
  <channel number="9999" id="CHRP" description="The C# Network"/>
  <channel number="0000" id="MDEW" description="The Mountain Dew Channel"/>
  <channel number="0001" id="VIDG" description="The video Game Network"/>
</sourcedata>
```

As you can see, it is a listing of cable or satellite stations. Next, we're going to create a little application that will read in this XML file into a DataSet. The DataSet will then add a new row and save out to another XML file. We'll take a look at that file when we're done. Here's the source code to our DiskData application:

```csharp
using System;
using System.Data;

namespace DiskData
{
  /// <summary>
  /// Summary description for DiskDemo.
  /// </summary>
  class DiskDemo
  {
    /// <summary>
    /// The main entry point for the application.
    /// </summary>
    STAThread]
    static void Main(string[] args)
    {
      DataSet cableChannels = new DataSet();
```

This next line is fairly straightforward. We're telling the DataSet to read the XML data contained in the sourcedata.xml file. What we don't see happening here is that the DataSet is going to *infer* the data structure and table structure from the XML file itself. We'll cover *schema inference* in the next chapter. For now, just consider it "magic" that we'll de-mystify in the next chapter.

```csharp
      cableChannels.ReadXml(@"..\..\sourcedata.xml");
      Console.WriteLine("Proposed Cable Channels:\n");
      foreach (DataRow channel in cableChannels.Tables["channel"].Rows)
      {
        Console.WriteLine("{0}/{1}: {2}", (string)channel["id"],
            (string)channel["number"],(string)channel["description"]);
      }
```

Here we're going to create a new `DataRow`, which we should be familiar with by now. Then, we'll add it to our table. Finally, we'll call the `WriteXml` method, which will take the entire contents of the `DataSet` and write it out to an XML file.

```
      DataRow newChannel = cableChannels.Tables["channel"].NewRow();
      newChannel["id"] = ".NET";
      newChannel["number"] = "0002";
      newChannel["description"] = "The .NET Show, All Day, All Night.";
      cableChannels.Tables["channel"].Rows.Add( newChannel );
      cableChannels.WriteXml(@"..\..\destdata.xml");
    }
  }
}
```

Finally, after we've built and run the application, we end up with an XML file (`destdata.xml`) that looks like this:

```
<?xml version="1.0" standalone="yes"?>
<sourcedata>
  <channel number="9997" id="SNOW" description="The snow channel. No
      reception. Ever." />
  <channel number="9998" id="WROX" description="The Wrox Network" />
  <channel number="9999" id="CHRP" description="The C# Network" />
  <channel number="0000" id="MDEW" description="The Mountain Dew Channel" />
  <channel number="0001" id="VIDG" description="The video Game Network" />
  <channel number="0002" id=".NET" description="The .NET Show, All Day, All
      Night." />
</sourcedata>
```

There is only a slight bit of difference between the way I handwrote the original XML file and the way the `DataSet` wrote the XML file back out. It interpreted the data structure from the XML file and used that same structure to create this new XML file.

Manual Population

Manual population of the `DataSet` is something that we should be pretty familiar with by now. We've seen a few examples of creating some new rows, and we've seen a couple of examples of creating tables. However, earlier in this chapter we conveniently skipped over the `FillOrders` method in our `DataRelations` example. We have saved the discussion of that method until now.

As I said, we've seen a couple of different ways to simply place data into a `DataSet`, but it can be more complex than that. For example, if there are keys and constraints already in place on the `DataSet`'s data structure, then any new row inserted must conform to those keys and constraints, otherwise the row will be flagged with an error, or an exception will be thrown.

In the example below, note that we create the parent rows *before* we create the child rows. This is because there is a foreign key constraint in place that prevents us from having any *orphan rows* (rows with no parent). Let's take a look at the source code to the `FillOrders` method:

```
private static void FillOrders(ref DataSet ordersData)
{
  DataTable orderMaster = ordersData.Tables["Orders"];
  DataTable orderItems = ordersData.Tables["OrderItems"];
  DataRow newOrder = orderMaster.NewRow();
  DataRow orderItem;

  newOrder["OrderId"] = "0001";
  newOrder["Customer"] = "Joan Doe";
  orderItem = orderItems.NewRow();
  orderItem["OrderId"] = "0001";
  orderItem["Amount"] = 12.45f;
  orderItem["SKU"] = "10101010";
  orderItem["Description"] = "Universal Fix-It All Product Device";
  orderItems.Rows.Add( orderItem );
  orderItem = orderItems.NewRow();
  orderItem["OrderId"] = "0001";
  orderItem["Amount"] = 2.99f;
  orderItem["SKU"] = "11111111";
  orderItem["Description"] = "Somewhat less universal do-it-all Device";
  orderItems.Rows.Add( orderItem );
  orderMaster.Rows.Add( newOrder );

  newOrder = orderMaster.NewRow();
  newOrder["OrderId"] = "0002";
  newOrder["Customer"] = "John Smith";
  orderMaster.Rows.Add( newOrder );
  orderItem = orderItems.NewRow();
  orderItem["OrderId"] = "0002";
  orderItem["Amount"] = 12.45f;
  orderItem["SKU"] = "1010101010";
  orderItem["Description"] = "Universal Fix-It All Product Device";
  orderItems.Rows.Add( orderItem );

  ordersData.AcceptChanges();
}
```

As you can see, each time we instantiate a new object and populate all of the relevant properties and information, we add it to the appropriate collection class. New child rows are added to the child table's Rows collection, new parent rows are added to the parent table's Rows collection. By now, you should have a fairly good idea of how to programmatically create DataTables, DataColumns, and DataRows, as well as relate multiple tables with constraints, keys, and relations.

Merging DataSets

Another extremely handy feature of the DataSet is the ability to *merge* a DataSet with other DataSets. Merging a DataSet essentially combines the data found in one DataSet with the data found in another DataSet, DataTable, or DataRow. Through the use of the missingSchemaAction and preserveChanges parameters you can determine how that data will be merged.

The following is a list of the possible values for the `MissingSchemaAction` enumeration:

- ❑ `Add` – Adds the columns necessary to support the new schema
- ❑ `AddWithKey` – Adds the columns necessary to support the new schema, as well as creates/adds primary key information
- ❑ `Error` – If the schemas of the items being merged do not match exactly, then an exception will be thrown
- ❑ `Ignore` – All extra columns in the merge will simply be ignored

To illustrate `DataSet` merging, we're going to create two `DataSet`s and merge them and then examine the results. To follow along, create a new C# **Console Application** called `Merge`. Also, rename or recreate the main class so that the class name is `MergeDemo` and the filename is `MergeDemo.cs`. The following is the code listing for the `MergeDemo` class:

```
using System;
using System.Data;

namespace Merge
{
  /// <summary>
  /// Summary description for MergeDemo.
  /// </summary>
  class MergeDemo
  {
    /// <summary>
    /// The main entry point for the application.
    /// </summary>
    [STAThread]
    static void Main(string[] args)
    {
```

First thing we're going to do is create our data structure. This should all look fairly familiar. We're going to create a table called `Books` in two different `DataSet`s. The first `DataSet`, `regularBooks`, will contain a `Books` table with two simple columns: `ISBN` and `Title`. The second `DataSet`, `bestsellers`, will contain a `Books` table with three columns: `ISBN`, `Title`, and `WeeksOnTop10`.

```
DataSet regularBooks = new DataSet("RegularBooks");
DataSet bestSellers = new DataSet("BestSellers");

DataTable regularTable = new DataTable("Books");
DataTable sellerTable = new DataTable("Books");

DataColumn newCol = new DataColumn("ISBN", typeof(string));
regularTable.Columns.Add( newCol );
newCol = new DataColumn("ISBN", typeof(string));
sellerTable.Columns.Add( newCol );
newCol = new DataColumn("Title", typeof(string));
regularTable.Columns.Add( newCol );
newCol = new DataColumn("Title", typeof(string));
sellerTable.Columns.Add( newCol );
```

```
newCol = new DataColumn("WeeksOnTop10", typeof(int));
newCol.DefaultValue = 0;
sellerTable.Columns.Add( newCol );
```

Now that we've created our data structure, we can start loading the `DataSets` with some data. We'll add two rows to the regular books `DataSet`, and two rows to the bestseller books `DataSet`.

```
DataRow newBook = regularTable.NewRow();
newBook["ISBN"] = "1861007000";
newBook["Title"] = ".NET Compact Framework";
regularTable.Rows.Add( newBook );
newBook = regularTable.NewRow();
newBook["ISBN"] = "1861005547";
newBook["Title"] = "Professional Windows Forms";
regularTable.Rows.Add( newBook );

// now add book to best seller table, which has an extra column.
newBook = sellerTable.NewRow();
newBook["ISBN"] = "0786687647";
newBook["Title"] = "Lucky Man: A Memoir";
newBook["WeeksOnTop10"] = 3;
sellerTable.Rows.Add( newBook );
newBook = sellerTable.NewRow();
newBook["ISBN"] = "0446530077";
newBook["Title"] = "Find Me";
newBook["WeeksOnTop10"] = 1;
sellerTable.Rows.Add( newBook );

regularBooks.Tables.Add( regularTable );
bestSellers.Tables.Add( sellerTable );
```

Here we finally get to see the `Merge` method put to use. We call the `Merge` method and indicate that we want to merge the `regularBooks DataSet` with the `bestSellers DataSet`. We want to preserve the changes made while merging, and we indicate that if one of the tables in one of the `DataSets` being merged is missing column definitions that other tables have, we will create those column definitions automatically. The idea here is that after we're done merging, all four books in our single `Books` table should have three columns, `ISBN`, `Title`, and `WeeksOnTop10`.

```
// now merge the regular books and the bestseller books.
regularBooks.Merge( bestSellers, true, MissingSchemaAction.Add );

// now display the new merged data.
foreach (DataRow book in regularTable.Rows)
{
  Console.WriteLine("{0}, ISBN: {1}, Weeks On Top 10: {2}",
      book["Title"].ToString(), book["ISBN"].ToString(),
      (int)book["WeeksOnTop10"]);
}
    }
  }
}
```

Let's compile this example and see if our guess about what the new `DataSet` looks like was accurate. The following is a screenshot of the console output when running this example:

It worked as we expected. The two books that didn't have the `WeeksOnTop10` column to begin with were given that column, and the `DefaultValue` for that column was used when adding that column to those two rows. The other books that originally had values for the `WeeksOnTop10` column retained that value. The result is a completely seamless merge of two similar `DataSets`.

Anytime you need to combine two sets of data, before you decide to write a complex loop that will manually add data or convert it, consider using the `Merge` method. Chances are, if you're combining virtually any kind of data, the `Merge` method can be a big help and a huge timesaver.

Putting It All Together

This chapter has been all about the functionality, flexibility, and power of ADO.NET's `DataSet` class. We've seen how you can programmatically create tables, columns, and even rows of data. We've also seen how we can add advanced data integrity management concepts such as constraints and keys. In addition, we've covered how we can relate data in one table to data in another table within the same `DataSet`.

This next code example is going to put all of those concepts together into one single application to show you at least one point of view on a practical application of all this information. It's one thing to learn the syntax for the `DataSet`, but it is far more useful to know when, where, *and* how to practically apply the techniques of working with a `DataSet`.

Our example that illustrates all of these concepts is an extremely stripped down contact/relationship management system. It tracks a list of people, and also allows you to keep track of various notes and conversations with those people. This is accomplished using a parent-child relationship.

We're going to create a Windows Forms application called `Contacts` this time around. We won't be going through each and every detail of the creation of the application. For that you can either take a look at the screenshots or download the code from the book's download area on Wrox's web site at www.wrox.com.

Our Windows Forms application is called `Contacts`. It consists of three forms: the main form (`frmMain`), a form to enter contact information (`frmContact`), and a form to log contact messages (`frmMessageLog`). The main form sports a bound `DataGrid` while the other forms use simple Windows controls. For more information on Windows Forms programming, consult the Wrox book *Professional Windows Forms* (ISBN: 1-86100-554-7).

Before we take a look at the forms, we'll take a look at a class we made called `GlobalData`. Essentially we borrowed the age-old object-oriented trick of getting around the lack of global variable space by making a class that contains only static members and using that class to 'house' our data. This allows us to maintain a single instance of our `DataSet` and give all of our forms easy access to that data. Here's the code listing for `GlobalData.cs`:

```
using System;
using System.Data;

namespace Contacts
{
  /// <summary>
  /// Summary description for GlobalData.
  /// </summary>
  public class GlobalData
  {
    static GlobalData()
    {
      contactsData = new DataSet("ContactsData");
      DataTable contacts = new DataTable("Contacts");
      DataColumn contactId = new DataColumn("ContactId", typeof(int));
      contactId.AutoIncrement = true;
      contacts.Columns.Add( contactId );
      contacts.PrimaryKey = new DataColumn[] { contactId };

      DataColumn contactName = new DataColumn("ContactName",
          typeof(string));
      contacts.Columns.Add( contactName );

      DataTable contactMessages = new DataTable("ContactMessages");
      DataColumn contactId2 = new DataColumn("ContactId", typeof(int));
      contactMessages.Columns.Add( contactId2 );
      DataColumn message = new DataColumn("Message", typeof(string));
      contactMessages.Columns.Add( message );
      DataColumn messageDate = new DataColumn("MessageDate",
          typeof(DateTime));
      contactMessages.Columns.Add( messageDate );

      contactsData.Tables.Add( contacts );
      contactsData.Tables.Add( contactMessages );

      DataRelation relContactMessages = new DataRelation(
          "ContactMessages", contactId, contactId2, true);
      contactsData.Relations.Add( relContactMessages );
    }

    public static DataSet contactsData;
  }
}
```

In the class we just listed, we create the data structure for our table each time we load our application. This is done in the `GlobalData` class to keep the code neat and organized. It is a shame that we have to manually define the data structure for the `DataSet` each time, but we'll discover an answer to that problem in the next chapter.

We'll take a look at the code behind each of the forms and explain what we're doing at each point. The first form is the main form, `frmMain`. The following is the code listing for that form, which is found in `frmMain.cs`:

```csharp
using System;
using System.Drawing;
using System.Collections;
using System.ComponentModel;
using System.Windows.Forms;
using System.Data;

namespace Contacts
{
    /// <summary>
    /// Summary description for Form1.
    /// </summary>
    public class frmMain : System.Windows.Forms.Form
    {
        private System.Windows.Forms.DataGrid dgContacts;
        private System.Windows.Forms.MainMenu mainMenu1;
        private System.Windows.Forms.MenuItem menuItem1;
        private System.Windows.Forms.MenuItem menuItem2;
        private System.Windows.Forms.MenuItem menuItem3;
        private System.Windows.Forms.MenuItem menuItem4;
        private System.Windows.Forms.Button button1;
        private System.Windows.Forms.Button button2;
        private System.Windows.Forms.MenuItem menuItem5;
        private System.Windows.Forms.MenuItem menuItem6;
        private System.Windows.Forms.DataGridTableStyle dataGridTableStyle1;
        private System.Windows.Forms.DataGridTextBoxColumn
            dataGridTextBoxColumn1;
        private System.Windows.Forms.DataGridTableStyle dataGridTableStyle2;
        private System.Windows.Forms.DataGridTextBoxColumn
            dataGridTextBoxColumn2;
        private System.Windows.Forms.DataGridTextBoxColumn
            dataGridTextBoxColumn3;

        /// <summary>
        /// Required designer variable.
        /// </summary>
        private System.ComponentModel.Container components = null;

        public frmMain()
        {
            //
            // Required for Windows Form Designer support
            //
            InitializeComponent();
```

This next line is responsible for binding the `DataGrid` to the `Contacts` table in our global `DataSet` instance. We've configured the `DataGrid` to neatly display all of the columns that we want displayed, as well as the child columns in the parent-child relationship.

```
    //
    // TODO: Add any constructor code after InitializeComponent call
    //
    dgContacts.DataSource = GlobalData.contactsData.Tables["Contacts"];
    dgContacts.Refresh();
}

/// <summary>
/// Clean up any resources being used.
/// </summary>
protected override void Dispose( bool disposing )
{
  if( disposing )
  {
    if (components != null)
    {
      components.Dispose();
    }
  }
  base.Dispose( disposing );
}
```

To keep this listing under 10 pages, we decided to snip out all of the control-initialization code that normally hides in the "Windows Form Designer generated code" region. This code is available in the code download for this chapter, available at the Wrox web site (www.wrox.com).

```
#region Windows Form Designer generated code
// cut out for clarity...
#endregion

/// <summary>
/// The main entry point for the application.
/// </summary>
 [STAThread]
static void Main()
{
  Application.Run(new frmMain());
}
```

Here we see some of the disk access that we learned about earlier in the chapter. These two menu items are responsible for loading and saving the in-memory cache of data to an XML file that resides in our main project directory, called `contacts.xml`.

```
private void menuItem2_Click(object sender, System.EventArgs e)
{
  GlobalData.contactsData.ReadXml(@"..\..\contacts.xml");
  dgContacts.Refresh();
}
```

```
  // the "Accept Changes" button on the main form
  private void button1_Click(object sender, System.EventArgs e)
  {
    GlobalData.contactsData.AcceptChanges();
  }

  private void button2_Click(object sender, System.EventArgs e)
  {
    GlobalData.contactsData.RejectChanges();
    dgContacts.Refresh();
  }
```

This next event handler responds to the **Add Contact** menu item. It creates an instance of the contact information form, displays it, and if the user clicked **OK**, saves that contact into the in-memory database. The `DataGrid` will immediately reflect those changes.

```
  private void menuItem6_Click(object sender, System.EventArgs e)
  {
    using (frmContact contactForm = new frmContact())
    {
      if (contactForm.ShowDialog() == DialogResult.OK)
      {
        DataTable contacts = GlobalData.contactsData.Tables["Contacts"];
        DataRow newContact = contacts.NewRow();
        newContact["ContactName"] = contactForm.ContactName;
        contacts.Rows.Add( newContact );
        dgContacts.Refresh();
      }
    }
  }
```

This event handler responds to the **Add Contact Message** menu item. Typically this would be to take note of a conversation with the contact. It creates an instance of the message logging form, displays it, and if the user clicked **OK**, it will save that new message to the `ContactMessages` child table. The `DataGrid` immediately reflects the changes (if they are visible to the user at the time):

```
  private void menuItem3_Click(object sender, System.EventArgs e)
  {
    GlobalData.contactsData.WriteXml(@"..\..\contacts.xml");
  }

  private void menuItem7_Click(object sender, System.EventArgs e)
  {
    if (GlobalData.contactsData.Tables["Contacts"].Rows.Count == 0)
      return;

    using (frmMessageLog messageLog = new frmMessageLog())
    {
      if (messageLog.ShowDialog() == DialogResult.OK)
      {
        // add contact message log.
        DataRow newMessage =
```

```
                GlobalData.contactsData.Tables["ContactMessages"].NewRow();
        newMessage["Message"] = messageLog.MessageText;
        newMessage["MessageDate"] = messageLog.MessageDate;
        newMessage["ContactId"] = messageLog.ContactId;
        GlobalData.contactsData.Tables["ContactMessages"].Rows.Add(
            newMessage );
        dgContacts.Refresh();
      }
    }
  }

  private void frmMain_Load(object sender, System.EventArgs e)
  {

  }
 }
}
```

Now that we've taken a look at the main form, which is pretty straightforward, we can take a look at the other forms. We'll strip out the redundant code and display that you would find in any Windows Form and just show you the pertinent event handlers.

First we'll look at the code behind the frmContact form:

```
    private void btnOk_Click(object sender, System.EventArgs e)
    {
      this.Close();
    }

    private void btnCancel_Click(object sender, System.EventArgs e)
    {
      this.Close();
    }
```

The above two event handlers are pretty simple. If you click either the OK or the Cancel button, the form closes. Typically, if there were additional form validation to be done, it would take place there. This next little piece of code may not have much to do with ADO.NET or DataSets, but I've found that it is an invaluable best practice when working with Windows Forms. I like to encapsulate the controls that I am working with on the form in properties that hide the actual implementation. This allows me to change the way in which a form queries a user for a piece of data without having to break all other code that depends on that form. If I make a change, I just have to make a change to the property that encapsulates the control and not all of the forms that depend on it. Granted, in a small application this extra little bit of effort may seem like a waste of time – but in larger applications, it becomes an incredibly handy tool.

```
    // Its always a good idea to abstract the controls and not allow other
    // portions of the program to access them directly.
    public string ContactName
    {
      get
      {
```

```
          return txtContactName.Text;
      }
      set
      {
        txtContactName.Text = value;
      }
    }
  }
}
```

Finally, we'll take a look at the form that performs queries for a new contact message log. That code can be found in frmMessageLog.cs. The important bits are included below:

```
public frmMessageLog()
{
  //
  // Required for Windows Form Designer support
  //
  InitializeComponent();

  //
  // TODO: Add any constructor code after InitializeComponent call
  //
  cboContact.DataSource = GlobalData.contactsData.Tables["Contacts"];
  cboContact.DisplayMember = "ContactName";
  cboContact.ValueMember = "ContactId";
}
```

The above is the default constructor for the frmMessageLog form class. It uses data binding to populate a drop-down list ComboBox with a list of all of the contacts in our global data. This ComboBox is used to select which contact was the subject of the message/conversation being logged.

We also encapsulated this form's controls in the form of public properties. I've included the code for those below:

```
public DateTime MessageDate
{
  get {
    return dtpMessageDate.Value;
  }
  set {
    dtpMessageDate.Value = value;
  }
}

public string MessageText
{
  get
  {
    return txtMessage.Text;
  }
```

```
    set {
      txtMessage.Text = value;
    }
  }

  public int ContactId
  {
    get {
      if (cboContact.SelectedIndex > -1 && cboContact.Items.Count > 0)
        return (int)cboContact.SelectedValue;
      else
        return -1;
    }
  }
}
```

Well, now that we've seen most of the code that drives this little application, let's take a look at a couple of screenshots of it in action. This first screenshot shows the application after I've drilled down onto the list of messages for John Q Customer. To get to this, I added John Q Customer as a Contact (from the Contact menu), and then added three Message Logs (again from the Contact menu) with the data you see below. Also note that if you load contacts twice in a row, the program will break (this is a code sample, not a commercial app!). Binding to a DataGrid took an enormous amount of user interface coding and work out of our hands. It automatically handles and provides users the ability to navigate through parent-child relationships in a tree-like fashion.

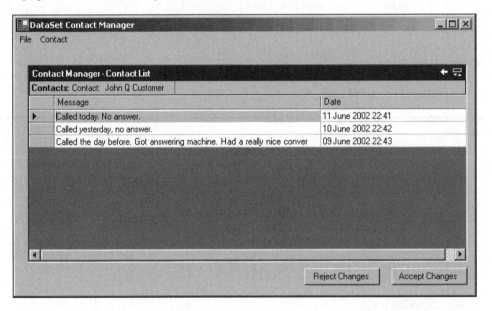

Here's a look at the contact management software while looking at the top-level list of contacts within the DataGrid. Note that we have added two new Contacts compared with the previous screen shot. As you can see, the grid knows that there are child rows and automatically provides a "+" symbol next to each one to allow the user to expand the list of children to get a view like the previous one.

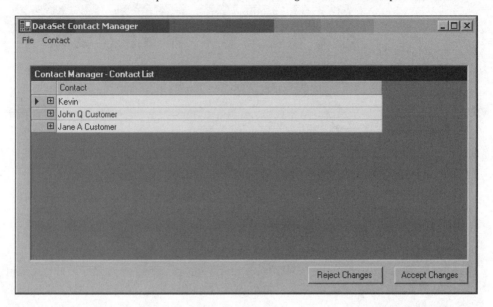

Our little contact manager application isn't exactly an example of a real-world, robust Windows Forms application. However, it does demonstrate the usefulness and versatility of the DataSet. We can use it to store related, hierarchical, table-style data in memory with very little overhead and extra programming work. The DataSet is also easy to bind to both Windows and ASP.NET Forms controls.

Summary

This chapter has been packed full of useful information on the DataSet. We've discussed the hierarchy of the "innards" of the DataSet, including DataTables, DataColumns, and DataRows. We delved even further and took a look at keys, constraints, and even how to relate multiple tables together within the same DataSet. Finally, we started to round out the discussion with some information on how to get data in and out of the DataSet and even looked at an example of merging the data for two varied DataSets into one.

This chapter should have given you a really good look at how the DataSet works, what it is composed of, and how to use it practically to solve your problems. This chapter is also a preparation for the next, where we'll get into some more advanced topics and discuss some very powerful features of the DataSet that we didn't cover here.

3

Strongly Typed DataSets

In our last chapter we learned about DataSets and where they fit within the ADO.NET hierarchy. We learned about tables, rows, columns, keys, constraints, relations, and more. This chapter continues on from the solid knowledge of DataSets given in Chapter 2, to discuss a specialized version of the DataSet, the (strongly) typed DataSet. We'll take a look at a definition of the DataSet, and then move on to a discussion of how XML Schemas relate to DataSets, and how typed DataSets make use of them. Finally, we'll take a look at how to annotate DataSet Schemas (and why we would want to). At the end of the chapter we'll wrap up our discussion by re-writing the previous chapter's contact manager sample using typed DataSets.

This chapter relies heavily on the reader having previous knowledge of XML. A little bit of knowledge of XML Schemas and/or DTDs is helpful, but not necessary to get the main points of the chapter. If you need a good resource for generic XML reference and information, check out Wrox's *Professional XML* (ISBN: 1-86100-505-9) or better yet, *Professional XML for .NET Developers* (ISBN: 1-86100-531-8). Another book that might prove very useful as a companion resource to this chapter is *Professional XML Schemas* (ISBN: 1-86100-547-4), also published by Wrox Press.

What is a Typed DataSet?

As we saw in the previous chapter, the DataSet provides a generic way for accessing and manipulating disconnected data in memory. However, it doesn't come with any way of enforcing strongly-typed member access. Any time you retrieve the value of a column, you retrieve that value as type Object. One way to enforce strongly-typed member access on a DataSet is to create a new class that inherits from the DataSet, and provides properties and methods as *wrappers* to the standard Object-based accessors. Not only does this provide a way to enforce type-safe access to various column values, but it also allows you to access tables and columns directly by name, rather than by supplying string-based collection indices. This has the added benefit of providing member-listing information to the IntelliSense technology that allows you to get a design-time pop-up window of properties and methods.

This is all good, but we still haven't finished explaining *why* you would want to use a typed DataSet. We've already mentioned that it allows for type-safe data access and access to tables and columns by name. If you'll recall from the previous chapter, in our samples we had to dynamically build the data structure (or schema) each and every time we start the application. With the typed DataSet, the schema (including tables, relationships, columns, and much more) is all pre-built into the derived class itself. That means that once you've built your typed DataSet at design time, you don't need to do anything at run time to build the data structure.

Another, and slightly more subtle, benefit of the use of typed DataSets is that they provide a way to standardize and enforce data structures. For example, if an application architect wants to make sure that every time a certain piece of data is manipulated, it is done with specific data types and in a specific data structure, that architect can simply create a typed DataSet and indicate that the programmers on the team have to use that typed DataSet for all access to that data.

The use of typed DataSets also gives us more readable, clear, and understandable code. With all of the members of a typed DataSet being accessed as actual members (rather than collection indices), the compiler will actually make type mis-match checks for us at compile time, rather than throwing exceptions at run time when a row value is used improperly.

DataSet Schemas (XSD)

XML is a hierarchical organization of data, which is grouped into tags. The beauty of XML is that it is easy to read and understand for both humans and programs. An XML is document is made up of tags structured in a tree format, with elements and sub-elements all belonging to a single root element. An element can contain other elements or be empty (though no element can contain the root element). Elements can have attributes, which can be used to put constraints, names, and other qualifiers pertaining to the XML document in the data.

The data structure for DataSets and typed DataSets alike can be represented by an **XML Schema Definition (XSD)**. This is an XML-based standard for describing hierarchical data structures in a standardized and generic way. XSD is a standard created by the World-Wide Web Consortium (W3C) and has been adopted as the method for determining the data structure for the DataSet class (and thus all classes that inherit from it). Microsoft was part of the team that originally defined the XSD standard. You can find the most current reference for this standard on the Web at: http://www.w3.org/XML/Schema.

We won't be going into a tremendous amount of detail on all of the various definitions and details of XSD itself. Instead, we'll learn about some of the more relevant aspects of XSD while we go through other topics in this chapter. For more information on XSD and using XML Schemas in your applications, we suggest you take a look at *Professional XML Schemas* (ISBN: 1-86100-547-4) from Wrox Press.

Building Schemas

Each element of a `DataSet` data structure can be represented by a corresponding section of XML in an XSD schema. XSD can represent tables, columns, relationships, keys, and constraints. We've already seen how to programmatically build a data structure into our `DataSet`. What we didn't mention is that as we do that, we are also modifying the `DataSet`'s schema. We can examine the schema (XSD) of the `DataSet` at any time programmatically by asking for it with a method.

Rather than bog you down with an XSD reference at this point, we'll instead take a look at a data structure we built in the last chapter. Then, we'll take a look at what that data structure looks like in the form of an XML Schema.

For this example, we're just going to copy the `ManualData` directory from the Chapter 2 code to the Chapter 3 code. We'll re-list the `DataMain.cs` file and highlight the change we've made to create a text file containing the `DataSet` schema:

```csharp
using System;
using System.Data;

namespace ManualData
{
  /// <summary>
  /// DataMain Class
  /// Demonstrates manually creating a DataTable, DataColumns, and DataRows
  /// </summary>
  class DataMain
  {
    /// <summary>
    /// The main entry point for the application.
    /// </summary>
    [STAThread]
    static void Main(string[] args)
    {
      DataSet ds = new DataSet();
      DataTable quotes = new DataTable("Quotes");
      DataColumn symbol = new DataColumn("Symbol");
      symbol.DataType = typeof(string);
      symbol.MaxLength = 4;
      DataColumn description = new DataColumn("Description");
      description.DataType = typeof(string);
      description.MaxLength = 50;
      quotes.Columns.Add( symbol );
      quotes.Columns.Add( description );
      ds.Tables.Add( quotes );
```

```
            // Now add some data to the table.
            DataRow newQuote = quotes.NewRow();
            newQuote["Symbol"] = "MSFT";
            newQuote["Description"] = "Microsoft Corporation";
            quotes.Rows.Add( newQuote );

            // Now display it to make sure the data is in the table.
            Console.WriteLine("Stock Quote");
            Console.WriteLine("Symbol: {0}, Description: {1}",
                quotes.Rows[0]["Symbol"].ToString(),
                quotes.Rows[0]["Description"].ToString());

            // Added the following to examine the schema (XSD) of the DataSet.
            ds.WriteXmlSchema(@"..\..\StockQuote.xsd");
            ds.WriteXml(@"..\..\StockQuote.xml");
        }
    }
}
```

The `WriteXmlSchema` method creates a text file that contains the XML Schema for the `DataSet`. Let's take a look at the output produced in `StockQuote.xsd`, which you can now find in the project directory for this example:

```
<?xml version="1.0" standalone="yes"?>
<xs:schema id="NewDataSet" xmlns="" xmlns:xs="http://www.w3.org/2001/XMLSchema"
xmlns:msdata="urn:schemas-microsoft-com:xml-msdata">
  <xs:element name="NewDataSet" msdata:IsDataSet="true" msdata:Locale="en-
      GB">
    <xs:complexType>
      <xs:choice maxOccurs="unbounded">
        <xs:element name="Quotes">
          <xs:complexType>
            <xs:sequence>
              <xs:element name="Symbol" minOccurs="0">
                <xs:simpleType>
                  <xs:restriction base="xs:string">
                    <xs:maxLength value="4" />
                  </xs:restriction>
                </xs:simpleType>
              </xs:element>
              <xs:element name="Description" minOccurs="0">
                <xs:simpleType>
                  <xs:restriction base="xs:string">
                    <xs:maxLength value="50" />
                  </xs:restriction>
                </xs:simpleType>
              </xs:element>
            </xs:sequence>
          </xs:complexType>
        </xs:element>
      </xs:choice>
    </xs:complexType>
  </xs:element>
</xs:schema>
```

The document may look intimidating to some of you. For those of you used to working with XML or even older XML **Document Type Definitions (DTDs)** it should be a little easier to read.

In the example above, the outermost element shows us that the document contains a schema. The root element for this schema is called NewDataSet. That is essentially the type definition for the root node of the XML representation of our DataSet's data. That root element contains a sub-element called Quotes. That sub-element then contains two more sub-elements, Symbol and Description. Again, for more information on XML and XSD, consult the W3C standards document or a book on the subject.

The above schema is essentially the type definition for all of the data that can be contained by that DataSet. When represented in XML, the data we created in the sample program looks like this:

```
<?xml version="1.0" standalone="yes"?>
<NewDataSet>
  <Quotes>
    <Symbol>MSFT</Symbol>
    <Description>Microsoft Corporation</Description>
  </Quotes>
</NewDataSet>
```

Before we move on any further, we'll go over the bare minimum of some of the components of a standard XML Schema.

element

The <element> element is a type definition for an element that will occur in the **instance document**. An instance document is the XML *data* that corresponds to the XML *schema*. Just as an object variable is considered an instance of a class, the XML data itself is considered to be an instance of the schema to which it corresponds. We won't go into too much detail on the various ways in which this element can be used, but the following is an excerpt from Microsoft's .NET Framework Reference guide on the syntax for this element:

```
<element
  abstract = Boolean : false
  block = (#all | List of (extension | restriction | substitution))
  default = string
  final = (#all | List of (extension | restriction))
  fixed = string
  form = (qualified | unqualified)
  id = ID
  maxOccurs = (nonNegativeInteger | unbounded) : 1
  minOccurs = nonNegativeInteger : 1
  name = NCName
  nillable = Boolean : false
  ref = QName
  substitutionGroup = QName
  type = QName
  {any attributes with non-schema Namespace}...>
Content: (annotation?, ((simpleType | complexType)?, (unique | key |
keyref)*))
</element>
```

The `default` attribute allows you to specify the default value of an element if it is defined as a simple type. The `fixed` attribute prevents the use of the `default` attribute (the reverse is also true) and indicates the fixed, unchangeable value of the element if it is a simple element.

The `mixed` attribute for all applicable XSD elements indicates whether or not character data may appear between child elements of a complex type. The default for this value is `false`. If a `DataSet` is loading data from an XML document with mixed data and the schema does not allow it, all of that character data will be stripped out when loaded into the `DataSet`.

simpleType

A `simpleType` is an element that can contain attributes and cannot contain any elements. The type of the data within the simple type must be a derivation of one of the basic (also referred to as primitive) data types supported by XSD.

Primitive XML Data Types

The following is a list of the basic XML data types supported by XML Schemas:

Data Type	Description
anyURI	Represents a URI string as defined by RFC 2396. An `anyURI` can be an absolute or relative path.
base64Binary	Represents base-64 encoded binary data.
boolean	Standard Boolean true/false data type.
date	Represents a date.
dateTime	Represents a specific point in time.
decimal	Represents numbers with arbitrary, configurable precision.
double	Represents double-precision floating-point numbers (64-bit).
duration	Represents a time span in the format `PnYnMnDTnHnMnS` where `nY` is the number of years, `nM` is the number of months, `nD` is the number of days, `nH` is the number of hours, `nM` is the number of minutes, and `nS` is the number of seconds. The duration must always begin with the `P` and take the above listed format.
float	Represents single-precision floating-point numbers (32-bit).
gDay	Represents a specific day of a month on the Gregorian calendar.
gMonthDay	Represents a specific date of a specific month on the Gregorian calendar.
gYear	Represents a Gregorian year.
gYearMonth	Represents a specific month and year within the Gregorian calendar.
hexBinary	Represents hex-encoded binary data.

Data Type	Description
NOTATION	Represents a NOTATION attribute type, which is a set of Qnames.
QName	Represents a qualified name. A qualified name is a namespace URI prefix, followed by a colon, and then followed by a local name.
string	The standard character string type.
time	Represents a time of day (without regard to date).

complexType

The complexType element is a type definition element for elements that can contain nested elements as well as attributes. For example, the following is an instance of a complex type as far as XML Schema is concerned:

```
<customer id="2212101">
  <name>John Doe</name>
  <rank>1</rank>
</customer>
```

Actually, to be entirely accurate, the customer element is a complexType and the name and rank elements are both simpleTypes. The following is the excerpt from Microsoft's Reference guide on the syntax of complexType:

```
<complexType
  abstract = Boolean : false
  block = (#all | List of (extension | restriction))
  final = (#all | List of (extension | restriction))
  id = ID
  mixed = Boolean : false
  name = NCName
  {any attributes with non-schema Namespace…}>
Content: (annotation?, (simpleContent | complexContent | ((group | all |
choice | sequence)?, ((attribute | attributeGroup)*, anyAttribute?))))
</complexType>
```

As with most XSD elements, the abstract attribute functions the same way as the abstract keyword might function on a C# class definition. If this value is true, then the instance document (XML DOM) cannot contain that element directly, but must instead use elements that derive from the abstract element.

Inferring Schemas

In the last example, we looked at manually building the data structure of a DataSet and then using that to generate an XML Schema. However, there is another way to generate the XML Schema called schema **inference**. This is basically a set of rules that are used to analyze a set of data (usually found in an XML instance document) and use that data to *guess* or *infer* what the data structure should be. This process is fairly useful, but is not always 100% accurate and sometimes the results may not be exactly what you want them to be.

Oftentimes, when trying to build a schema for a `DataSet`, programmers will *infer* a schema from the data they would like to work with, and then make minor tweaks and changes to the inferred schema to make it a perfect fit to the expected data. In general, schema inference should only be considered a back-up tool, or a starting point. Programmers will often infer a schema from a sample of their data to look at what a schema for it might look like. Generally it is preferred to explicitly specify the XSD for a given typed `DataSet` rather than infer.

Before we take a look at a sample application that infers an XML schema from pre-existing data, let's cover the rules that the `DataSet` follows to infer a schema from XML instance data.

Inference Rules

The following is a list of the rules that the `DataSet` uses to infer tables, columns, relations, and element text from an existing XML document. This is not only important to know to help you determine what your result will be if you infer a schema, but it also helps understand more fully the relationship between the `DataSet` hierarchy and the hierarchy of data in an XML document. When the data structure of a `DataSet` is inferred, it identifies XML structures that represent tables, columns, and relationships, in that order.

Inferring Tables

The following is a list of XML structures that will result in the inference of a `DataTable`:

Elements with Attributes

A set of repeating elements that contain attributes will be inferred as a `DataTable`. For example, take a look at the following example:

```
<DocumentElement>
  <Customer id="1001" name="Joe"/>
  <Customer id="1002" name="John"/>
</DocumentElement>
```

The above XML will result in a `DataTable` named `Customer` with two columns, `id` and `name`.

Elements with Child Elements

Another XML structure that will result in a table being created in the `DataSet` is a repeating set of elements that contain other child elements. An element that contains elements is also considered a `complexType`. Consider the following XML:

```
<DocumentElement>
  <Customer>
    <id>1001</id>
    <name>Joe</name>
  </Customer>
  <Customer>
    <id>1002</id>
    <name>John</name>
  </Customer>
<DocumentElement>
```

Because the `Customer` element is a repeated element, and it contains child elements `<id>` and `<name>`, a table will be created. This table will be called `Customer`, with two columns, `id` and `name`. The `DataSet` resulting will be identical to the first example we looked at.

Repeating Simple Elements

The last way to infer a table is to identify a pattern of repeating simple elements that contain plain text. Consider the following XML:

```
<DocumentElement>
  <Customer>Joe 1001</Customer>
  <Customer>John 1002</Customer>
</DocumentElement>
```

This will result in a table being created called `Customer`. The column created will be called `Customer_Text`.

Inferring Columns

`DataColumns` are inferred after all of the structures in the XML document representing tables have been identified. The following is a list of the XML structures that will be identified and used to create columns within tables:

Attributes

As we said, an element with attributes will be considered a table. The attributes on that element will then become columns. The following XML will create a table with two columns:

```
<DocumentElement>
  <Table column1="value1" column2="value2"/>
</DocumentElement>
```

Elements without Attributes or Child Elements

If an element has no child elements, or has no attributes, it will be inferred as a column. The following XML illustrates attributeless, child elements being inferred as columns:

```
<DocumentElement>
  <Table>
    <Column1>Value1</Column1>
    <Column2>Value2</Column2>
  </Table>
</DocumentElement>
```

This will infer a table called `Table`, and two columns: `Column1` and `Column2`.

Limitations of Inference

One of the biggest problems with Schema Inference is that it is very possible that two different instance documents based on the same data structure could possibly result in two very different schemas. For example, if there is only one row of data within a non-nested table, then by the rules of inference, that single column in the single row will end up being considered a table rather than a column. For instance:

```
<DocumentElement>
  <Book>Professional ASP.NET 1.0</Book>
</DocumentElement>
```

Because `Book` is a single child element of the `DocumentElement` element, the inference rules dictate that `DocumentElement` become a table, while `Book` is listed as a column. Unfortunately, that may not be the behavior you were looking for, especially if you planned on having multiple books:

```
<DocumentElement>
  <Book>Professional ASP.NET 1.0</Book>
  <Book>Professional ADO.NET</Book>
</DocumentElement>
```

Now we end up with a table called `Book` (because `Book` is a repeating element) with a column called `Book_Text` to handle the inner text of the element itself. What this means is that you could possibly break your code simply by having one less row of data in your XML document.

The other main limitation of schema inference is that there is no data type conversion. All columns that are inferred are inferred as unlimited-length strings with no constraints or boundaries. This is more than likely not what your application will end up needing. After all – why enjoy the type-safe benefits of a typed `DataSet` if all of the types are unrestrictive strings?

To get around these problems, many programmers will use inference to get a good "guess" at what the schema should look like for a particular set of data (either using their own tools or the XSD tool to infer schema information from a valid document) and then tweak the schema themselves to provide integers, range requirements, and nullability requirements.

Inference Sample

We'll take a quick look at what inference looks like by demonstrating a common use for schema inference: obtaining a "nearly perfect" schema from an existing XML document. As we said, there are some limitations to schema inference, but inferring a schema from existing data is also an extremely useful tool that should not be underestimated.

For example, consider the following XML document:

```
<MyDataSet>
  <StockItem>
    <ProductId>11101</ProductId>
    <Description>A Product</Description>
    <Price>21.99</Price>
    <QtyOnHand>12</QtyOnHand>
    <QtyInWareHouse>48</QtyInWareHouse>
  </StockItem>
  <StockItem>
    <ProductId>11021</ProductId>
    <Description>Another Product</Description>
    <Price>18.95</Price>
    <QtyOnHand>8</QtyOnHand>
```

```
    <QtyInWareHouse>12</QtyInWareHouse>
  </StockItem>
</MyDataSet>
```

This XML document is saved as `SourceDocument.xml` in a folder, `Inference`, inside the `FTrackADONET\Chapter03` directory.

It looks pretty straightforward. If we were to put this in a `DataSet`, we would probably want a single table called `StockItem` with the columns `ProductId`, `Description`, `Price`, `QtyOnHand`, and `QtyInWareHouse`.

Let's take a look at what an inferred schema for this data might look like. To do that, we'll drop to a Visual Studio .NET command prompt (so we know we have the tools in our path) and type the following:

So now we actually have an XSD file that should hopefully represent the data structure that we're trying to create. Let's take a look at this `SourceDocument.xsd` file:

```xml
<?xml version="1.0" encoding="utf-8"?>
<xs:schema id="MyDataSet" xmlns=""
    xmlns:xs="http://www.w3.org/2001/XMLSchema" xmlns:msdata="urn:schemas-
    microsoft-com:xml-msdata">
  <xs:element name="MyDataSet" msdata:IsDataSet="true"
     msdata:Locale="en-GB">
    <xs:complexType>
      <xs:choice maxOccurs="unbounded">
        <xs:element name="StockItem">
          <xs:complexType>
            <xs:sequence>
              <xs:element name="ProductId" type="xs:string" minOccurs="0" />
              <xs:element name="Description" type="xs:string"
                  minOccurs="0" />
              <xs:element name="Price" type="xs:string" minOccurs="0" />
              <xs:element name="QtyOnHand" type="xs:string" minOccurs="0" />
              <xs:element name="QtyInWareHouse" type="xs:string"
                  minOccurs="0" />
            </xs:sequence>
          </xs:complexType>
        </xs:element>
      </xs:choice>
    </xs:complexType>
  </xs:element>
</xs:schema>
```

It looks pretty good, and it looks like it will do what we want, but there are a few problems. The first and most obvious is that all of our data types are string, and none of the elements (columns) are required. We want a schema that has strong type definitions, as well as requiring that every single stock item have a product ID. Just to make it even more interesting, we also want to make sure that the product ID is always exactly seven characters long.

To make the changes we want to make, we'll open up the SourceDocument.xsd file in FTrackADONET\Chapter03\Inference inside Visual Studio .NET. The main reason for this is that VS .NET knows exactly how to modify XSD and can give you IntelliSense and interactive help while building the schema.

To restrict a specific data type to do something like only allowing exactly seven characters, we need to derive a new simpleType based on the original basic type of string. So, let's look at the opened file in VS .NET. First we need to change the type of ProductId from string to ProductIdType. Simply type ProductIdType in over the top of string in your table, in the ProductId row. So your screen should now look like this:

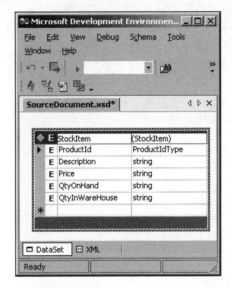

Now, we create the simpleType. Simply right-click anywhere on the design page and a menu will appear. Select Add and then New simpleType. Another table should now appear on the design page.

Rename **simpleType1** to `ProductIdType` and right-click on **Add**. There will only be one choice available, **New facet**. Select this.

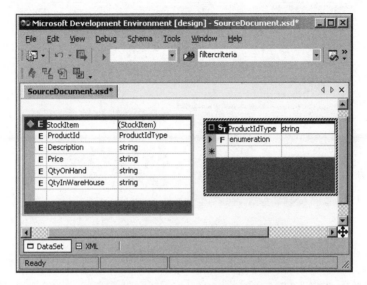

Enumeration is one of a series of options. Click on it, and a drop-down box should show others. Select length, and under the string column enter 7. In the **Properties** window, set the **fixed** property to **true**.

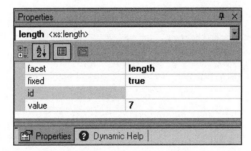

Now, for the other elements, change **Price** to **float**, and **QtyOnHand** and **QtyInWareHouse** to **nonNegativeInteger**.

This is what it looks like in the Visual Studio .NET designer after we've made our schema changes:

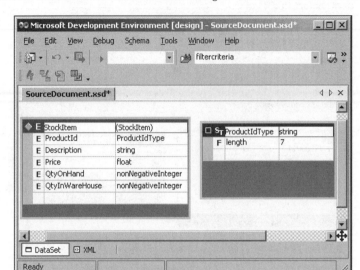

You can see that we have a new `simpleType` called `ProductIdType`. There is a facet (essentially a rule or constraint for a particular type in the schema) attached to that type that says we must have exactly seven characters in any instance data of that type. And now let's see what the XML view of the schema looks like:

```xml
<?xml version="1.0" encoding="utf-8" ?>
<xs:schema id="MyDataSet" xmlns=""
    xmlns:xs="http://www.w3.org/2001/XMLSchema"
    xmlns:msdata="urn:schemas-microsoft-com:xml-msdata">
  <xs:element name="MyDataSet" msdata:IsDataSet="true">
    <xs:complexType>
      <xs:choice maxOccurs="unbounded">
        <xs:element name="StockItem">
          <xs:complexType>
            <xs:sequence>
              <xs:element name="ProductId" type="ProductIdType"
                  minOccurs="1" />
              <xs:element name="Description" type="xs:string"
                  minOccurs="0" />
              <xs:element name="Price" type="xs:float" minOccurs="0" />
              <xs:element name="QtyOnHand" type="xs:nonNegativeInteger"
                  minOccurs="0" />
              <xs:element name="QtyInWareHouse"
                  type="xs:nonNegativeInteger" minOccurs="0" />
            </xs:sequence>
          </xs:complexType>
        </xs:element>
      </xs:choice>
    </xs:complexType>
  </xs:element>
  <xs:simpleType name="ProductIdType">
```

```
      <xs:restriction base="string">
        <xs:length fixed="true" value="7"></xs:length>
      </xs:restriction>
    </xs:simpleType>
  </xs:schema>
```

You can see that what we've essentially done here is create a new type of data called `ProductIdType`. All Product IDs should then be of that data type, and should all follow the same restrictions as all other Product IDs. In our case, the `ProductIdType` is a fixed, 7-character long string. There is an enormous amount of configurability in using XML schemas to fine-tune the way in which you deal with data in a `DataSet`. This is just the tip of the iceberg. If you really want to see the other kinds of advanced things you can do with XML Schemas, I definitely suggest you read *Professional XML Schemas* (ISBN: 1-86100-547-4) published by Wrox Press.

Building Typed DataSets

So far we've taken a quick look at the fact that `DataSet` data structures can be represented as XML Schema. We also took a brief look at how XML Schemas can be built, as well as how they can be inferred from existing XML data.

So, why exactly is all this important? This chapter is about building strongly-typed `DataSets` and how they can be used easily and practically. In order to build a strongly-typed `DataSet`, whichever method you plan on using to build your typed `DataSets` will need to know what data structure is required. This data structure is obtained from an XML Schema Definition (XSD).

There are two main ways to build a typed `DataSet`: using Visual Studio .NET or using a command-line tool called `XSD`.

Using Visual Studio .NET

In our previous example involving editing the XML Schema Definition file (XSD) within Visual Studio .NET, we took advantage of the fact that VS.NET knows exactly how to deal with XSD files. There are many types of files that Visual Studio .NET knows how to edit and validate, including XSD files designed to create typed `DataSets`.

Visual Studio .NET has various built-in templates for creating specific types of classes, controls, and various other projects. To demonstrate creating a `DataSet` within Visual Studio .NET, we'll create a new C# **Console Application** called `TypedDataSet1`. This project can be found in the code download, in the `FTrackADONET\Chapter03\TypedDataSet1` folder. To add a new typed `DataSet` to this project, right-click the project and click **Add** and then choose **Add Class**. Select the `DataSet` template from the **Add new Item** dialog and give it an appropriate name (we chose `Books` for ours).

You should be presented with a blank XML Schema designer screen. Open up the **Toolbox** tray and drag an **Element** from the toolbox onto the designer surface. We call our element `WroxBooks` and create two attributes on that element called `ISBN` and `Description`. It should look very similar to the following screenshot:

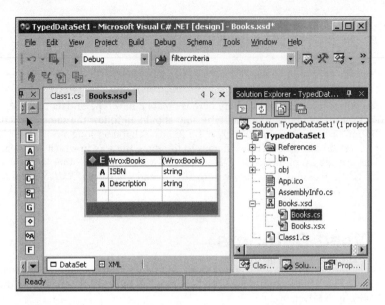

When you build this project, you will have a class called Books that will inherit from the standard DataSet class. You will be able to access the ISBN and Description columns by name, rather than by indexer or string properties. Not only that, but they will be provided as string properties rather than properties that return data of type Object.

You'll notice that at the bottom of the visual designer tool that there are two tabs, one called DataSet and one called XML. This allows you to switch back and forth between the "diagram" view of the DataSet and the view of the actual XSD. If you click over to view the XML source for the DataSet's schema, it will look as follows:

```xml
<?xml version="1.0" encoding="utf-8" ?>
<xs:schema id="Books" targetNamespace="http://tempuri.org/Books.xsd"
    elementFormDefault="qualified" attributeFormDefault="qualified"
    xmlns="http://tempuri.org/Books.xsd"
    xmlns:mstns="http://tempuri.org/Books.xsd"
    xmlns:xs="http://www.w3.org/2001/XMLSchema" xmlns:msdata="urn:schemas-
    microsoft-com:xml-msdata">
  <xs:element name="Books" msdata:IsDataSet="true">
    <xs:complexType>
      <xs:choice maxOccurs="unbounded">
        <xs:element name="WroxBooks">
          <xs:complexType>
            <xs:sequence />
            <xs:attribute name="ISBN" type="xs:string" />
            <xs:attribute name="Description" type="xs:string" />
          </xs:complexType>
        </xs:element>
      </xs:choice>
    </xs:complexType>
  </xs:element>
</xs:schema>
```

If you compare this schema to the schema we inferred at the beginning of the chapter, you'll notice that there are some very visible similarities. If you want to flip back to the reference section on XSD and examine this schema in more detail it might help make things more clear.

Using the XSD Tool

The XSD.exe tool is a multi-purpose utility for dealing with XML Schemas. It allows you to generate classes based on a schema or generate a typed DataSet (it refers to that as a "sub-classed" DataSet). There are several options that you can use so that you can select only a portion of an XML Schema to use to generate the DataSet. Other configurable options include the source-code language to be used (such as VB.NET and C#). It also allows you to generate a schema based on an existing, compiled data type residing in an Assembly. In addition, the XSD utility allows you to automatically infer a schema based on an existing XML document file.

If you type XSD on its own at the command prompt (assuming you're using a command prompt that has XSD in its path; for instance, in our installation this is C:\Program Files\Microsoft Visual Studio .NET\FrameworkSDK\Bin\xsd.exe) you will be presented with a list of all the options available to you. To accomplish essentially the same thing as the previous example that involved Visual Studio.NET, we'll copy the .xsd file we created inside VS .NET to a new XSD directory for testing.

Enter the following command, all on one line, and we will produce a C# class that sub-classes the DataSet class, just like the class created by Visual Studio .NET in the last example:

```
C:\FTrackADONET\Chapter03\XSD>xsd /d C:\FTrackADONET\Chapter03\TypedDataset1\
Books.xsd
```

This command line creates the classes required to create a typed DataSet in the default language (C#), based on the schema contained in the Books.xsd file.

Hello, Typed DataSet

Now that we've taken a look at the mechanics of actually constructing the class that makes up a typed DataSet, let's take a quick look at how we might use one. We'll see more detailed examples of typed DataSets as we get into the support for relations, but for now, it is appropriate to illustrate a simple "Hello World" type example utilizing a typed DataSet.

To follow along with this project, create a new **Console Application** (C#) called TypedDS2. Then, add a new DataSet to the Visual Studio .NET project just as we did earlier in the chapter. Now, create the same DataSet structure as in the above example, making sure that the name of your main element is not the same name as the XSD file (for instance, you cannot have an element named <Books> in a file named Books.xsd because of the rules followed by the class generator, so we have called our element <WroxBooks>).

Build the application once to make sure that the typed DataSet generation is working properly, and to make sure that IntelliSense knows about the new methods and properties on that class. The following is the listing for the main class of this application (HelloMain.cs):

```
using System;

namespace TypedDS2
{
  /// <summary>
  /// Summary description for HelloMain.
  /// </summary>
  class HelloMain
  {
    /// <summary>
    /// The main entry point for the application.
    /// </summary>
     [STAThread]
    static void Main(string[] args)
    {
      Books books = new Books();
      Books.WroxBooksRow newBook;

      newBook = books.WroxBooks.NewWroxBooksRow();
      newBook.ISBN = "186100527X";
      newBook.Description = "Professional ADO.NET";
      books.WroxBooks.AddWroxBooksRow( newBook );

      newBook = books.WroxBooks.NewWroxBooksRow();
      newBook.ISBN = "1861007035";
      newBook.Description = "Professional ASP.NET 1.0";
      books.WroxBooks.AddWroxBooksRow( newBook );

      books.WriteXml(@"..\..\Books.XML");
      Console.WriteLine("Book 1 is {0} (ISBN:{1})",
        books.WroxBooks[0].Description,
        books.WroxBooks[0].ISBN);
    }
  }
}
```

After building and running this "Hello World" type application, we generate an XML file and receive the following console output:

The XML file, which is just an XML representation of the data we put in the DataSet, looks like this:

```
<?xml version="1.0" standalone="yes"?>
<Books xmlns="http://tempuri.org/Books.xsd">
  <WroxBooks d2p1:ISBN="186100527X" d2p1:Description="Professional ADO.NET"
      xmlns:d2p1="http://tempuri.org/Books.xsd" />
  <WroxBooks d2p1:ISBN="1861007035" d2p1:Description="Professional ASP.NET
      1.0" xmlns:d2p1="http://tempuri.org/Books.xsd" />
</Books>
```

With the addition of a couple of namespace qualifiers on the elements created by the `DataSet`, it is pretty much as we expected and have seen before.

Relational Data Model Support

Now that we've seen some code for creating a simple "Hello World" application that uses the basic functionality of a typed `DataSet`, we can take that one step further and look at how to deal with relational data within the typed `DataSet`. We already know that the `DataSet` itself contains support for relations, constraints, and keys. All of that information for a standard `DataSet` either has to be added at run time by the programmer or has to be inferred from the data itself, which may or may not work properly.

Another one of the large benefits of a typed `DataSet` is that the relations, constraints, and keys can be placed in the source schema, which means that the sub-class for the typed `DataSet` will already know about all of the relations and will actually create type-safe member accessors for dealing with those relations.

We've already seen how data relations are managed in regular `DataSets`, so we'll now go into an example on how the code looks when managing relational data with a typed `DataSet`. To do this, we're going to start with a project called `BookReviews`, which will be a C# **Console Application**.

What we're going to do is create a simple application that deals with relational data in a typed `DataSet`. The first thing we'll do when building our application is create our `DataSet`. Just as we did earlier, right-click the project and click **Add**. Then click **Add Class** and choose the **DataSet** template from the right-hand side of the dialog box. Click over to the XML tab of the editor and put in the following schema information (this XSD file already exists in the code for this project in `FTrackADONET\Chapter03\BookReviews\BookReviewsData.xsd`):

```xml
<?xml version="1.0" standalone="yes" ?>
<xs:schema id="BookReviewsData" xmlns=""
    xmlns:xs="http://www.w3.org/2001/XMLSchema"
    xmlns:msdata="urn:schemas-microsoft-com:xml-msdata">
  <xs:element name="BookReviewsData" msdata:IsDataSet="true">
    <xs:complexType>
      <xs:choice maxOccurs="unbounded">
        <xs:element name="Books">
          <xs:complexType>
            <xs:sequence>
              <xs:element name="ISBN" type="xs:string" />
              <xs:element name="Description" type="xs:string"
                  minOccurs="0" />
            </xs:sequence>
          </xs:complexType>
        </xs:element>
        <xs:element name="Reviews">
          <xs:complexType>
            <xs:sequence>
              <xs:element name="ISBN" type="xs:string" minOccurs="0" />
              <xs:element name="Author" type="xs:string" minOccurs="0" />
              <xs:element name="Rating" type="xs:int" minOccurs="0" />
              <xs:element name="Text" type="xs:string" minOccurs="0" />
```

```
            </xs:sequence>
          </xs:complexType>
        </xs:element>
      </xs:choice>
    </xs:complexType>
    <xs:unique name="Constraint1" msdata:PrimaryKey="true">
      <xs:selector xpath=".//Books" />
      <xs:field xpath="ISBN" />
    </xs:unique>
    <xs:keyref name="BookReviews" refer="Constraint1">
      <xs:selector xpath=".//Reviews" />
      <xs:field xpath="ISBN" />
    </xs:keyref>
  </xs:element>
</xs:schema>
```

This may look a little complex, but if you go through it line by line it should become more clear. If you remember the rules of inference, complex elements with child elements are inferred as tables. So, by looking at this schema, seeing two definitions for complex element types, we know that we're creating two tables: Books and Reviews. The Books table has an ISBN and a Description column, both of type string. The Reviews table has an ISBN (foreign key), an Author, a Rating (integer), and the Text of the review.

Looking at this schema in the design view, we see something like this:

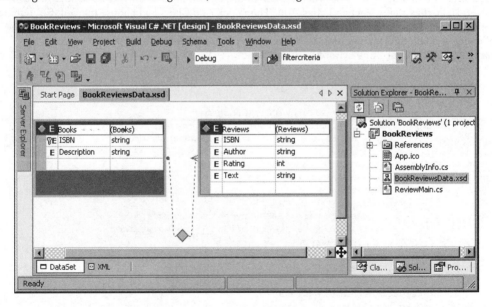

To see the details of the relationship that you can see between the two tables, double-click the diamond icon and you will see the relation detail dialogue shown next:

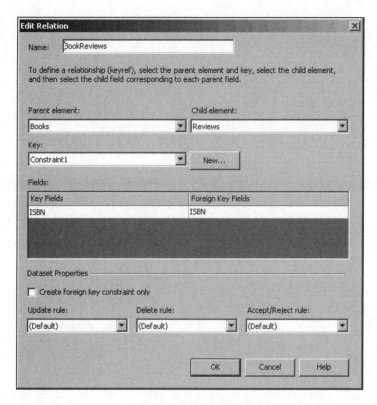

As usual, we build the application once first to make sure that the typed DataSet is working properly and that IntelliSense is going to give us accurate information when we expect it.

Before we look at the code for our main class, let's look at the BookReviews.xml file that we will need to include in our C:\FTrackADONET\Chapter03\BookReviews directory.

```xml
<?xml version="1.0" standalone="yes"?>
<BookReviewsData>
  <Books>
    <ISBN>186100527X</ISBN>
    <Description>Professional ADO.NET</Description>
  </Books>
  <Books>
    <ISBN>1861007035</ISBN>
    <Description>Professional ASP.NET 1.0</Description>
  </Books>
  <Reviews>
    <ISBN>1861007035</ISBN>
    <Author>Joe</Author>
    <Rating>5</Rating>
    <Text>Best book on ASP.NET available!!</Text>
  </Reviews>
  <Reviews>
    <ISBN>186100527X</ISBN>
```

```
      <Author>John Smith from Somewhere, IL</Author>
      <Rating>3</Rating>
      <Text>Pretty good book.</Text>
    </Reviews>
    <Reviews>
      <ISBN>1861007035</ISBN>
      <Author>Jayne Dowe</Author>
      <Rating>4</Rating>
      <Text>I loved this book. A real page-turner!</Text>
    </Reviews>
</BookReviewsData>
```

The following is the code for our main class, the `ReviewMain.cs` file:

```
using System;
using System;
using System.Data;

namespace BookReviews
{
  /// <summary>
  /// Summary description for ReviewMain.
  /// </summary>
  class ReviewMain
  {
    /// <summary>
    /// The main entry point for the application.
    /// </summary>
     [STAThread]
    static void Main(string[] args)
    {
      //
      // TODO: Add code to start application here
      //
```

Rather than instantiate a new `DataSet` class, we're actually creating a new instance of the `BookReviewsData` class, which we created by supplying the appropriate XML Schema.

```
      BookReviewsData bookReviews = new BookReviewsData();
      bookReviews.ReadXml(@"..\..\BookReviews.XML");

      float avgRating;
      int ratingTotal;
      foreach (BookReviewsData.BooksRow book in bookReviews.Books.Rows)
      {
        ratingTotal = 0;
```

Here we're using the `ReviewsRow` class (nested within the `BookReviewsData` class) rather than the generic `DataRow`. This allows us type-safe and pre-named access to the column names. Also, note that instead of using `GetChildRows()` with the name of the relationship we want to invoke, we're actually calling a method created in the `BooksRow` class called `GetReviewsRows()` that knows the name of the relationship to invoke at design time:

```
foreach (BookReviewsData.ReviewsRow review in book.GetReviewsRows())
{
  ratingTotal += review.Rating;
}
```

As usual, the typed `DataSet` allows us to write extremely readable code. The following couple of lines of code compute and print out the average rating value for a given book. Notice that we are using named members such as `Description` and `ISBN` and not using string-indexed array properties that return `Object` type data:

```
avgRating = (float)ratingTotal /
    (float)book.GetReviewsRows().Length;
Console.WriteLine("{0} ({1}) - {2} avg. Rating",
    book.Description, book.ISBN, avgRating);
}
Console.WriteLine("\nType the ISBN of the book you want details on:");
string inputISBN = Console.ReadLine();
```

This is one of my personal favorite features of the typed `DataSet`. If a primary key has been defined on the `DataSet`'s schema, then the tool (be it Visual Studio .NET or `XSD.exe`) that generated the sub-class will actually create a search method that retrieves a sub-classed row of data by searching the data on that primary key. In the example below, we use the auto-generated method `FindByISBN`:

```
BookReviewsData.BooksRow selBook =
    bookReviews.Books.FindByISBN(inputISBN);
if (selBook == null)
{
  Console.WriteLine("That book doesn't exist in the DataSet.");
}
else
{
  foreach (BookReviewsData.ReviewsRow review in
      selBook.GetReviewsRows())
  {
    Console.WriteLine("{0} : {1} stars.\n{2}\n\n",
        review.Author, review.Rating, review.Text);
  }
}
}
}
}
```

So, when we build and run this application, we get the following console output:

Typed DataSet Annotation

By now you should have a good idea of how to use the typed DataSet, and hopefully *why* you would use the typed DataSet to solve many data-related problems. However, in addition to all of the things we have seen that can be done with a typed DataSet, there is more still that we can do.

In our previous example, our schema-generated typed DataSet had tables called Books and Reviews, but the XML elements for a single book and a single review were also called <Books> and <Reviews>. Also, the method used to retrieve the list of reviews for a given book was called GetReviewsRows. When we generated this DataSet, the sub-classes that represented a single row of each table were called ReviewsRow and BooksRow. While these are fairly readable and useful, they can be even more readable and even more useful. Through the use of something called **DataSet schema annotation**, we can control how our custom typed DataSet class is generated at design time. We can control the names of the accessors for the columns, relations, and much more. This next section will take you through some of the things that you can do with annotation.

Aside from the convenience of being able to create meaningfully-named accessors to your data through annotation, annotation also allows you to keep those meaningful names separate from the underlying physical structure of the data itself. This means that you can create a typed DataSet with meaningful, readable names for columns that could be cryptically named things like A1, A2, C3, etc. within the data source that originally supplied the data.

codegen

The codegen namespace prefix within an XML Schema for a typed DataSet allows you to configure how the names of various objects in the DataSet will be generated. The following is a list of the various codegen options for DataSet annotations.

typedName

typedName is an attribute that you can place on any element within the XML Schema that will be converted into an object. The value of this attribute indicates the name of a single instance of that object. For example:

```
<xs:element name="Books" codegen:typedName="Book">
```

Adding this little bit of XML will change the name of the `BooksRow` sub-class created in the previous example from `BooksRow` to simply, `Book`. Notice that the element itself can still retain its original name and data structure, all we're doing is modifying the name used when creating the `DataSet` sub-class.

typedPlural

The `typedPlural` codegen attribute allows us to manually set the name of the collection of objects. So, in our previous example, that would have been the collections called `BooksRows` and `ReviewsRows`. We can change that using a piece of XML that looks like this:

```
<xs:element name="Books" codegen:typedName="Book" typedPlural="Books">
```

This makes things much easier to read when coding, and much more natural because the typed `DataSet` really should be the "human-readable" form of our data, and does not need to retain any confusing, cryptic, or archaic naming conventions established by the data source itself.

typedParent

The `typedParent` codegen attributes allows us to configure the name of the object when it is referred to as the parent in a parent-child relationship. This attribute is usually found in the definition of the `keyref` element that defines the parent-child relationship in the XML Schema. The following is just a single-line piece of such a definition:

```
<xs:keyref name="BookReviews" codegen:typedParent="Book">
```

This indicates that anytime a specific row of type `Review` is instantiated, its parent row will always be examinable via a type-safe accessor property called `Book`.

typedChildren

The `typedChildren` codegen attribute allows us to configure the name of the method that will be used to obtain the list of child rows based on the relationship we have already defined. This means that we can replace the previous example's `GetReviewsRows` method with something more appropriate, such as `Reviews` or `GetReviews`:

```
<xs:keyref name="BookReviews" codegen:typedParent="Book"
codegen:typedChildren="GetReviews">
```

nullValue

The `nullValue` specifies the value that will be retrieved when queried if the actual underlying value is the value `DBNull`. This value is either a replacement value of the same type as the column on which this attribute is placed, or it is one of the following specific attribute values:

- ❏ _throw
  This value indicates that if the value of this column is queried, and the underlying value is `DBnull`, then an exception will be thrown. If nothing is specified for the `nullValue` attribute, this is the default.

❑ _null
This value indicates that a null reference should be returned, or if the data type of the column is a primitive type (like `string`, or `int`) then an exception will be thrown.

❑ _empty
For strings this will return the `String.Empty` constant, otherwise it will return an object created by an empty constructor. Again, if a primitive type is encountered (other than a string), then an exception will be thrown.

The msdata Namespace

The `msdata` namespace prefix allows for even more configuration and annotation of the `DataSet`. It allows you to manipulate the names and behaviors of constraints, indicate the updating and deleting rules for relationships, and specify relationships without having to use the `key`/`keyref` syntax.

ConstraintName

This attribute is found on the `<xs:key>` element to further annotate a given constraint or relationship. This allows you to specify a name for the constraint that is something other than the name of the XSD `key` or `keyref`. The following bit of XSD illustrates the use of this attribute:

```
<xs:key msdata:ConstraintName="KeyOrderId" name="KeyOrdersKey">
  <xs:selector path=".//Orders"/>
  <xs:field path="OrderId"/>
</xs:key>
```

ConstraintOnly

The `ConstraintOnly` msdata attribute indicates that *only* the constraint should be created in the `DataSet`. So, for example, if the attribute is applied to a `keyref` on a relationship, then only the actual constraint will be created (no `DataRelation` will be created).

UpdateRule

If this attribute is supplied in the schema, its value is applied to the `UpdateRule` constraint property in the `DataSet`. Otherwise, the default value of `Cascade` is used when the typed `DataSet` is built, which will be used to maintain referential integrity.

DeleteRule

If this attribute is supplied in the schema, its value is applied to the `DeleteRule` constraint property in the `DataSet`. Otherwise, the default value of `Cascade` is used, which will be used to maintain referential integrity.

AcceptRejectRule

If this attribute is supplied in the schema, its value is applied to the `AcceptRejectRule` constraint property in the `DataSet`. Otherwise, the default value of `Cascade` is used for referential integrity.

PrimaryKey

This attribute indicates that the given key element on which this attribute is placed is either a primary key or isn't. If the attribute is left off, or is included and set to `false`, the key is not a primary key. If the value is `true`, then the `DataSet` will create a primary key for that particular key element. The following bit of XSD illustrates the use of the `PrimaryKey` attribute:

```
<xs:key msdata:ConstraintName="KeyOrderId" msdata:PrimaryKey="true">
  <xs:selector path=".//Orders"/>
  <xs:field path="OrderId"/>
</xs:key>
```

Relationship

The `Relationship` annotation allows you to specify an entire relationship between two tables without having to use the standard XSD `key`/`keyref` notation so long as the data is not nested. The following is an example of the syntax of defining a relationship using the `Relationship` attribute:

```
<msdata:Relationship name="RelationshipName"
     msdata:parent="parent"
     msdata:child="child"
     msdata:parentkey="parentkey"
     msdata:childkey="childkey" />
```

The parent attribute indicates the name of the element that represents the parent table in the `DataSet` structure. The child attribute indicates the name of the element that represents the child table in the `DataSet` structure. The `parentkey` and `childkey` attributes indicate the names of the fields/keys to be used when building the parent-child relationship.

Putting It All Together

Now that we've taken a look at the capabilities, power, and flexibility of the typed `DataSet`, let's take a look at a practical example of putting it to use. In our last chapter, we concluded the discussion of generic `DataSet`s by building a fairly crude contact manager. To illustrate just how much cleaner the code looks and works using a typed `DataSet`, we're going to upgrade the previous project to use a new typed `DataSet`.

The first step is to copy the entire solution folder (`Contacts`) from the Chapter 2 code to the Chapter 3 code. I renamed the folder `TypedContacts` just to make things clearer, but didn't mess with the solution or project filenames. This code is included in the download for this book in the `FTrackADONET\Chapter03\TypedContacts` folder.

Now we're going to add a typed `DataSet` to our project. To do this, I just made note of the data structure previously created in the other project's `GlobalData` class constructor and converted that into an XML Schema. As usual, right-click the project and add a new `DataSet` class. I called mine `ContactsData.xsd`. The following is a listing of that `DataSet`'s XML Schema Definition:

```
<?xml version="1.0" standalone="yes" ?>
<xs:schema id="ContactsData" xmlns=""
    xmlns:xs="http://www.w3.org/2001/XMLSchema"
```

```
        xmlns:msdata="urn:schemas-microsoft-com:xml-msdata"
        xmlns:codegen="urn:schemas-microsoft-com:xml-msprop">
  <xs:element name="ContactsData" msdata:IsDataSet="true">
    <xs:complexType>
      <xs:choice maxOccurs="unbounded">
```

On this element definition below, we're basically building the data structure for the Contacts table.
You can see that we've also annotated this element to provide our own custom name for the object and
a collection of those objects. Without this, we would end up with names like ContactsRow and
ContactsRows. Contact and Contacts seems far more readable and logical. Note the use of the
AutoIncrement msdata attribute on the ContactId column. This effectively turns on the
AutoIncrement property on the DataColumn object created.

```
        <xs:element name="Contacts" codegen:typedName="Contact"
            codegen:typedPlural="Contacts">
          <xs:complexType>
            <xs:sequence>
              <xs:element name="ContactId" msdata:AutoIncrement="true"
                  type="xs:int" />
              <xs:element name="ContactName" type="xs:string"
                  minOccurs="0" />
            </xs:sequence>
          </xs:complexType>
        </xs:element>
```

Now we're going to define the type definition for the child table. This table also contains a ContactId
column, but we don't do anything to the definition of it at this point. Also again note the use of annotation
to provide clearer and more understandable names for the objects created relating to this table.

```
        <xs:element name="ContactMessages"
            codegen:typedName="ContactMessage"
            codegen:typedPlural="ContactMessages">
          <xs:complexType>
            <xs:sequence>
              <xs:element name="ContactId" type="xs:int" minOccurs="0" />
              <xs:element name="Message" type="xs:string" minOccurs="0" />
              <xs:element name="MessageDate" type="xs:dateTime"
                  minOccurs="0" />
            </xs:sequence>
          </xs:complexType>
        </xs:element>
      </xs:choice>
    </xs:complexType>
    <xs:unique name="Constraint1" msdata:PrimaryKey="true">
      <xs:selector xpath=".//Contacts" />
      <xs:field xpath="ContactId" />
    </xs:unique>
    <xs:keyref name="ContactMessages" refer="Constraint1">
      <xs:selector xpath=".//ContactMessages" />
      <xs:field xpath="ContactId" />
    </xs:keyref>
  </xs:element>
</xs:schema>
```

Build the project once to get a compiled version of the typed `DataSet`. Now all we have to do is make a few minor changes to the project's code and we should be up and running. If you'll recall from the previous chapter's example, we had a good deal of code stuffed into the `GlobalData` class's constructor in order to initialize the data structure of the `DataSet`.

Now that the data structure of our `DataSet` is actually "burned" into the typed `DataSet`'s class definition itself, we no longer need to have any code that builds data structure at run time. That work has all been done for us by Visual Studio .NET and the schema we built.

Let's take a look at the source code listing for our revised `GlobalData.cs` file:

```csharp
using System;
using System.Data;

namespace Contacts
{
  /// <summary>
  /// Summary description for GlobalData.
  /// </summary>
  public class GlobalData
  {
    static GlobalData()
    {
      contactsData = new ContactsData();
    }

    public static ContactsData contactsData;
  }
}
```

Looks just a bit smaller, doesn't it? Instead of creating a public, static instance of a generic `DataSet`, we're creating a public instance of our typed `DataSet`, which, as we said, knows how to build and enforce its own data structure.

With that out of the way, let's take a look at the revised version of the `frmMain.cs` code listing for the main form of the application. This is the section of code that does all of the work. Fortunately for us, we put all of the "business logic" for this application in the same place so we only had to modify the main form code to update the application:

```csharp
using System;
using System.Drawing;
using System.Collections;
using System.ComponentModel;
using System.Windows.Forms;
using System.Data;

namespace Contacts
{
/// <summary>
/// Summary description for Form1.
/// </summary>
public class frmMain : System.Windows.Forms.Form
{
```

```
private System.Windows.Forms.DataGrid dgContacts;
private System.Windows.Forms.MainMenu mainMenu1;
private System.Windows.Forms.MenuItem menuItem1;
private System.Windows.Forms.MenuItem menuItem2;
private System.Windows.Forms.MenuItem menuItem3;
private System.Windows.Forms.MenuItem menuItem4;
private System.Windows.Forms.Button button1;
private System.Windows.Forms.Button button2;
private System.Windows.Forms.MenuItem menuItem5;
private System.Windows.Forms.MenuItem menuItem6;
private System.Windows.Forms.DataGridTableStyle dataGridTableStyle1;
private System.Windows.Forms.DataGridTextBoxColumn dataGridTextBoxColumn1;
private System.Windows.Forms.DataGridTableStyle dataGridTableStyle2;
private System.Windows.Forms.DataGridTextBoxColumn dataGridTextBoxColumn2;
private System.Windows.Forms.DataGridTextBoxColumn dataGridTextBoxColumn3;
private System.Windows.Forms.MenuItem menuItem7;
/// <summary>
/// Required designer variable.
/// </summary>
private System.ComponentModel.Container components = null;

public frmMain()
{
//
// Required for Windows Form Designer support
//
InitializeComponent ();
```

This is the first noticeable change. Rather than refer to the collection of tables within the contactsData DataSet, we can directly refer to the Contacts table as a property:

```
//
// TODO: Add any constructor code after InitializeComponent call
//
dgContacts.DataSource = GlobalData.contactsData.Contacts;
dgContacts.Refresh();
}

/// <summary>
/// Clean up any resources being used.
/// </summary>
protected override void Dispose( bool disposing )
{
  if( disposing )
  {
    if (components != null)
    {
      components.Dispose();
    }
  }
  base.Dispose( disposing );
}

#region Windows Form Designer generated code
```

As usual, to keep things clear and easy to read, we've cut out the Windows Form Designer code that initializes the various properties of the controls on the form.

```
#endregion

    /// <summary>
    /// The main entry point for the application.
    /// </summary>
    [STAThread]
    static void Main()
    {
        Application.Run(new frmMain());
    }
```

Even though we are dealing with a typed `DataSet`, we can still use methods that are part of the base `DataSet` class, such as `ReadXml` and `WriteXml`:

```
    private void menuItem3_Click(object sender, System.EventArgs e)
    {
        GlobalData.contactsData.WriteXml(@"..\..\contacts.xml");
    }

    private void menuItem2_Click(object sender, System.EventArgs e)
    {
        GlobalData.contactsData.ReadXml(@"..\..\contacts.xml");
        dgContacts.Refresh();
    }

    private void button1_Click(object sender, System.EventArgs e)
    {
        GlobalData.contactsData.AcceptChanges();
    }

    private void button2_Click(object sender, System.EventArgs e)
    {
        GlobalData.contactsData.RejectChanges();
        dgContacts.Refresh();
    }
```

This next method shows off some more of the power of the typed `DataSet`. Rather than using the `NewRow` method of a generic item within the collection of tables, the typed `DataSet` has actually created a new method called `NewContact` that actually returns an object of type `Contact`, which is a class nested within our typed `DataSet`. It is called `Contact` because of our annotation, and would have been called `ContactsRow` otherwise:

```
    private void menuItem6_Click(object sender, System.EventArgs e)
    {
        using (frmContact contactForm = new frmContact())
        {
            if (contactForm.ShowDialog() == DialogResult.OK)
            {
```

```
        ContactsData.ContactsDataTable contacts =
            GlobalData.contactsData.Contacts;
        ContactsData.Contact newContact = contacts.NewContact();
        newContact.ContactName = contactForm.ContactName;
        contacts.Rows.Add( newContact );
        dgContacts.Refresh();
      }
    }
  }
```

Much like the previous method, this one also adds a new row to a table. The ContactMessages table
also has a method that returns a strongly-typed row of type ContactMessage, which is also a nested
class within our typed DataSet class. When we add this row, it will enforce the parent-child
relationship. In other words, we couldn't add this row unless a row with the same contact ID already
existed in the parent table.

```
    private void menuItem7_Click(object sender, System.EventArgs e)
    {
      if (GlobalData.contactsData.Contacts.Rows.Count == 0) return;
        using (frmMessageLog messageLog = new frmMessageLog())
        {
          if (messageLog.ShowDialog() == DialogResult.OK)
          {
            // add contact message log
            ContactsData.ContactMessage newMessage =
                GlobalData.contactsData.ContactMessages.NewContactMessage();
            newMessage.Message = messageLog.MessageText;
            newMessage.MessageDate = messageLog.MessageDate;
            newMessage.ContactId = messageLog.ContactId;
            GlobalData.contactsData.ContactMessages.Rows.Add( newMessage );
            dgContacts.Refresh();
          }
        }
      }
    }
  }
```

When this application is complete, it should run and look exactly like the previous example from the
end of the DataSet chapter. The main differences between this application and the one from the
previous chapter should be very, very noticeable. The first and foremost being that our GlobalData
class did not have to build the data structure at run time. Secondly, everything reads a lot easier and in
a much more object-oriented fashion. Finally, we know that if we attempt to place incorrect or badly
typed data in our typed DataSet, an exception will be thrown. In the previous example, a typecast
would have been attempted since the rows of a DataSet store all the column values as type Object.

Summary

In this chapter we've thrown quite a bit of material at you. We mentioned XML Schemas and how they relate to the internal data structure of a `DataSet`, but we don't have enough room in this chapter or book to cover every aspect of XSD. Once through XSD we looked at how to infer and build schemas using various tools that come with Visual Studio .NET. Then we finally got into the meat of typed `DataSets` and explained the practical *when, why,* and *how* of using them. We also covered making the typed `DataSet` even more programmer-friendly through the use of `DataSet` annotation.

This chapter should be read as if it was part two of Chapter 2. Without good, solid knowledge of the `DataSet` itself, this chapter would mean very little. Hopefully through reading these two chapters you have learned what you need to know about one of the core components of ADO.NET – the `DataSet`.

4

XML and ADO.NET

In today's world of complex enterprise applications and Web applications, access to data is fairly commonplace. Any mention of data access typically brings to mind applications like SQL Server, Oracle, or Microsoft Access. With all of that data functionality available, it is often easy to forget that XML, too, is a useful and viable source of data.

This chapter will explore the various ways that .NET supports XML. We'll discuss .NET's native support for the **XML Document Object Model (DOM)**. In addition, we'll take a look at the extensive support for XML that is built into ADO.NET and several of its core components. This includes support for concepts such as XPath, XSL transformations, treating an XML document as relational data and much, much more. We'll also see how you can use XML within ADO.NET for non-relational data, such as data for reports or business-to-business document exchange.

Finally, we'll round out the chapter with a discussion of some of the more advanced techniques available to you with the combination of XML and ADO.NET. This chapter assumes a basic knowledge of what XML is and what it looks like, and some familiarity with the different aspects of the DOM.

DOM in .NET

The .NET Framework has native support for the W3C DOM (World Wide Web Consortium Document Object Model). In the COM world, this support is encapsulated within the MSXML component (currently at version 4.0). The .NET Framework provides the same access to the XML DOM through the System.Xml namespace and the various classes contained within it. Two of the more noteworthy classes in this namespace are the XmlDocument and XmlDataDocument, which we will spend some time talking about.

XmlDocument

The XmlDocument class is an object-oriented representation of the W3C DOM. In other words, it represents an XML document. It contains methods for loading itself from disk or from various streams. It also contains methods for saving to disk or to streams, as well as those required to traverse the document model itself and other useful methods.

Just to demonstrate the ease with which you can manipulate a standard XML document, we'll write a little sample program that creates an XML document. After that we'll move on to how this relates to ADO.NET. We suggest that you set up the directory structure C:\FTrackADONET\Chapter04 to store the examples in this chapter. The code download will also be available in this format.

For the sample program, create a new C# Console Application called HelloXml. The code listing for the main file of the application (HelloMain.cs) looks like this:

```
using System;
using System.Xml;

namespace HelloXml
{
  /// <summary>
  /// Summary description for HelloMain
  /// </summary>
  class HelloMain
  {
    /// <summary>
    /// The main entry point for the application.
    /// </summary>
    [STAThread]
    static void Main(string[] args)
    {
      //
      // TODO: Add code to start application here
      //
      XmlDocument newDoc = new XmlDocument();
      XmlElement documentElement = newDoc.CreateElement("HelloDocument");
      // create the document element.
      newDoc.AppendChild( documentElement);
      XmlElement greeting = newDoc.CreateElement("Greeting");
      greeting.InnerText = "Hello World";
      documentElement.AppendChild( greeting );
      Console.WriteLine("Our XML Document:\n{0}", newDoc.InnerXml);
    }
  }
}
```

As you can see, this program uses methods that should look familiar to anyone who has had any experience with Microsoft's COM implementation of the DOM (MSXML). XmlElement, for instance, is an object that represents an element. We start off by creating the document element. Then, we append a greeting element and set the inner text to "Hello World". Here's a screenshot of the output of the program:

```
C:\WINNT\System32\cmd.exe                                    _ □ ×
Microsoft Windows 2000 [Version 5.00.2195]
(C) Copyright 1985-2000 Microsoft Corp.

C:\FTrackADONET\Chapter04\HelloXml\obj\Debug>helloxml
Our XML Document:
<HelloDocument><Greeting>Hello World</Greeting></HelloDocument>

C:\FTrackADONET\Chapter04\HelloXml\obj\Debug>_
```

XmlDataDocument

This chapter is all about using XML and ADO.NET together to provide for easy, robust data access and manipulation. While being able to manipulate XML in its native DOM format with the `XmlDocument` class is extremely useful and handy, it doesn't have all that much to do with ADO.NET.

The `XmlDataDocument` class, on the other hand, has a direct relationship with the `DataSet`, the core component of ADO.NET. The `DataSet`, as we've seen in previous chapters, is an in-memory relational cache capable of maintaining and manipulating multiple related tables of data without bias toward any particular data source. This class is an extension of the `XmlDocument` class. It allows the programmer to manipulate either relational data or XML data using the W3C DOM.

The DOM is essentially a hierarchical tree of XML `Node` objects. This class allows you to work with both XML data and relational data using the same access paradigm. We'll take a look at how to use the `XmlDataDocument` for working with XML data, and then we'll look at using it to work with relational data. Finally, we'll wrap up this section of the chapter by showing how to work with both relational and hierarchical XML data at the same time.

The following is a quick reference guide to the `XmlDataDocument` class that will help us through some of the examples we're going to be developing in this section of the chapter. We've taken out some of the methods that are inherited directly from the `XmlDocument` class to make things clearer.

XmlDataDocument Quick Reference Guide	
Property	**Description**
DataSet	Gets the `DataSet` that provides a relational representation of the XML contained within the `XmlDataDocument`.
Method	
CloneNode	Creates a copy of the current node.
CreateNavigator	Creates a new `XPathNavigator` object for navigating the document. The navigator's starting position is on the `<Document>` element of the `XmlDataDocument`.
GetElementFromRow	Retrieves the XML element associated with a particular `DataRow` object from the `DataSet` linked with the `XmlDataDocument`.

Table continued on following page

XmlDataDocument Quick Reference Guide	
Method	**Description**
GetRowFromElement	Retrieves a DataRow object associated with the specified XmlElement instance.
Load	Loads the XmlDataDocument using the specified data source, *and* synchronizes the associated DataSet with the loaded data.

Obviously this is an oversimplification of an extremely powerful, versatile, and complex class. What we've listed are the additions or major changes to the class over its parent, XmlDocument. There are obviously some changes in the internal implementation of some of the methods and properties that belong to the XmlDocument class, such as the fact that the XmlDataDocument does not support entity references and the XmlDocument does.

Using the XMLDataDocument for XML Data

Because the XmlDataDocument class inherits from the XmlDocument class, the way it allows access to XML data via the DOM is identical to that of the XmlDocument. To show you that you can use an XmlDataDocument class in almost every situation where you used an XmlDocument, we'll rewrite our previous HelloXml sample using the XmlDataDocument.

To do that, we'll create a new C# Console Application, and call our new project HelloDataXml. Note that the only lines that have changed are the ones highlighted in gray. The following is the code listing for our new project:

```csharp
using System;
using System.Xml;

namespace HelloDataXml
{
  /// <summary>
  /// Summary description for HelloMain.
  /// </summary>
  class HelloMain
  {
    /// <summary>
    /// The main entry point for the application.
    /// </summary>
    [STAThread]
    static void Main(string[] args)
    {
      //
      // TODO: Add code to start application here
      //
      XmlDataDocument newDoc = new XmlDataDocument();
      XmlElement documentElement =
          newDoc.CreateElement("HelloDataDocument");
      // create the document element.
      newDoc.AppendChild( documentElement );
```

```
            XmlElement greeting = newDoc.CreateElement("Greeting");
            greeting.InnerText = "Hello XmlDataDocument World";
            documentElement.AppendChild( greeting );
            Console.WriteLine("Our XmlDataDocument XML:\n{0}", newDoc.InnerXml);
        }
    }
}
```

As you can see, even though we're using a specialized class designed to be synchronized with a `DataSet`, we can still use it to manipulate XML documents the same way we can with the `XmlDocument` class:

This is all well and good, but why would anyone use the `XmlDataDocument` for standard XML manipulation when they can just use the `XmlDocument` class? Well, one of the main reasons for that is the use of XPath. The `XmlDataDocument` class is optimized for performing XPath queries against its underlying data.

XPath

XPath is a query language that allows for the search and retrieval of data in an XML document. It allows you to select nodes that have various properties. More complex XPath statements allow you to select nodes that fit in a certain place in a certain hierarchy with specific data values or attributes. It is an incredibly powerful tool and allows you query-level access to XML data that you might only expect to be able to accomplish with an RDBMS like SQL Server or Oracle. There isn't enough room in this chapter or this book to go into detail on what exactly XPath is. For more information on XPath, there are several Wrox books including *Professional XML* (ISBN: 1-86100-505-9) or *Professional XML for .NET Developers* (ISBN: 1-86100-531-8).

Both the `XmlDocument` and the `XmlDataDocument` allow you to retrieve a list of XML nodes based on an XPath expression with the `SelectSingleNode` and `SelectNodes` methods. Knowledge of XPath and how to use it is essential for some of the more advanced features available with the `XmlDataDocument` class.

We'll quickly illustrate how to select some nodes from an XML document using an XPath expression so you can see what it looks like and get a feel for some of the extra functionality available with XML, which you might not have been aware of. Create a new C# Console Application called `XPathDemo`. This application, like all of the others, is also available in the code download in the `FTrackADONET\Chapter04` folder. This application is going to use Microsoft's sample XML file, which comes with the MSXML 4.0 SDK. This file is also included with the download for this chapter in the same folder.

101

This file, `books.xml`, is an XML list of books and their properties, including ISBN, price, genre, title, author, and other information. We'll write a simple application that runs two XPath queries against this file to show how we can achieve extremely robust search-and-retrieve functionality using XPath against XML. Before we get working on the actual application, let's take a look at Microsoft's sample XML file. This file will need to be included in the `Chapter04` folder along with `XPathDemo` in order for the application to work.

```xml
<?xml version="1.0"?>
<catalog>
    <book id="bk101">
        <author>Gambardella, Matthew</author>
        <title>XML Developer's Guide</title>
        <genre>Computer</genre>
        <price>44.95</price>
        <publish_date>2000-10-01</publish_date>
        <description>An in-depth look at creating applications
        with XML.</description>
    </book>
    <book id="bk102">
        <author>Ralls, Kim</author>
        <title>Midnight Rain</title>
        <genre>Fantasy</genre>
        <price>5.95</price>
        <publish_date>2000-12-16</publish_date>
        <description>A former architect battles corporate zombies,
        an evil sorceress, and her own childhood to become queen
        of the world.</description>
    </book>
    <book id="bk103">
        <author>Corets, Eva</author>
        <title>Maeve Ascendant</title>
        <genre>Fantasy</genre>
        <price>5.95</price>
        <publish_date>2000-11-17</publish_date>
        <description>After the collapse of a nanotechnology
        society in England, the young survivors lay the
        foundation for a new society.</description>
    </book>
    <book id="bk104">
        <author>Corets, Eva</author>
        <title>Oberon's Legacy</title>
        <genre>Fantasy</genre>
        <price>5.95</price>
        <publish_date>2001-03-10</publish_date>
        <description>In post-apocalypse England, the mysterious
        agent known only as Oberon helps to create a new life
        for the inhabitants of London. Sequel to Maeve
        Ascendant.</description>
    </book>
    <book id="bk105">
        <author>Corets, Eva</author>
        <title>The Sundered Grail</title>
        <genre>Fantasy</genre>
        <price>5.95</price>
```

```
         <publish_date>2001-09-10</publish_date>
         <description>The two daughters of Maeve, half-sisters,
         battle one another for control of England. Sequel to
         Oberon's Legacy.</description>
   </book>
   <book id="bk106">
         <author>Randall, Cynthia</author>
         <title>Lover Birds</title>
         <genre>Romance</genre>
         <price>4.95</price>
         <publish_date>2000-09-02</publish_date>
         <description>When Carla meets Paul at an ornithology
         conference, tempers fly as feathers get ruffled.</description>
   </book>
   <book id="bk107">
         <author>Thurman, Paula</author>
         <title>Splish Splash</title>
         <genre>Romance</genre>
         <price>4.95</price>
         <publish_date>2000-11-02</publish_date>
         <description>A deep sea diver finds true love twenty
         thousand leagues beneath the sea.</description>
   </book>
   <book id="bk108">
         <author>Knorr, Stefan</author>
         <title>Creepy Crawlies</title>
         <genre>Horror</genre>
         <price>4.95</price>
         <publish_date>2000-12-06</publish_date>
         <description>An anthology of horror stories about roaches,
         centipedes, scorpions  and other insects.</description>
   </book>
   <book id="bk109">
         <author>Kress, Peter</author>
         <title>Paradox Lost</title>
         <genre>Science Fiction</genre>
         <price>6.95</price>
         <publish_date>2000-11-02</publish_date>
         <description>After an inadvertant trip through a Heisenberg
         Uncertainty Device, James Salway discovers the problems
         of being quantum.</description>
   </book>
   <book id="bk110">
         <author>O'Brien, Tim</author>
         <title>Microsoft .NET: The Programming Bible</title>
         <genre>Computer</genre>
         <price>36.95</price>
         <publish_date>2000-12-09</publish_date>
         <description>Microsoft's .NET initiative is explored in
         detail in this deep programmer's reference.</description>
   </book>
   <book id="bk111">
         <author>O'Brien, Tim</author>
         <title>MSXML3: A Comprehensive Guide</title>
```

```
        <genre>Computer</genre>
        <price>36.95</price>
        <publish_date>2000-12-01</publish_date>
        <description>The Microsoft MSXML3 parser is covered in
        detail, with attention to XML DOM interfaces, XSLT processing,
        SAX and more.</description>
    </book>
    <book id="bk112">
        <author>Galos, Mike</author>
        <title>Visual Studio 7: A Comprehensive Guide</title>
        <genre>Computer</genre>
        <price>49.95</price>
        <publish_date>2001-04-16</publish_date>
        <description>Microsoft Visual Studio 7 is explored in depth,
        looking at how Visual Basic, Visual C++, C#, and ASP+ are
        integrated into a comprehensive development
        environment.</description>
    </book>
</catalog>
```

Change the code for the main class of the XPathDemo project to the following (XPathMain.cs). We'll go through it as we go along.

```csharp
using System;
using System.Xml;
using System.Xml.XPath;

namespace XPathDemo
{
  /// <summary>
  /// Summary description for Class1
  /// </summary>
  class XPathMain
  {
    /// <summary>
    /// The main entry point for the application
    /// </summary>
     [STAThread]
    static void Main(string[] args)
    {
      //
      // TODO: Add code to start application here
      //
      XmlDataDocument docBooks = new XmlDataDocument();
      XmlNodeList results;

      docBooks.Load(@"..\..\..\books.xml");
      XmlElement rootNode = docBooks.DocumentElement;
```

The `SelectNodes` method, as we can see below, is the one that's doing all the work here. The XPath expression that we're passing, translated roughly to English means: "Select all `book` nodes that are children of the `catalog` node that have a child node `price` whose value is less than 6.00." So we've just retrieved all of the books in our XML file that are cheaper than $6.00.

```
results = rootNode.SelectNodes("/catalog/book[number(price) < 6.00]");
DisplayResults(results);
```

For a slightly more complex XPath expression, we attempt to retrieve a list of all of the science fiction and fantasy books in the document. To do this, we use the XPath | operator. You can think of this operator as functionally similar to the SQL UNION operator. A key thing to remember is that with a UNION operator, the default operation is to remove duplicate rows. The | operator does something very similar. If a single node appears in the result set for more than one XPath expression combined with the | operator, it will only appear *once* in the final result set.

```
    // now get all fantasy books and sci-fi books.
    results = rootNode.SelectNodes("/catalog/book[genre='Fantasy'] |
        /catalog/book[genre='Science Fiction']");
    DisplayResults(results);
}
```

This next method is used to display the results to the console. We use the default iterator on an `XmlNodeList` type to iterate through the list of XML nodes returned as results. We also use the `SelectSingleNode` method with some simple node-selection XPath expressions to print out the values of the title, price, and genre nodes.

```
    static void DisplayResults(XmlNodeList results)
    {
      if (results == null)
      {
        Console.WriteLine("No results matched XPath criteria.");
      }
      else
      {
        Console.WriteLine("{0} books matched.", results.Count);
        foreach (XmlElement book in results)
        {
          Console.WriteLine("{0} sells for ${1} ({2})",
              book.SelectSingleNode("title").InnerText,
              book.SelectSingleNode("price").InnerText,
              book.SelectSingleNode("genre").InnerText);
        }
        Console.WriteLine();
      }
    }
  }
}
```

When we build and run this application from the console, our output looks like this:

We can see that our application successfully selected seven books under the price of $6.00, and 5 books that belonged to either the fantasy or science fiction genres.

XPathNavigator

The XPathNavigator is a specialized class that is optimized for traversing XML documents to evaluate XPath expressions. One of the biggest advantages of the XPathNavigator is that it allows you to use XPath expressions against *any* data store. As its name implies, it is designed for navigation only, and therefore allows only read-only access to the underlying data.

In addition to providing you random-access, read-only traversal of the underlying data using an XPath model, the XPathNavigator class supports transformations using XSLT. Because the XmlDataDocument allows us to create an XPathNavigator with the CreateNavigator method, we can therefore use XSLT to transform XML data or DataSet data due to the linked nature of the XmlDataDocument.

To illustrate this, we're going to transform the books.xml document into an HTML page. To do this, we're going to load the books document into an XmlDataDocument and then transform it using an XPathNavigator. This example not only illustrates that we can transform an XML document, but we can also transform any data residing in a DataSet (because the DataSet can be linked to the XmlDataDocument, which we'll show in the next section of this chapter).

Our C# Console Application, BooksTransform, consists of one main class file (TransformMain.cs). This code is available in the code download, in the FTrackADONET\Chapter04\BooksTransform folder. The code listing for this file is below:

```
using System;
using System.Xml;
using System.Xml.XPath;
using System.Xml.Xsl;

namespace BooksTransform
{
```

```
/// <summary>
/// Summary description for TransformMain.
/// </summary>
class TransformMain
{
  /// <summary>
  /// The main entry point for the application.
  /// </summary>
  [STAThread]
  static void Main(string[] args)
  {
    //
    // TODO: Add code to start application here
    //
    XmlDataDocument docBooks = new XmlDataDocument();
    docBooks.Load(@"..\..\..\books.xml");
    XPathNavigator xpnBooks = docBooks.CreateNavigator();
    XslTransform xt = new XslTransform();
    xt.Load(@"..\..\BooksToHTML.xslt");

    XmlTextWriter xtw = new XmlTextWriter(@"..\..\books.html", null);
    xt.Transform( docBooks, null, xtw );

  }
 }
}
```

The code here is fairly simple. We load an `XmlDataDocument` with XML (but we could have just as easily synchronized it with a pre-loaded `DataSet` from an RDBMS like SQL or Oracle). Then we create an `XPathNavigator` from the `XmlDataDocument` and transform it using an XSLT file. Without going into too much detail on how exactly XSLT works, here's the listing for our XSLT file (`BooksToHTML.xslt`). The `XslTransform` class transforms XML data using a XSLT stylesheet. You will need to include this in the `FTrackADONET\Chapter04\BooksTransform` application directory for this example to work.

```
<?xml version="1.0"?>
<xsl:stylesheet version="1.0"
    xmlns:xsl="http://www.w3.org/1999/XSL/Transform">
<xsl:template match="/">          .
<HTML>
<HEAD>
<TITLE>Books to HTML Sample</TITLE>
</HEAD>
<BODY style="font-family:Arial, helvetica, sans-serif; font-size:11pt;
    background-color:#FFFFFF">
<table width="650" border="0" cellspacing="0" cellpadding="3">
<tr bgcolor="#eeeeee">
  <td>
    <b>Title</b>
  </td>
  <td>
    <b>Genre</b>
  </td>
```

```
        <td>
          <b>Author</b>
        </td>
        <td>
          <b>Price</b>
        </td>
      </tr>
      <tr bgcolor="#eeeeee">
        <td colspan="4"
          style="border: solid; border-width:1px; border-color:#000000; border-top:0px;
              border-left:0px; border-right:0px;">
          <b>Description</b>
        </td>
      </tr>
      <xsl:for-each select="//book">
        <tr>
          <xsl:if test="position() mod 2 > 0">
            <xsl:attribute name="bgcolor">#c0c0c0</xsl:attribute>
          </xsl:if>
          <td>
            <xsl:value-of select="title"></xsl:value-of>
          </td>
          <td>
            <xsl:value-of select="genre"></xsl:value-of>
          </td>
          <td>
            <xsl:value-of select="author"></xsl:value-of>
          </td>
          <td>
            $<xsl:value-of select="price"></xsl:value-of>
          </td>
        </tr>
        <tr>
          <xsl:if test="position() mod 2 > 0">
            <xsl:attribute name="bgcolor">#c0c0c0</xsl:attribute>
          </xsl:if>
          <td colspan="4">
            <xsl:value-of select="description"></xsl:value-of>
          </td>
        </tr>
      </xsl:for-each>
      </table>
      </BODY>
      </HTML>
      </xsl:template>
      </xsl:stylesheet>
```

One thing to keep in mind is that you should *not* let Visual Studio .NET create an XSLT file for you. When it does, it doesn't use the header that we've used above. The header it supplies actually causes all kinds of validation problems when using XSLT like we've used. When making your own XSLT files, make sure that your header looks like ours.

This is a screenshot of Internet Explorer viewing the HTML we generated through the `XmlDataDocument` and the `XslTransform` classes. To see this screen, you will need to run the `books.html` file in the `FTrackADONET\Chapter04\BooksTransform` directory. This file will be created when the application is run.

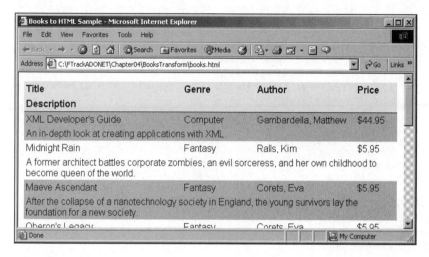

Relational View

So far we've taken a look at how to work with XML using the `XmlDocument` class to conform to the DOM specification. Then we took a look at some of the things that we can accomplish by using the `XmlDataDocument` with standard XML data, allowing an XML view of the underlying data.

Now we're going to explore the other side of the `XmlDataDocument`: the relational view. The `XmlDataDocument` allows us to load an XML document and view the data contained in it relationally with a synchronized `DataSet`. This allows for a hierarchical XML structure to be viewed as a collection of related tables, columns, and rows.

To follow along with this next example, create a new C# Console Application project called `XMLRelational`. We're going to load up an `XmlDataDocument` with the contents of our `books.xml` file. Then, we're going to use the relational view of that document (a `DataSet`) to add a new book to that file. The code for this project is in the `FTrackADONET\Chapter04\XMLRelational` folder.

Before we look at the code listing for the main class of our application, here is the `books.xsd` file that you will need to include in the `FTrackADONET\Chapter04` directory.

```
<?xml version="1.0" encoding="utf-8"?>
<xs:schema id="catalog" xmlns="" xmlns:xs="http://www.w3.org/2001/XMLSchema"
    xmlns:msdata="urn:schemas-microsoft-com:xml-msdata">
  <xs:element name="catalog" msdata:IsDataSet="true">
    <xs:complexType>
      <xs:choice maxOccurs="unbounded">
        <xs:element name="book">
          <xs:complexType>
            <xs:sequence>
```

```
                      <xs:element name="author" type="xs:string" minOccurs="0"
                         msdata:Ordinal="0" />
                      <xs:element name="title" type="xs:string" minOccurs="0"
                         msdata:Ordinal="1" />
                      <xs:element name="genre" type="xs:string" minOccurs="0"
                         msdata:Ordinal="2" />
                      <xs:element name="price" type="xs:float" minOccurs="0"
                         msdata:Ordinal="3" />
                      <xs:element name="publish_date" type="xs:date" minOccurs="0"
                         msdata:Ordinal="4" />
                      <xs:element name="description" type="xs:string" minOccurs="0"
                         msdata:Ordinal="5" />
                  </xs:sequence>
                  <xs:attribute name="id" type="xs:string" />
               </xs:complexType>
             </xs:element>
           </xs:choice>
        </xs:complexType>
     </xs:element>
</xs:schema>
```

The following is the code listing for the main class for the `XMLRelational` application. Once again, we will explain it as we go along.

```csharp
using System;
using System.Xml;
using System.Data;

namespace XMLRelational
{
  /// <summary>
  /// Summary description for RelationalMain
  /// </summary>
  class RelationalMain
  {
    /// <summary>
    /// The main entry point for the application
    /// </summary>
     [STAThread]
    static void Main(string[] args)
    {
      //
      // TODO: Add code to start application here
      //
```

One of the interesting things about the `DataSet` relationship with the `XmlDataDocument` that we'll learn more about later is that anything in the XML document that is not defined by the `DataSet`'s schema will be completely ignored. This means that if we fail to supply a schema in some way, *all* of the data in the XML document will be ignored. For this example, we used the XSD tool to infer a schema from the `books.xml` file and then modified it to include the appropriate data types.

```csharp
       XmlDataDocument docBooks = new XmlDataDocument();
       docBooks.DataSet.ReadXmlSchema(@"..\..\..\books.xsd");
```

Calling the `Load` method on the `XmlDataDocument` object not only populates the `XmlDataDocument` instance with all of the XML nodes, elements, and attributes in the file, but it synchronizes the data with the `DataSet` as well.

```
docBooks.Load(@"..\..\..\books.xml");
DataSet dataBooks = docBooks.DataSet;
```

Just so we can see for ourselves that our `DataSet` has an actual table and columns in it and the relationship between it and the `XmlDataDocument` isn't just an elaborate trick, we print out the columns and their data types:

```
Console.WriteLine("Tables in DataSet: {0}", dataBooks.Tables.Count);
foreach (DataColumn col in dataBooks.Tables[0].Columns)
{
  Console.WriteLine("{0} ({1})", col.ColumnName,
      col.DataType.ToString());
}
```

We're adding a new book here, but note that we're not doing it by adding an XML node or changing attributes. We're creating a new row. If you'll recall from the original `books.xml` file, the `"id"` of the book is an attribute, while all other data for the book is composed of child elements. Note that below, we're dealing with columns and rows at all times, and the format of the XML document itself has been completely hidden from us:

```
// now add a new book to the list.
DataTable booksTable = dataBooks.Tables[0];
DataRow newBook = booksTable.NewRow();
newBook["id"] = "bk113";
newBook["author"] = "Stephen King";
newBook["title"] = "The Shining";
newBook["genre"] = "Horror";
newBook["price"] = "7.99";
newBook["publish_date"] = System.Convert.ToDateTime("1997-01-01");
newBook["description"] = "The Overlook Hotel is more than just a home-
    away-from-home for the Torrance family. For Jack, Wendy, and their
    young son, Danny, it is a place where past horrors come to life.
    And where those gifted with the shining do battle with the darkest
    evils. Stephen King's classic thriller is one of the most
    powerfully imagined novels of our time.";
booksTable.Rows.Add( newBook );

// now save the dataset via XML to show that we can save the
// relational data via XML.
//dataBooks.WriteXml(@"..\..\..\books2.xml");
docBooks.Save(@"..\..\..\books2.xml");
    }
  }
}
```

Now, what we've just done is load up an XML document in a W3C DOM-compliant format (hierarchy of nodes). Next, we've examined a physical data structure and created a new data item using an entirely relational paradigm, without any knowledge of which pieces of data are attributes and which pieces are elements.

To prove that the XML is still in the same format and hasn't been ruined by what we just did, let's look at the books2.xml file we created. Again, you can view this by opening the file that has been created for us in the FTrackADONET\Chapter04 directory.

```xml
<?xml version="1.0"?>
<catalog>
  <book id="bk101">
    <author>Gambardella, Matthew</author>
    <title>XML Developer's Guide</title>
    <genre>Computer</genre>
    <price>44.95</price>
    <publish_date>2000-10-01T00:00:00.0000000+01:00</publish_date>
    <description>An in-depth look at creating applications
        with XML.</description>
  </book>
  <book id="bk102">
    <author>Ralls, Kim</author>
    <title>Midnight Rain</title>
    <genre>Fantasy</genre>
    <price>5.95</price>
    <publish_date>2000-12-16T00:00:00.0000000-00:00</publish_date>
    <description>A former architect battles corporate zombies,
        an evil sorceress, and her own childhood to become queen
        of the world.</description>
  </book>
  <book id="bk103">
    <author>Corets, Eva</author>
    <title>Maeve Ascendant</title>
    <genre>Fantasy</genre>
    <price>5.95</price>
    <publish_date>2000-11-17T00:00:00.0000000-00:00</publish_date>
    <description>After the collapse of a nanotechnology
        society in England, the young survivors lay the
        foundation for a new society.</description>
  </book>
  <book id="bk104">
    <author>Corets, Eva</author>
    <title>Oberon's Legacy</title>
    <genre>Fantasy</genre>
    <price>5.95</price>
    <publish_date>2001-03-10T00:00:00.0000000-00:00</publish_date>
    <description>In post-apocalypse England, the mysterious
        agent known only as Oberon helps to create a new life
        for the inhabitants of London. Sequel to Maeve
        Ascendant.</description>
  </book>
  <book id="bk105">
    <author>Corets, Eva</author>
    <title>The Sundered Grail</title>
```

```
    <genre>Fantasy</genre>
    <price>5.95</price>
    <publish_date>2001-09-10T00:00:00.0000000+01:00</publish_date>
    <description>The two daughters of Maeve, half-sisters,
        battle one another for control of England. Sequel to
        Oberon's Legacy.</description>
</book>
<book id="bk106">
  <author>Randall, Cynthia</author>
  <title>Lover Birds</title>
  <genre>Romance</genre>
  <price>4.95</price>
  <publish_date>2000-09-02T00:00:00.0000000+01:00</publish_date>
  <description>When Carla meets Paul at an ornithology
      conference, tempers fly as feathers get ruffled.</description>
</book>
<book id="bk107">
  <author>Thurman, Paula</author>
  <title>Splish Splash</title>
  <genre>Romance</genre>
  <price>4.95</price>
  <publish_date>2000-11-02T00:00:00.0000000-00:00</publish_date>
  <description>A deep sea diver finds true love twenty
      thousand leagues beneath the sea.</description>
</book>
<book id="bk108">
  <author>Knorr, Stefan</author>
  <title>Creepy Crawlies</title>
  <genre>Horror</genre>
  <price>4.95</price>
  <publish_date>2000-12-06T00:00:00.0000000-00:00</publish_date>
  <description>An anthology of horror stories about roaches,
      centipedes, scorpions  and other insects.</description>
</book>
<book id="bk109">
  <author>Kress, Peter</author>
  <title>Paradox Lost</title>
  <genre>Science Fiction</genre>
  <price>6.95</price>
  <publish_date>2000-11-02T00:00:00.0000000-00:00</publish_date>
  <description>After an inadvertant trip through a Heisenberg
      Uncertainty Device, James Salway discovers the problems
      of being quantum.</description>
</book>
<book id="bk110">
  <author>O'Brien, Tim</author>
  <title>Microsoft .NET: The Programming Bible</title>
  <genre>Computer</genre>
  <price>36.95</price>
  <publish_date>2000-12-09T00:00:00.0000000-00:00</publish_date>
  <description>Microsoft's .NET initiative is explored in
      detail in this deep programmer's reference.</description>
</book>
<book id="bk111">
```

```
    <author>O'Brien, Tim</author>
    <title>MSXML3: A Comprehensive Guide</title>
    <genre>Computer</genre>
    <price>36.95</price>
    <publish_date>2000-12-01T00:00:00.0000000-00:00</publish_date>
    <description>The Microsoft MSXML3 parser is covered in
        detail, with attention to XML DOM interfaces, XSLT processing,
        SAX and more.</description>
  </book>
  <book id="bk112">
    <author>Galos, Mike</author>
    <title>Visual Studio 7: A Comprehensive Guide</title>
    <genre>Computer</genre>
    <price>49.95</price>
    <publish_date>2001-04-16T00:00:00.0000000+01:00</publish_date>
    <description>Microsoft Visual Studio 7 is explored in depth,
        looking at how Visual Basic, Visual C++, C#, and ASP+ are
        integrated into a comprehensive development
        environment.</description>
  </book>
  <book id="bk113">
    <author>Stephen King</author>
    <title>The Shining</title>
    <genre>Horror</genre>
    <price>7.99</price>
    <publish_date>1997-01-01T00:00:00.0000000-00:00</publish_date>
    <description>The Overlook Hotel is more than just a home-away-from-home
        for the Torrance family. For Jack, Wendy, and their young son,
        Danny, it is a place where past horrors come to life. And where
        those gifted with the shining do battle with the darkest evils.
        Stephen King's classic thriller is one of the most powerfully
        imagined novels of our time.</description>
  </book>
</catalog>
```

There are two things that are noteworthy about this new document. The first is that we have created an entirely new book. Take a look at the "id" attribute. Even though we accessed that attribute as a column in a DataSet just like everything else, the DataSet still kept the "id" column as an attribute. The second thing to note is that the publish_date element has grown in size. This is because it has been typecast to the universal XML format for denoting an instance of time on a particular date. Also, if you'll remember the code listing, you'll see that we commented out the DataSet's WriteXml method and instead used the XmlDataDocument's Save method. The purpose for this was so that you could experiment by un-commenting one or the other. The end result is that you can use either the DataSet or the XmlDataDocument to save the results: the results will be identical.

Bridging the Gap

Our discussion of the `XmlDataDocument` so far has consisted of accessing either XML data or relational data. Now we're going to talk more about the synchronized nature of the `XmlDataDocument` and show you how you can make changes to the XML and have those changes appear in the `DataSet`. Conversely, changes made to the `DataSet` will appear in the XML document. We've already seen this in a limited fashion by creating a new book and having that book show up as part of the document for the `XmlDataDocument`.

Our next sample involves the use of the `GetRowFromElement` and `GetElementFromRow` methods of the `XmlDataDocument`. These methods allow you to determine "where you are" within the context of either the XML document or the `DataSet`. For any row in the `DataSet`, the `XmlDataDocument` knows how to find out what corresponding `XmlElement` it belongs to. Additionally, the `XmlDataDocument` can figure out which row in the `DataSet` belongs to a given XML element.

For our example, we're going to create another C# Console Application, called `XmlRelational2`. The code for this application is again available in `FTrackADONET\Chapter04\XMLRelational2`. The application we're going to build will illustrate how we can easily interchange the model through which we access our data depending on circumstances and need. At times it may be more convenient to access data using XML elements while at other times it might be more useful to access them with `DataRows`.

The following example (`XmlRelationalMain.cs`) illustrates how either method is perfectly viable and will not damage our data in any way:

```csharp
using System;
using System.Data;
using System.Xml;

namespace XmlRelational2
{
  class XmlRelationalMain
  {
    /// <summary>
    /// The main entry point for the application.
    /// </summary>
    [STAThread]
    static void Main(string[] args)
    {
      //
      // TODO: Add code to start application here
      //
      XmlDataDocument booksDoc = new XmlDataDocument();
      booksDoc.DataSet.ReadXmlSchema(@"..\..\..\books.xsd");
      booksDoc.Load(@"..\..\..\books.xml");
      DataSet booksData = booksDoc.DataSet;

      XmlElement pdxLostElement =
          (XmlElement)booksDoc.SelectSingleNode("//book[title='Paradox
          Lost']");
```

This next section of code prints out identical information from the `Paradox Lost` book. The first section of code prints out that information from the XML element and the second section of code prints out the same information from the `DataRow`.

```
Console.WriteLine("Paradox Lost Info from XML Element:");
Console.WriteLine("{0} by {1} for ${2}",
    pdxLostElement.SelectSingleNode("title").InnerText,
    pdxLostElement.SelectSingleNode("author").InnerText,
    pdxLostElement.SelectSingleNode("price").InnerText);

DataRow pdxLostRow = booksDoc.GetRowFromElement( pdxLostElement );
Console.WriteLine("Paradox Lost Info from DataRow:");
Console.WriteLine("{0} by {1} for ${2}",
    pdxLostRow["title"].ToString(), pdxLostRow["author"].ToString(),
    pdxLostRow["price"].ToString());
```

Here we'll make three changes to the book's information. The first change is through the element we retrieved using an XPath query. The second change is made through the `DataRow`, and the third change is through the XML element we retrieved via the `GetElementFromRow` method. This is to illustrate that even though we're modifying the data from three different points in three different ways, our resulting XML file should contain all three changes.

```
// now make some changes
XmlElement pdxLostElement2 = booksDoc.GetElementFromRow(pdxLostRow);
pdxLostElement2.SelectSingleNode("title").InnerText = "Pradxo Lsto";
pdxLostRow["author"] = "Krsse, Ptre";
pdxLostElement.SelectSingleNode("price").InnerText = "12.95";

// save those changes so we can see them.
booksDoc.Save(@"..\..\..\books3.xml");
    }
  }
}
```

Well, let's take a look at the entry in our `books3.xml` file for the modified `Paradox Lost` title information to see if our guess about the behavior of the `XmlDataDocument` was accurate:

```
...
</book>
<book id="bk109">
  <author>Krsse, Ptre</author>
  <title>Pradxo Lsto</title>
  <genre>Science Fiction</genre>
  <price>12.95</price>
  <publish_date>2000-11-02T00:00:00.0000000-00:00</publish_date>
  <description>After an inadvertant trip through a Heisenberg
    Uncertainty Device, James Salway discovers the problems
    of being quantum.</description>
</book>
...
```

Good news! We successfully inserted horrible typographical errors in the title and author fields and raised the price of the book.

Advanced Techniques

Now that we've taken a look at how to use the `XmlDataDocument` to expose both an XML view and a relational view of the same set of data, there are a few advanced techniques that we can use that can be used to produce some extremely handy results. Remembering back to the beginning of the relational view discussion on the `XmlDataDocument`, we mentioned that the synchronized `DataSet` will not load any data from the `XmlDataDocument` that is not explicitly described in that `DataSet`'s schema.

While that may sound like a limitation at first, it is actually a feature that we can take advantage of, to produce some very interesting and useful results.

Limiting a Relational View of an XML Document

The next sample that we're going to go through will show a more practical use for the `XmlDataDocument`. There are many cases in applications where different users may require different views of the same data.

One such example is in an enterprise application where more than one different application may access the same data source. As an example, consider the case of an online retailer. Its web site has direct access to the customer information, their orders, and all of the details of those orders. You could say that the web site's back-end has unlimited access to the data.

On the other hand, once an order has been created for a customer, that order needs to be transmitted to some other facility for fulfillment. Often, the order is transmitted to a warehouse so that workers in the warehouse know what items to ship. The warehouse does not need (and should not have) access to the customer's credit card information, or other personal information. The warehouse should have access to enough information to find the items ordered such as SKUs (Stock Keeping Unit) and product IDs, and should have access to the address information in order to ship the order. Once the order in the warehouse has been processed, the warehouse should be able to modify the order status and update the main web site's backend.

We are simplifying an incredibly complex process by assuming that the back-end process will be accomplished by simply copying XML files around, but it is indicative enough to be used as a practical example of some of the powerful features of limiting access to relational views of XML via the `XmlDataDocument` and XML Schemas.

Now that we have our hypothetical situation set up, let's take a look at the two specific uses for our data: unlimited access to the data for the web site itself and a limited view for the warehouse application. The data itself can be passed around in its complete form, but the warehouse application will be unable to see and modify anything that we decide it shouldn't have access to.

Rather than actually build an example of an entire web site that illustrates a web site that has complete access to the data contained within the orders XML file, we'll simply show a console application that has that kind of access. Then, we'll show another application that has limited access.

To start the first application, we'll create a C# Console Application and call it `OrderTaker`, a stripped-down hypothetical application designed to take orders from a web site or from a customer service representative. To do this, we're going to create an XML Schema that defines an XML document that contains customers, orders, and order items. Here is that schema (`Orders.xsd`):

```xml
<?xml version="1.0" standalone="yes" ?>
<xs:schema id="OrdersData" xmlns=""
    xmlns:xs="http://www.w3.org/2001/XMLSchema"
    xmlns:msdata="urn:schemas-microsoft-com:xml-msdata">
  <xs:element name="Orders" msdata:IsDataSet="true">
    <xs:complexType>
      <xs:choice maxOccurs="unbounded">
        <xs:element name="Customers">
          <xs:complexType>
            <xs:sequence>
              <xs:element name="CustomerId" type="xs:integer"
                  minOccurs="1" />
              <xs:element name="CustomerName" type="xs:string"
                  minOccurs="0" />
              <xs:element name="EmailAddress" type="xs:string"
                  minOccurs="0" />
              <xs:element name="Address1" type="xs:string" minOccurs="0" />
              <xs:element name="Address2" type="xs:string" minOccurs="0" />
              <xs:element name="City" type="xs:string" minOccurs="0" />
              <xs:element name="State" type="xs:string" minOccurs="0" />
              <xs:element name="Zip" type="xs:string" minOccurs="0" />
            </xs:sequence>
          </xs:complexType>
        </xs:element>
        <xs:element name="Order">
          <xs:complexType>
            <xs:sequence>
              <xs:element name="OrderId" type="xs:integer" minOccurs="1" />
              <xs:element name="CustomerId" type="xs:integer"
                  minOccurs="0" />
              <xs:element name="OrderStatus" type="xs:string"
                  minOccurs="0" />
              <xs:element name="ShipTo" type="xs:string" minOccurs="0" />
              <xs:element name="ShipAddress" type="xs:string"
                  minOccurs="0" />
              <xs:element name="ShipAddress2" type="xs:string"
                  minOccurs="0" />
              <xs:element name="ShipCity" type="xs:string" minOccurs="0" />
              <xs:element name="ShipState" type="xs:string" minOccurs="0" />
              <xs:element name="ShipZip" type="xs:string" minOccurs="0" />
            </xs:sequence>
          </xs:complexType>
        </xs:element>
        <xs:element name="OrderItems">
          <xs:complexType>
            <xs:sequence>
              <xs:element name="OrderId" type="xs:integer" minOccurs="0" />
              <xs:element name="SKU" type="xs:string" minOccurs="0" />
              <xs:element name="Price" type="xs:float" minOccurs="0" />
```

```
            <xs:element name="Qty" type="xs:int" minOccurs="0" />
          </xs:sequence>
        </xs:complexType>
      </xs:element>
    </xs:choice>
  </xs:complexType>
  <xs:unique name="Constraint2" msdata:PrimaryKey="true">
    <xs:selector xpath=".//Customers" />
    <xs:field xpath="CustomerId" />
  </xs:unique>
  <xs:unique name="Constraint1" msdata:PrimaryKey="true">
    <xs:selector xpath=".//Order" />
    <xs:field xpath="OrderId" />
  </xs:unique>
  <xs:keyref name="OrderItems" refer="Constraint1">
    <xs:selector xpath=".//OrderItems" />
    <xs:field xpath="OrderId" />
  </xs:keyref>
  <xs:keyref name="CustomerOrders" refer="Constraint2">
    <xs:selector xpath=".//Order" />
    <xs:field xpath="CustomerId" />
  </xs:keyref>
  </xs:element>
</xs:schema>
```

What we have here is the `Customers` table. This table has a relation to the `Orders` table. The `Orders` table, in turn, has a relation to the `OrderItems` table. This gives us a good hierarchy for our data that also happens to model a fairly common hierarchy among e-commerce applications.

Here is the XML document (`Orders.xml`) that we will use. Remember to include both this and the `Orders.xsd` file in your `FTrackADONET\Chapter04` directory.

```
<?xml version="1.0"?>
<Orders>
  <Customers>
    <CustomerId>1</CustomerId>
    <CustomerName>John Q Customer</CustomerName>
    <EmailAddress>john@some.anonymous.place.com</EmailAddress>
    <Address1>1 John St</Address1>
    <Address2></Address2>
    <City>Anonymous</City>
    <State>IL</State>
    <Zip>11111</Zip>
  </Customers>
  <Order>
    <OrderId>1</OrderId>
    <CustomerId>1</CustomerId>
    <OrderStatus>Shipped</OrderStatus>
    <ShipTo/>
    <ShipAddress/>
    <ShipAddress2/>
    <ShipCity/>
    <ShipState/>
```

```
        <ShipZip/>
    </Order>
    <Order>
        <OrderId>2</OrderId>
        <CustomerId>1</CustomerId>
        <OrderStatus>Backordered</OrderStatus>
        <ShipTo/>
        <ShipAddress/>
        <ShipAddress2/>
        <ShipCity/>
        <ShipState/>
        <ShipZip/>
    </Order>
    <OrderItems>
        <OrderId>1</OrderId>
        <SKU>801010</SKU>
        <Price>24.99</Price>
        <Qty>12</Qty>
    </OrderItems>
    <OrderItems>
        <OrderId>2</OrderId>
        <SKU>905612</SKU>
        <Price>8.99</Price>
        <Qty>1</Qty>
    </OrderItems>
    <OrderItems>
        <OrderId>2</OrderId>
        <SKU>905613</SKU>
        <Price>7.99</Price>
        <Qty>1</Qty>
    </OrderItems>
</Orders>
```

As our "sample" application, we'll just write a little application that proves that we have relational (DataSet) access to all of the data included in the above schema. Here's the source code listing for our main class (TakerMain.cs) in the OrderTaker project:

```csharp
using System;
using System.Data;
using System.Xml;

namespace OrderTaker
{
    /// <summary>
    /// Summary description for Class1.
    /// </summary>
    class TakerMain
    {
        /// <summary>
        /// The main entry point for the application.
        /// </summary>
        [STAThread]
        static void Main(string[] args)
```

```
    {
      //
      // TODO: Add code to start application here
      //
      float price;
      int qty;
      float total;
      XmlDataDocument ordersDoc = new XmlDataDocument();
      DataSet ordersData = ordersDoc.DataSet;
      ordersData.ReadXmlSchema(@"..\..\..\Orders.xsd");

      ordersDoc.Load(@"..\..\..\Orders.XML");

      Console.WriteLine("We have access to customers and their orders:");
      foreach (DataRow customer in ordersData.Tables["Customers"].Rows)
      {
        Console.WriteLine("{0}: {1}", customer["CustomerId"].ToString(),
            customer["CustomerName"].ToString());
        foreach (DataRow order in customer.GetChildRows("CustomerOrders"))
        {
          Console.WriteLine("Order {0}. Status: {1}",
              order["OrderId"].ToString(),order["OrderStatus"].ToString());
          foreach (DataRow item in order.GetChildRows("OrderItems"))
          {
            price = System.Convert.ToSingle(item["Price"]);
            qty = System.Convert.ToInt32(item["Qty"]);
            total = price * qty;
            Console.WriteLine("   --  {0}. {1} @ ${2}. Total ${3}",
                item["SKU"].ToString(), item["Qty"].ToString(), price,
                total);
          }
        }
      }
    }
  }
}
```

When we build and run this application, we get screen output that looks like this:

The other half of our example was a stripped-down prototype of a warehouse application. The warehouse application has less access to information than the web site itself does. The only things the warehouse should be able to do is to see shipping information, and order details.

Now, we removed the billing address information from the Customers table in the schema, and we removed the pricing information from the OrderItems table. This new, limited schema is stored in the Orders_Warehouse.XSD file:

```xml
<?xml version="1.0" standalone="yes" ?>
<xs:schema id="OrdersData" xmlns="" xmlns:xs="http://www.w3.org/2001/XMLSchema"

xmlns:msdata="urn:schemas-microsoft-com:xml-msdata">
<xs:element name="Orders" msdata:IsDataSet="true">
  <xs:complexType>
    <xs:choice maxOccurs="unbounded">
      <xs:element name="Customers">
        <xs:complexType>
          <xs:sequence>
            <xs:element name="CustomerId" type="xs:integer" minOccurs="1" />
            <xs:element name="CustomerName" type="xs:string"
                minOccurs="0" />
          </xs:sequence>
        </xs:complexType>
      </xs:element>
      <xs:element name="Order">
        <xs:complexType>
          <xs:sequence>
            <xs:element name="OrderId" type="xs:integer" minOccurs="1" />
            <xs:element name="CustomerId" type="xs:integer" minOccurs="0" />
            <xs:element name="OrderStatus" type="xs:string" minOccurs="0" />
            <xs:element name="ShipTo" type="xs:string" minOccurs="0" />
            <xs:element name="ShipAddress" type="xs:string" minOccurs="0" />
            <xs:element name="ShipAddress2" type="xs:string"
                minOccurs="0" />
            <xs:element name="ShipCity" type="xs:string" minOccurs="0" />
            <xs:element name="ShipState" type="xs:string" minOccurs="0" />
            <xs:element name="ShipZip" type="xs:string" minOccurs="0" />
          </xs:sequence>
        </xs:complexType>
      </xs:element>
      <xs:element name="OrderItems">
        <xs:complexType>
          <xs:sequence>
            <xs:element name="OrderId" type="xs:integer" minOccurs="0" />
            <xs:element name="SKU" type="xs:string" minOccurs="0" />
            <xs:element name="Qty" type="xs:int" minOccurs="0" />
          </xs:sequence>
        </xs:complexType>
      </xs:element>
    </xs:choice>
  </xs:complexType>

  <xs:unique name="Constraint2" msdata:PrimaryKey="true">
    <xs:selector xpath=".//Customers" />
    <xs:field xpath="CustomerId" />
  </xs:unique>
  <xs:unique name="Constraint1" msdata:PrimaryKey="true">
    <xs:selector xpath=".//Order" />
```

```
        <xs:field xpath="OrderId" />
    </xs:unique>
    <xs:keyref name="OrderItems" refer="Constraint1">
      <xs:selector xpath=".//OrderItems" />
      <xs:field xpath="OrderId" />
    </xs:keyref>
    <xs:keyref name="CustomerOrders" refer="Constraint2">
      <xs:selector xpath=".//Order" />
      <xs:field xpath="CustomerId" />
    </xs:keyref>
  </xs:element>
</xs:schema>
```

Here's the source code listing for the limited "warehouse" version of the application using the XmlDataDocument to limit the view of data. Create a C# Console Application and call it OrderWarehouse. Remember to also include the Orders_Warehouse.XSD file in the FTrackADONET\Chapter04 folder.

```
using System;
using System.Xml;
using System.Data;

namespace OrderWarehouse
{
  /// <summary>
  /// Summary description for Class1
  /// </summary>
  class WarehouseMain
  {
    /// <summary>
    /// The main entry point for the application
    /// </summary>
    [STAThread]
    static void Main(string[] args)
    {
      //
      // TODO: Add code to start application here
      //
      XmlDataDocument ordersDoc = new XmlDataDocument();
      DataSet ordersData = ordersDoc.DataSet;
      ordersData.ReadXmlSchema(@"..\..\..\Orders_warehouse.xsd");
      ordersDoc.Load(@"..\..\..\Orders.XML");

      Console.WriteLine("We have limited access to customer data.");
      foreach (DataRow customer in ordersData.Tables["Customers"].Rows)
      {
        Console.WriteLine(customer["CustomerName"]);
        foreach (DataRow order in customer.GetChildRows("CustomerOrders"))
        {
          Console.WriteLine("{0}: {1}", order["OrderId"].ToString(),
            order["OrderStatus"].ToString());
          foreach (DataRow orderitem in order.GetChildRows("OrderItems"))
          {
```

```
                   Console.WriteLine(" -- {0}: {1} ordered.",
                      orderitem["SKU"].ToString(), orderitem["Qty"].ToString());
```

If you want to prove to yourself that this `DataSet` cannot possibly make any changes to data that it doesn't have any access to, uncomment the `Console.WriteLine()` call below and watch the exception that occurs. The `DataSet` will report that it has no such column named "Price".

```
              // if we try and access the price field, an exception will be
              // thrown because the DataSet doesn't know about it.
              // Console.WriteLine(" -- Price Paid: ${0}",
              //        orderitem["Price"].ToString());
            }
          }
        }

        // now we'll change some data to show that we can change the data
        //we're allowed to change without harming the restricted data.
        DataRow firstCustomer = ordersData.Tables["Customers"].Rows[0];
        firstCustomer["CustomerName"] = "Kevin Hoffman";
        ordersDoc.Save(@"..\..\..\Orders2.xml");
      }
    }
  }
```

In the last section of code, we made a change to the first customer and then saved the file to disk. We didn't have any access whatsoever to the customer's billing information or to the prices of items on their orders, but that information is *still* retained in the file itself. The data itself has maintained *integrity* even though we've limited the access to that data.

If you've tried a similar experiment by loading XML into a `DataSet` directly that doesn't contain schema entries for particular columns, you'll have noticed that when you have that `DataSet` back to disk, all of that information that you didn't have access to has been erased. With the intervention of the `XmlDataDocument`, we can limit access to XML data, *and* maintain data integrity.

Let's take a look at the XML for the first customer in our updated `Orders2.xml` file:

```
<?xml version="1.0"?>
<Orders>
  <Customers>
    <CustomerId>1</CustomerId>
    <CustomerName>Kevin Hoffman</CustomerName>
    <EmailAddress>john@some.anonymous.place.com</EmailAddress>
    <Address1>1 John St</Address1>
    <Address2></Address2>
    <City>Anonymous</City>
    <State>IL</State>
    <Zip>11111</Zip>
  </Customers>
```

Take a close look at this record. The first thing to notice is that we did manage to successfully change the customer's name. More importantly, the address for that customer is accurate and has been saved, even though we didn't have access to it through the `DataSet`.

> Even though the `DataSet` cannot actually see all of the data in the underlying XML document, it is still there and will still be there even after changes have been made to the `DataSet`.

Limiting a Relational View of XML with a Typed DataSet

In the last chapter, we discussed the benefits and mechanics of using strongly typed `DataSet`s. They provide a strongly typed data access model for columns, rows, and relationships. In addition, they provide the data structure at design time, so there is no need to constantly load the schema for the data. This makes for fewer programming errors due to forgetting to load the schema, and also prevents different versions of the same schema from being loaded from multiple places (such as two different directories on disk or two different URLs).

The above example illustrated limiting data access to information by providing an XML Schema to the underlying `DataSet` for the `XmlDataDocument` instance. One way to provide that schema is to load the schema from a disk file, which we illustrated.

The other way to provide that schema is to create a typed `DataSet`, which has its schema built into it at design time. This way, you don't need to worry about deploying XSD files to various different application sites – the application distribution itself contains the appropriate `DataSet`. For example, the developers of the application would send one typed `DataSet` to the web site distribution, and they would send a limited version of that typed `DataSet` to the application distribution running in the warehouse.

The following is a modification of the limited-access demo from above. The difference between the previous approach and this next method is that this application is using a typed `DataSet` and we don't need to load the XSD file at the beginning of the program. As well, the `DataSet` itself will *not* have any member definitions for information that isn't contained in the schema. This means that the typed `DataSet` will not have member definitions for the customer billing information or for the pricing information on the order detail records.

To build this project, we first create a C# Console Application and call it `OrderWarehouse_Typed`. (Once again, the pre-built code for this application is in the code download in the `FTrackADONET\Chapter04\OrderWarehouse_Typed` folder.) From there, we add a new `DataSet` to the project (right-click the project, choose **Add**, then add a class and choose **DataSet** from the list of available class templates) and paste in the limited schema from the `Orders_Warehouse.XSD` file. We have already seen the listing for this in our previous example.

Here's the code listing for the main class for our `OrderWarehouse_Typed` application:

```
using System;
using System.Xml;
using System.Data;

namespace OrderWarehouse_Typed
{
    /// <summary>
    /// Summary description for Class1.
    /// </summary>
```

```
class WarehouseMain
{
  /// <summary>
  /// The main entry point for the application.
  /// </summary>
  [STAThread]
  static void Main(string[] args)
  {
    //
    // TODO: Add code to start application here
    //
    Orders ordersData = new Orders();
    XmlDataDocument ordersDoc = new XmlDataDocument( ordersData );
    ordersDoc.Load(@"..\..\..\Orders.XML");

    // display the customers.
    foreach (Orders.CustomersRow customer in ordersData.Customers.Rows)
    {
      Console.WriteLine(customer.CustomerName);
```

Again, just to prove the point that the typed `DataSet` does not have access to the information that is missing from the schema, if you uncomment the indicated line of code, an exception will occur as that class does not have a property definition for the `Address1` field.

```
    // uncomment to cause an exception
    //Console.WriteLine(customer.Address1);
    // display the customer's orders
    foreach (Orders.OrderRow order in customer.GetOrderRows())
    {
      Console.WriteLine("{0}: Status {1}", order.OrderId,
          order.OrderStatus);
      // display the order's items
      foreach (Orders.OrderItemsRow orderitem in
          order.GetOrderItemsRows())
      {
        Console.WriteLine(" -- {0}: {1} Ordered.", orderitem.SKU,
            orderitem.Qty);
      }
    }
  }

  // modify the first customer
  Orders.CustomersRow firstCustomer = ordersData.Customers[0];
  firstCustomer.CustomerName = "Kevin Hoffman";
  ordersDoc.Save(@"..\..\..\Orders2.xml");
  }
 }
}
```

The following screenshot shows what it looks like when we build and run this application. We can see that the hierarchy of the data is still in place, and even though we didn't specifically load a schema, the schema is being enforced by the typed `DataSet`:

The examples that we've seen here are examples that illustrate that you can limit access to data by "hiding" information from the schema for the particular `DataSet` that you're planning on using to access the data. There is actually more to it than that.

Any information that does not match or verify against the schema will not be visible to the `DataSet`. This means that not only can you exclude columns and tables and relations from the `DataSet`'s view of the data, but also you can actually limit particular rows!

For example, if your schema indicates that the numeric type for the `OrderId` only has a valid range of 1-100, then only orders 1 through 100 will appear in any `DataSet` using that schema as a "window" into the `XmlDataDocument`'s XML data. You can see that the possibilities here are endless. Rather than working with simple XML files, hook up this concept of data limitation to an enormous, multi-site enterprise application with a vast back-end network of data sources, and you can take a lot of the extremely hard, painful, and laborious details out of data limitation simply by providing schemas to the various different application development teams and using the advanced techniques we've described here to not only limit the view of available data, but to preserve the integrity of any data that is not included in the schema.

Summary

This chapter has covered some varied and advanced topics. The use of XML for data representation is becoming more and more commonplace, and will gain even more momentum as the push toward Web Services gains more strength.

We took a brief look at how the .NET Framework contains native, managed code that supports the W3C DOM standard. Then we took that discussion further and took a look at how to use the `XmlDataDocument`, not only as a way of accessing XML data, but as a way of providing a relational view to XML hierarchical data. Finally, we wrapped up the chapter by discussing the advanced concepts of using XML Schemas and typed `DataSets`. We looked at how you can limit not only the view of data, but access to that data, simply by providing a schema that did not contain information about the secured data.

By the time you've finished this chapter and the ones preceding it, you should now have a mastery of the concepts involved in the `DataSet`, the typed `DataSet`, and how to use all of that knowledge and more to use XML easily, effectively, and practically within the .NET Framework and more specifically within ADO.NET.

5

DataReaders

In the last two chapters, you have learned about the power and flexibility of the ADO.NET `DataSet`. While the `DataSet` provides essentially an in-memory subset of the underlying data store, its power and flexibility come with a price. A `DataSet` object generally carries more information than just the data. It may contain schema information about the underlying data store. For instance, if a table in the `DataSet` represents a database table, it must also contain the metadata about the table itself.

A `DataSet` is a good candidate for caching data in-memory to be used by an application. Such an application typically manipulates the cached data in disconnected mode and only updates the underlying data store at certain times. For instance, a Windows Form application may present a collection of customer records and allow users to make changes to them. It pushes the changes to the data store only when the user asks or when a specific event occurs, such as a designated period of time lapses.

It is also common for an application to load a collection of records from a database but not modify them. For instance, an online bookshop application may display a list of books as the result of a user search. The user doesn't modify any of the book information. Instead, they may choose several books from the list and consider ordering them later. In such cases, loading data in a `DataSet` is not the most efficient solution. The application doesn't need the data to be cached in-memory, neither does it need any table schema information. For an application designed to support a large number of users, caching a `DataSet` for each user is an expensive exercise as it consumes a huge portion of system memory and may cause the server to run out of memory. This is a typical scenario of applications, especially web applications, where most data access operations are essentially read-only operations.

ADO.NET provides an efficient solution for such situations. It defines `DataReader` classes to facilitate forward-only and read-only access to data stores. A data reader is highly efficient for retrieving a set of data as the result of a read operation, and then extracting it in one pass. It is especially suitable to read a large amount of data because it doesn't cache the data in the memory. The list below summarizes the data reader features discussed in this chapter.

❑ How data readers fit in the .NET data provider object model

❑ How to use `Command` objects to execute SQL statements and stored procedures

❑ How to specify run-time search criteria using parameters

❑ How to extract data from a data reader

❑ How to retrieve binary data

❑ How to read data using output parameters

❑ How to run multiple queries and access results

❑ How to retrieve hierarchical result sets

❑ How to retrieve column schema information using a data reader

The next section presents an overview of ADO.NET data provider architecture. The rest of this chapter then discusses various aspects of the data readers.

Connecting to the Database

In order to access data in a database, you must connect to the database and then perform appropriate database operations. The .NET data access architecture uses data providers to access different types of data sources. Each data provider contains a collection of well-defined and inter-related classes that perform operations such as connecting to databases, executing commands, and processing results. To provide a uniform interface among classes in different data providers, each class in a data provider must implement an interface defined in the `System.Data` namespace. Among other things, each data provider defines each of the following:

❑ `Connection` class implementing the `IDbConnection` interface. This class is responsible for establishing and managing connections to underlying data stores.

❑ `Command` class implementing the `IDbCommand` interface. This class is responsible for executing commands against the underlying data stores.

❑ `DataReader` class implementing the `IDataReader` interface. This class is responsible for holding results returned from command executions.

❑ `DataAdapter` class implementing the `IDataAdapter` interface. The next chapter will cover this class in detail.

❑ `Transaction` class implementing the `IDbTransaction` interface. This class will also be discussed in the next chapter.

The .NET Framework includes two .NET data providers, SQL Server .NET Data Provider and OLE DB .NET Data Provider. Microsoft has also developed another data provider, ODBC .NET Data Provider, and offers it for free download at http://msdn.microsoft.com/downloads (search for "ODBC .NET Data Provider" at the site, because the links change!). At the time of writing this chapter, Microsoft is also developing an Oracle .NET Data Provider. Various third-party database vendors have released or are in the process of creating .NET Data Providers for their products. For instance, CoreLab Software Development has released a .NET Data Provider for MySQL, MySqlDirect.NET (http://crlab.com/mysqlnet/). The figure below illustrates the data providers and their object hierarchy related to data readers. The `DataAdapter` and `Transaction` classes are the subjects of the next chapter; therefore they are omitted from the hierarchy here.

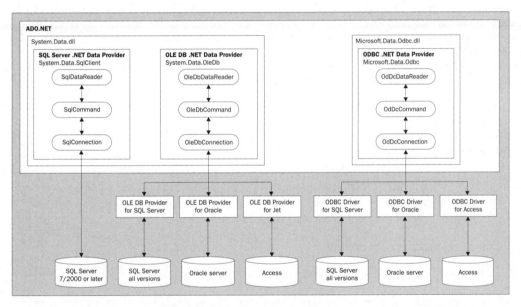

All three data providers implement a similar set of functionalities, such as connecting to a data store, executing a command, and so forth. I will start by briefly discussing each provider in the next few sections. In later sections, I will base the discussion on the SQL Server .NET Data Provider as most of the features and issues also apply to the other two data providers. When there are differences among the data providers, or when certain features are only available to some of the data providers, I will point out the differences in the text.

Connections to SQL Server

The SQL Server .NET Data Provider offers optimized access to SQL Server 7 and 2000. To connect to SQL Server 6.5 or earlier, you will need to use the OLE DB .NET Data Provider and the OLE DB Provider for SQL Server. In this chapter, the term SQL Server will refer to SQL Server 7 or later.

The SQL Server .NET Data Provider is specifically designed to provide efficient access to SQL Server, and therefore is the preferred choice for applications that use SQL Server as the backend database. It directly calls the SQL Server API functions to perform database operations. The above figure shows that it has one less layer of abstraction than the other two data providers, which use either a database-specific OLE DB Data Provider or ODBC driver to execute database commands. While you can use the OLE DB or ODBC .NET Data Providers to access SQL Server, their performances may not be as good as the SQL Server .NET Data Provider. In practice, you will only use OLE DB .NET Data Provider to access SQL Server if you need to take advantage of the features provided by OLE DB that are not available in the SQL Server .NET Data Provider. One such feature is the OLE DB chapter, which allows you to retrieve a hierarchical, or shaped, result set.

The SQL Server .NET Data Provider is defined in the `System.Data.SqlClient` namespace, which is contained in the `System.Data` DLL assembly. If you use Visual Studio.NET to develop applications, this assembly is automatically referenced for most types of projects. While you can reference classes in this namespace using fully qualified names such as:

```
System.Data.SqlClient.SqlConnection cn =
    new System.Data.SqlClient.SqlConnection(ConnectionString)
```

it will be much easier if you import this namespace in your classes:

```
using System.Data.SqlClient;

SqlConnection cn = new SqlConnection(ConnectionString)
```

All examples in this and the next chapters assume that you have included the `using` directive, and therefore will not qualify `SqlClient` class names with namespace identifiers.

The SqlConnection Class

To connect to a SQL Server, you instantiate a `SqlConnection` object and invoke its `Open` method. When you no longer need the connection, you call its `Close` method to close it. The `SqlConnection` class defines two constructors; one takes no argument, and the other accepts a connection string. Therefore you can instantiate a connection in either of the following two ways:

```
// Passing in the connection string to the constructor
SqlConnection cn = new SqlConnection(ConnectionString);
cn.Open();
```

or:

```
// Using the default constructor and assign the connection string.
SqlConnection cn = new SqlConnection();
cn.ConnectionString = ConnectionString;
cn.Open();
```

Obviously the first form requires less typing and you will probably use it in most situations. The second form is useful in cases where you want to reuse the `Connection` object to connect using a different identity or to different databases.

```
SqlConnection cn = new SqlConnection();
cn.ConnectionString = ConnectionString1;
cn.Open();
// Do something
cn.Close();
```

or:

```
cn.ConnectionString = ConnectionString2;
cn.Open();
// Do something else
cn.Close();
```

Please note that you can only assign a different connection string to a `Connection` object when it is closed. As illustrated in the above code snippet, you must close the connection before modifying its connection string. You can find out whether or not a connection is open by checking its `State` property, which can be either `Open` or `Closed`. This property can have other values such as `Executing` or `Broken`, but the current versions of the SQL Server, OLE DB, and ODBC Data Providers don't support them as yet.

A standard disclaimer before we dive in – in order to focus on the data reader features, I don't include any exception handling in sample code. In a production application, you should try to catch and handle any exceptions raised when connecting to databases and processing data. Failing to connect to a database falls into the category of exceptions and should be handled as such.

SQL Server Connection Strings

The SQL Server .NET Data Provider connection string contains a collection of property name-value pairs. Each property name-value pair is separated by a semicolon.

```
PropertyName1=Value1;PropertyName2=Value2;...;PropertyNameN=ValueN
```

Also, a connection string must contain the SQL server instance name:

```
Data Source=ServerName
```

The downloadable sample project for this chapter uses a local SQL Server (`localhost`). If you intend to run it with a remote server, you should assign the correct server to the `Data Source` property in the sample object. You must also specify one of the two supported authentication methods – Windows authentication or SQL Server authentication. Windows authentication uses your Windows login user identity to connect to the database, while the SQL authentication requires you to explicitly specify the SQL Server user ID and password. To use Windows authentication, you include the `Integrated Security` property in the connection string.

```
Data Source=ServerName;Integrated Security=True
```

By default, the `Integrated Security` property is `False`, which disables Windows authentication. If you don't explicitly set this property to `True`, the connection will use SQL Server authentication and therefore you must supply a SQL Server user ID and password. The only other recognized value of the `Integrated Security` property is `SSPI`, which stands for **Security Support Provider Interface**. It is supported on all Windows NT operating systems, including Windows NT 4.0, 2000, and XP. This is the only interface used to connect to SQL Server using Windows authentication, and is treated exactly the same as `Integrated Security` property value equals `True`.

> *For more information on SSPI, please read the subject on MSDN:*
> http://msdn.microsoft.com/library/en-us/security/security/sspi.asp

In the Windows authentication mode, SQL Server uses the Windows security subsystem to validate a user connection. It doesn't examine the connection string for user ID and password, even if you explicitly specify them. The fact that only Windows NT, 2000, and XP support SSPI implies that you can only use Windows integrated security to connect to SQL Server if you are running those operating systems. In other systems, you must use SQL Server authentication. Regardless of which operation systems you use, you must specify a user ID and a password in the connection string when using SQL Server authentication:

```
Data Source=ServerName;User ID=donaldx;Password=unbreakable
```

By default, the SQL Server .NET Data Provider connects to the specified user's default database, which can be set when you create the user in the database. You can also modify a user's default database at any time. For instance, the system administrator's default database is `master`. If you want to connect to a different database, you should specify the database name:

```
Data Source=ServerName;Integrated Security=SSPI;Initial Catalog=Northwind
```

Each authentication method has its advantages and disadvantages. Windows authentication uses a single source of user repository and therefore eliminates the need to configure users for database access separately. The connection string doesn't contain a user ID and password, and therefore eliminates the risk of revealing them to unauthorized users. You can manage users and their roles in the Active Directory without having to explicitly configure their properties in the SQL Server.

The downside of Windows authentication is that it requires the client to connect to the SQL Server over a secured channel supported by Windows' security subsystem. If an application needs to connect to a SQL Server over an unsecured network such as the Internet, Windows authentication will not work. It also partially moves the responsibility of managing database access control from DBAs to system administrators, which may be an issue in established environments.

In general, common application design practices strengthen the case for using Windows authentication. Most corporate databases are hosted on more robust Windows server operating systems, which all support Windows authentication. The separation of the data access layer from the presentation layer also promotes the idea of encapsulating data-access code in middle-tier components, which typically run inside an internal network with the database server. This design removes the need to establish database connections over unsecured channels. In addition, Web Services also reduces the need to directly connect to databases in different domains. Chapter 8 will discuss techniques and issues for using ADO.NET with Web Services.

Don't Forget to Close Connections

Database connections are valuable resources, but they are expensive because they consume precious system resources such as memory and network bandwidth. In distributed applications that are designed to serve a large number of users, it is of paramount importance to close a connection when you no longer need it. This is even truer in ADO.NET, where a connection is not closed automatically when the `Connection` object goes out of scope.

This fact has an undesired effect on connection pooling. By default, .NET creates a connection pool for each process that connects to a database. When the process requests to open a database connection, the .NET Data Provider will try to pick an existing connection from the pool and pass it to the requesting process. That connection will only be returned to the connection pool when it is closed. When a connection goes out of scope, the garbage collector may collect the collection. However, the garbage collection does not close the connection, and therefore doesn't return the connection to the pool. When the process requests another collection, the .NET Data Provider can't reuse that connection.

To close a connection, you call its `Close` method. If you have a data reader attached to the connection, you should close the data reader first. Let's be explicit about this – we must always close a connection when it's no longer needed. Not closing unneeded connections has a significantly negative effect on the scalability of applications. Not only may other clients have to wait for the idle connection to become available, but also those that manage to connect may have less than ideal server resources when there are many open connections. While we, as developers, don't have control over how many simultaneous connections may happen, especially on high traffic applications, we must do our best to ensure that our applications don't use more resources than absolutely necessary. Closing connections as soon as possible is an easy and very effective practice to help us achieve this goal.

Connections to OLE DB Data Sources

The OLE DB .NET Data Provider is designed to connect to databases using their OLE DB providers. For instance, if your application uses Oracle, you will need to connect to it using the OLE DB .NET Data Provider together with either a Microsoft or an Oracle OLE DB provider for Oracle databases. The OLE DB .NET data provider is defined in the `System.Data.OleDbClient` namespace, which is also contained in `System.Data.dll`.

While the OLE DB .NET Data Provider is designed to communicate with native OLE DB Providers, it provides an almost identical interface to the SQL Server .NET Data Provider in connecting to client applications. For instance, like the `SqlConnection` class, the `OleDbConnection` class also defines two constructors. One constructor takes no argument, and the other accepts a connection string. Therefore, you can replace `SqlConnection` with `OleDbConnection` in the code snippet used in the `SqlConnection` class section, and use it to connect to an OLE DB data source.

There is one difference though. Because you can use the OLE DB .NET Data Provider to connect to different OLE DB providers, you must specify the underlying database-specific OLE DB Provider in the connection string. For instance, the following connection string can be used to connect to an Oracle database using Microsoft OLE DB Provider for Oracle:

```
Provider=MSDAORA;Data Source=ServerName;
User ID=donaldx;Password=unbreakable;Initial Catalog=MyAppDB
```

Note that Microsoft OLE DB Provider for SQL Server supports Windows authentication, so you can use it when connecting to SQL Server. For other databases, you will need to specify a user ID and password in your connection strings.

Connections to ODBC Data Sources

The ODBC .NET Data Provider provides applications with access to databases through their ODBC drivers. For instance, if your application connects to an Ingres database through an ODBC connection, you can use ADO.NET to access the database using the ODBC .NET Data Provider.

As I mentioned earlier, the ODBC .NET Data Provider is not a part of the .NET Framework. Instead, Microsoft releases it as a separate product. So it's probably not surprising to find that it is not defined in the `System.Data` namespace. Instead, it's defined in the `Microsoft.Data.Odbc` namespace, which is contained in `Microsoft.Data.Odbc.dll`. In your application, you will need to add a reference to this assembly, after downloading it from the MSDN site (see above).

The connection strings for the ODBC .NET Data Provider consist of property name-value pairs different from those for the SQL Server or OLE DB .NET Data Providers. For instance, to connect to the Northwind Access database through a DSN named `Northwind`, the connection string looks like this:

```
Driver={Microsoft Access Driver (*.mdb)};DSN=Northwind;
DBQ=D:\Microsoft Office\Office10\Samples\Northwind
```

The OLE DB .NET Data Provider reference documentation contains a list of sample connection strings for several databases. If you need to connect to other ODBC data sources, please check the documentation for data source-specific connection string formats.

To create a connection to an ODBC data source, you follow the same pattern as for SQL Server or OLE DB data sources. The code snippet below is an example:

```
OdbcConnection cn = new OdbcConnection(ConnectionString);
cn.Open();
```

Executing Commands

Once a database connection is established, you can perform data access and manipulation operations. Database gurus typically summarize such operations as CRUD – Create, Read, Update, and Delete. ADO.NET defines `Command` classes to perform those operations. Unlike in ADO, where you can execute commands directly from `Connection` objects, ADO.NET mandates the use of `Command` objects to execute database commands. As this chapter is about data readers, which are used for reading data only, we will look at how to perform read operations using `Command` objects. The other three operations will be the subject of the next chapter.

The `OleDbCommand` and `SqlCommand` classes are very similar, except that `OleDbCommand` does not have an `ExecuteXmlReader` method. This is also true of the other data provider-specific classes covered in this chapter.

The SqlCommand Class

In order to execute commands, you need to create a `Command` object. A `Command` object requires a `Connection` object and the `CommandText` to be executed. The `SqlCommand` class defines four constructors. The first is the default constructor that takes no parameters:

```
SqlCommand cmd = new SqlCommand();
cmd.Connection = ConnectionObject;
cmd.CommandText = CommandText;
```

The above code snippet creates a `SqlCommand` object using the default constructor. It then assigns an existing `Connection` object and a command text to the `Command` object's `Connection` and `CommandText` properties, respectively.

A typical method to retrieve data from databases involves using SQL `SELECT` statements. Therefore a command text may be a SQL `SELECT` query:

```
string CommandText = "SELECT CategoryID, CategoryName FROM Categories";
```

In addition, many relational databases, such as SQL Server and Oracle, support stored procedures to execute a group of SQL statements. You can specify a stored procedure name as the command text. I will explain more about executing a stored procedure in a moment.

The second constructor accepts a command text:

```
SqlCommand cmd = new SqlCommand(CommandText);
cmd.Connection = ConnectionObject;
```

This instantiates a `Command` object and initializes its `CommandText` property with the given command text. It then assigns the `Command` object's `Connection` property with an existing `Connection` object.

The third constructor accepts a `Connection` object and a command text:

```
SqlCommand cmd = new SqlCommand(CommandText, ConnectionObject);
```

The last constructor adds a third parameter, a `SqlTransaction` object. You don't need a transaction to read data from the database, so I will leave this constructor to the next chapter, which covers the database update operations.

In all cases, the `Connection` object doesn't have to be open when you attach a `Command` object to it. However, if it is not open, you must open it before executing the command. The `SqlCommand` object provides four execution methods:

- ❑ ExecuteNonQuery
- ❑ ExecuteScalar
- ❑ ExecuteReader
- ❑ ExecuteXmlReader

The `ExecuteNonQuery` method executes a command that doesn't return a result. You usually use it to execute insert, update, or delete queries. You will see more about this method in the next chapter.

The `ExecuteReader` method executes a command and populates a `DataReader` object with the results. As data readers are the main subject of this chapter, we will come back to this method after we briefly explain the other two methods.

The ExecuteScalar Method

The `ExecuteScalar` method executes a command that returns a single value. For instance, if you want to get the total number of products in your system, you use this method to execute a SQL query `SELECT Count(*) FROM Products`.

```
SqlCommand cmd = new SqlCommand("SELECT Count(*) FROM Products", cn);

cn.Open();
int ProductCount = (int)cmd.ExecuteScalar();
MessageBox.Show("Product count = " + ProductCount.ToString());
cn.Close();
```

Note that you don't have to ensure that the parent command returns only a single value. If the command returns more results, the `ExecuteScalar` method will return the value of the first field in the first row. All other values are not accessible and will be discarded. To obtain the best performance, it's worth constructing your `SELECT` query properly, so that its result set contains as little extra data as possible. This method is the preferred choice if you are only interested in a single return value such as the result of aggregate methods such as `COUNT`, `SUM`, and `MAX`.

> The **ExecuteScalar** method is a programming shortcut for retrieving a single value from a database. It does not offer any performance advantage over the **ExecuteReader** method. Therefore you should construct your query carefully so that it does not return unwanted data.

The ExecuteXmlReader Method

The `ExecuteXmlReader` method executes a command that will return an XML string. It will return a `System.Xml.XmlReader` object containing the returned XML.

> If you connect to SQL Server 2000 through any of the .NET Data Providers, you can execute a **SELECT** statement containing the **FOR XML** directive. You can also execute a **SELECT** statement that returns an XML string such as a field containing a raw XML string. For other databases, please consult the relevant documentation for XML-related query requirements.

Details about the `XmlReader` class are beyond this chapter. If you want to know more about this class and the `ExecuteXmlReader` method, please read *Professional ADO.NET* (ISBN: 1-86100-527-X) by Wrox Press, which covers this subject in greater detail.

Data Readers

When you execute a command that returns a result set, you need a way to extract data out of the result set. There are two methods to process result sets – using a data reader or a data adapter in conjunction with an ADO.NET `DataSet`. You already know a lot about the `DataSet` itself and will learn more about data adapters in the next chapter. In this section, we will focus on using data readers to process command results.

The DataReader Classes

ADO.NET data readers are the top classes in the ADO.NET class hierarchy. Each .NET Data Provider defines a `DataReader` class, which sits on top of the `Command` class in the same data provider. A `DataReader` class uses its corresponding `Command` class to retrieve data from the underlying data store.

Creating a DataReader Object

You never explicitly create a `DataReader` object in ADO.NET using its constructor. In fact, none of the `DataReader` classes exposes a public constructor. Instead, you always invoke the `Command` class's `ExecuteReader`, which returns a `DataReader` object. The code snippet below illustrates how you create a `SqlDataReader` object:

```
SqlCommand cmd = new SqlCommand(CommandText, ConnectionObject);
SqlDataReader dr = cmd.ExecuteReader();
```

The most common use of `DataReader` classes is to retrieve records returned by a SQL query or a stored procedure. The previous section showed how you assign a SQL query to the `Command` object. Once the `ExecuteReader` method returns, the resulting data reader provides you with a channel to the collection of qualified records.

A `DataReader` is often referred as a connected, forward-only, and read-only result set. That is, you must keep the connection open while accessing the data reader. In addition, you can traverse through the records only from the beginning to the end, and once only. You can't stop at a record and move backwards. The records are also read-only; therefore data reader classes don't provide a means to modify the records in the database. If you are familiar with ADO, this corresponds to a server-side forward-only record set.

> **Data readers use the underlying connection exclusively. When a data reader is open, you cannot use the connection to perform other tasks such as executing another command. Remember to close a data reader when you have read through its records or when you no longer need it.**

Specifying Data Reader Characteristics with Command Behavior

The `ExecuteReader` method has an overloaded version that accepts a command behavior parameter. While the command text specifies the query that returns a result set, you can provide some indications as to how you intend to use the result by specifying a command behavior. ADO.NET defines the `CommandBehavior` enumeration in the `System.Data` namespace.

If you use a connection to create a data reader and don't intend to use the connection for other tasks, you can instruct ADO.NET to close the connection when you close the data reader.

```
SqlDataReader dr = cmd.ExecuteReader(CommandBehavior.CloseConnection);
```

This is especially useful when you marshal a data reader to other parts of your application. The client object may not have access to the connection and therefore cannot explicitly close it, or it may have been developed by other programmers who may have inadvertently forgotten to close the connection explicitly. When the client closes the data reader, the connection is implicitly closed. Please note that while this behavior instructs the data reader to close the connection once all data has been processed, it does not close the data reader itself. The client object is still responsible for closing the data reader.

If your query only returns a single row, or you are only interested in the first row of a result set potentially containing multiple rows, you pass `CommandBehavior.SingleRow` to the `ExecuteReader` method. Specifying this behavior will help to improve the performance of your application. Depending on the implementation of this behavior by the data provider, even queries expected to return a single row may yield a better performance. Please note that this behavior applies to the data reader only; the `ExecuteScalar` method doesn't support such behavior. Therefore if a result set contains multiple rows, using `ExecuteReader(CommandBehaviorSingleRow)` is more efficient than using `ExecuteScalar` because the former only returns the first row.

Similarly, if you need only a first result set in a query that potentially returns multiple result sets, you can specify this with the `CommandBehavior.SingleResult`. We will discuss how you can use data readers to return multiple result sets later on.

There are other useful features here. For instance, you can use `SequentialAccess` when working with binary data such as graphics. If you want to read column schema information using a data reader, you can specify `SchemaOnly` to prevent the command returning any records. This subject is covered in further detail in the *Retrieving Schema Information* section. Please refer to the ADO.NET documentation for more information on the `CommandBehavior` enumeration.

Traversing the Records in a Data Reader

When the `ExecuteReader` method returns a `DataReader` object, the current cursor position is right before the first record. You must call the reader's `Read` method to move the cursor to the first record, which becomes the current record. If the reader contains at least one record, the `Read` method returns a Boolean value of `true`. To move to the next record, you call the `Read` method again. You can repeat this process until you run past the last record, at which point the `Read` method returns `false`. A common technique is to traverse through the records in a `while` loop:

```
while (dr.Read())
{
    // Do something with the current record
}
```

Whenever the `Read` method returns `true`, you can access the fields contained in the current record. If you perform potentially time-consuming operations for each record, the reader must be open for a long time. Consequently, the underlying connection must remain open for a long time. In such cases, using a disconnected `DataSet` may be a better option.

Accessing Field Values

ADO.NET provides two ways to access fields in a record. The first is the `Item` property, which returns the value of a field specified by either the field index or the field name. The second is the `Get` methods, which return a typed value of a field specified by the field index. Let's take a look at how you use these methods to retrieve field values.

The Item Property

Each `DataReader` class defines an `Item` property that returns an object representing the value of a field. In C#, the `Item` property is the indexer for the `DataReader` class. Like all .NET CLR collections, the `Item` property is always zero based. So you will treat it as an index to the current record in the `DataReader` object:

```
object FieldValue = dr[FieldName];
object FieldValue = dr[FieldIndex];
```

You can pass in either a string containing the name of the field, or a 32-bit integer specifying the index of the field. For instance, if the command text is a SQL SELECT query:

```
SELECT CategoryID, CategoryName FROM Categories
```

you can get the values of the two returned fields using either:

```
object ID   = dr["CategoryID"];
object Name = dr["CategoryName"];
```

or:

```
object ID   = dr[0];
object Name = dr[1];
```

In most cases, you will want to retrieve the field value in the appropriate type. For instance, the `CategoryID` field in the Northwind database is a 32-bit integer, while the `CategoryName` field is a `string`. Therefore you can cast the value returned by the `Item` property to C# `int` and `string` data types as illustrated below.

```
int    ID   = (int)dr[0];
string Name = (string)dr[1];
```

It's your responsibility to ensure that the type casting is valid. If you try to cast a field value to an incompatible type, such as a non-numeric string to an integer, you will throw a `System.InvalidCastException` at run time.

The Get Methods

Each `DataReader` class defines a set of `Get` methods that return typed values. For instance, the `GetInt32` method returns the value of a field as a .NET CLR 32-bit integer. The `Get` methods automatically convert the native data types in the data source to the corresponding .NET data types. Each `Get` method accepts the index of a field. For instance, in the above example, you can retrieve the values of `CategoryID` and `CategoryName` fields using the code snippet overleaf.

141

```
int ID = dr.GetInt32(0);
string Name = dr.GetString(1);
```

Although those methods convert data from data source types to .NET data types, they don't perform other data conversions such as converting a 16-bit integer to a 32-bit integer. Therefore you must use the correct `Get` method that matches the field type. If you use an incorrect `Get` method, for instance, using `GetInt32` on a SQL `smalltint` (16 bit) field, an `InvalidCastException` will be thrown.

The main drawback of the `Get` methods, however, is that you can't specify a field with the field name. This generally produces code that is less readable, and consequently harder to maintain. I personally think this is a feature Microsoft should have implemented. Before Microsoft gets around to doing it, however, we will have to live with this shortcoming. A possible workaround is to define a set of field index constants and use them for the `Get` methods.

```
const int IdFieldIndex   = 0;
const int NameFieldIndex = 1;

int    ID   = dr.GetInt32(IdFieldIndex);
string Name = dr.GetString(NameFieldIndex);
```

You can also define a field index `enum` and cast them into integers:

```
enum CategoryFields {ID = 0, Name};
int    ID   = dr.GetInt32((int)CategoryFields.ID);
string Name = dr.GetString((int)CategoryFields.Name);
```

Needless to say, neither of them is perfect. However, they are both better than using the magic field index numbers all over the place. A third approach is to use the `GetOrdinal` method to retrieve a field index and then use it to retrieve field values.

```
int    NameFieldIndex = dr.GetOrdinal("Name");
string Name           = dr.GetString(NameIndex);
```

This may seem cumbersome, as you need to make two method calls. However, this approach is very efficient when you need to loop through a large result set in the reader because you only need to retrieve the index or indices once.

```
int IdFieldIndex   = dr.GetOrdinal("ID");
int NameFieldIndex = dr.GetOrdinal("Name");
while (dr.Read())
{
    int    ID   = dr.GetInt32(IdFieldIndex);
    string Name = dr.GetString(NameFieldIndex);
}
```

The trick is to store the indices in local variables and use those variables in the loop.

> **SqlDataReader** only: if you use SQL Server .NET Data Provider, you can retrieve
> field values in native SQL Server data types using any of the **GetSql** methods. Those
> methods don't perform conversions from SQL Server data types to .NET CLR data
> types. Using those methods with native SQL types defined in the
> **System.Data.SqlTypes** namespace results in slightly more efficient code. To take
> advantage of such efficiency, you must ensure that you don't inadvertently convert
> them by assigning the return value of a **GetSql** method to a .NET CLR data type.

Retrieving Data – A Simple Example

Let's take a look at an example. The code snippet below is a simple example of retrieving database
records using a data reader. It uses a SQL SELECT query to read all records in the Categories table in
the sample Northwind database.

```
public void ReadTable()
{
    const string SelectQuery =
            "SELECT CategoryID, CategoryName, Description FROM Categories";
    SqlConnection cn = new SqlConnection(DbConnectionString);
    SqlCommand cmd = new SqlCommand(SelectQuery, cn);

    cn.Open();
    SqlDataReader dr = cmd.ExecuteReader();

    listBox1.Items.Clear();
    while (dr.Read())
    {
        int    ID   = dr.GetInt32(0);
        string Name = dr.GetString(1);
        string Desc = dr.GetString(2);
        listBox1.Items.Add(ID.ToString() + '\t' + Name + '\t' + Desc);
    }

    dr.Close();
    cn.Close();
}
```

The DbConnectionString is a Windows Form-level constant containing the database connection string.

```
private static string DbConnectionString =
        "Data Source=(local);Initial Catalog=Northwind;" +
        "User ID=sa;password=";
```

After executing the SELECT command, this method moves through the records in the data reader and
displays them in a listbox. The downloadable sample project contains a complete list of this method that
includes code for using the Item property and other techniques discussed above.

Retrieving Data with Parameterized Queries

The last example demonstrates a common flow of using a `DataReader` to retrieve data from the database. It uses a simple `SELECT` query to return all of the records in a table. In real applications, you will often need to retrieve only a subset of the records based on certain selection criteria. For instance, you may want to retrieve all products in a category.

```
SELECT ProductID, ProductName FROM Products WHERE CategoryID = 1
```

Typically, the category ID comes from a result of other operations, such as a user selecting a category from a list. The ID value, therefore, is often unknown at design time. How do you manage such queries containing parts that are variable at run time? In ADO.NET, you can use a feature called the **parameterized query**. This is an area where the SQL Server .NET Data Provider differs from the other two .NET data providers. Let's take a look at each.

Specifying Parameters in SQL Server .NET Data Provider

SQL Server .NET Data Provider supports named parameters. When you specify a `SELECT` query in the command text, you must indicate that parts of it will only be set at run time. Each of those variable parts is called a parameter, and has the @ prefix.

```
SELECT ProductID, ProductName FROM Products
  WHERE CategoryID = @CategoryID
    AND ProductID < @MaxProductID
```

This query specifies that the value of the `CategoryID` and the `ProductID` range are changeable at run time. Here, `@CategoryID` is the name of the parameter that will contain the category ID value, and the `@MaxProductID` is the name of the parameter that will contain the largest product ID value. A parameter name always contains the @ prefix.

You create the `Command` object as usual:

```
const string SelectQuery = "SELECT ProductID, ProductName FROM Products" +
                           " WHERE CategoryID = @CategoryID" +
                           "   AND ProductID < @MaxProductID";
SqlConnection cn  = new SqlConnection(DbConnectionString);
SqlCommand    cmd = new SqlCommand(SelectQuery, cn);
```

Now you have a `Command` object containing a parameterized query. What you need to do now is to create a `Parameter` object for each parameter in the query. The `SqlCommand` class exposes a `Parameters` collection property that stores all parameters for the command. You add a new parameter to the collection by calling its `Add` method.

```
cmd.Parameters.Add("@CategoryID", CategoryIDValue);
cmd.Parameters.Add("@MaxProductID", MaxProductIDValue);
```

The first argument in the `Add` method is the name of the parameter, which is `@CategoryID` for the first parameter and `@MaxProductID` for the second. The second argument is the value of the parameter. In the first line above, it's a variable named `CategoryIDValue`. The `Add` method creates a new parameter, adds it to the parent `Parameters` collection, and returns a reference to the newly created parameter.

Alternatively, you can manually create a `Parameter` object and then add it to the collection.

```
SqlParameter param = new SqlParameter("@CategoryID", CategoryID);
cmd.Parameters.Add(param);
```

As you would expect, there are several overloaded versions of the `Add` method. They accept different arguments such as the type and size of the parameter. Please read the ADO.NET documentation at http://msdn.microsoft.com/library/en-us/cpref/html/frlrfSystemDataSqlClientSqlParameterCollection ClassAddTopic.asp in MSDN for more details.

The order in which you add a parameter to the command's `Parameters` collection is not significant. That is, you don't have to add parameters in the order they appear in the parameterized query. Once you have done that, just go ahead and execute the command.

```
cn.Open();
SqlDataReader dr = cmd.ExecuteReader();
```

Specifying Parameters in OLE DB and ODBC .NET Data Providers

Neither the OLE DB .Net Data Provider nor the ODBC .NET Data Provider supports named parameters. Instead, you use the question mark (?) as a placeholder in the query to indicate where the parameters appear in the query. The following `SELECT` query demonstrates the same parameterized query as used in the last section.

```
SELECT ProductID, ProductName FROM Products
  WHERE CategoryID = ?
    AND ProductID < ?
```

As parameters are not named, you must add `Parameter` objects to the command's `Parameters` collection in the order they appear in the query. For instance, if the `SelectQuery` variable contains the above SQL `SELECT` query, the code snippet below is valid.

```
OleDbCommand cmd = new OleDbCommand(SelectQuery, cn);
cmd.Parameters.Add("CatID", CategoryIDValue);
cmd.Parameters.Add("MaxProductID", MaxProductIDValue);
```

However, reversing the order the parameters are added will assign `MaxProductIDValue` to the first parameter and `CategoryIDValue` to the second. You won't receive a compile error since they are of the same type, but the result will not be what you intended.

Please note that as parameters are not named, parameter names are ignored by the data provider. You can even pass in an empty string to the `Add` method.

Each of the three forms in the downloadable sample code contains the complete list of a method called `ReadParamQuery` that executes a parameterized query using each data provider. You can enter a category ID and click the **Read Param Query** button. A list of products belonging to the specified category and with an ID number of less than 10 will show in the listbox.

Retrieving Data with Stored Procedures

While using a parameterized query solves the problem of retrieving data based on run time conditions, running plain SQL queries is not very efficient. When executing a SQL query, the database must dynamically create an execution plan for the query. To create an execution plan, the database engine must examine the query and work out the best strategy to execute it. This process generally takes time.

Stored procedures, on the other hand, have the advantage of passing on the possible execution scenario to the database engine. In general, the database engine can create an execution plan when the procedure is created. It can therefore save the generated execution plan at design time. When an application executes the stored procedure, the database engine can use the generated execution plan without having to go through the process of figuring out how to do it at run time. We commonly refer to the ability to generate execution plans for stored procedures at design time as **compilation**. So you often hear people saying that the stored procedures can be compiled. This results in better data operation performance on subsequent calls.

In addition to the ability to be compiled, stored procedures can also return query results through the return values and output parameters of the stored procedures. When a query returns only one record, it's more efficient to return the values of queried fields as output parameters of stored procedures. The client applications can use those values directly without having to obtain a result set, which typically carries extra information, such as schema metadata.

All three .NET Data Providers support the use of stored procedures. However, such support only materializes if the underlying database supports stored procedures. While most databases implement stored procedures in some form, not all of them do. An example is Microsoft Access, which doesn't provide such capability. If you work with databases that support stored procedures, consider using them for all data manipulation operations.

To execute stored procedures in ADO.NET applications, you assign the stored procedure name to the command text. You must also set the command's CommandType as a stored procedure. If the stored procedure returns a value or has any parameters, you must also create the parameters and add them to the command's Parameters collection.

The Northwind database has a stored procedure, CustOrderHist, that calculates and returns the total order quantity of each product a given customer has ordered. To execute this stored procedure, you can create a Command object and pass in the name of the stored procedure to its constructor.

```
SqlConnection cn = new SqlConnection(DbConnectionString);
SqlCommand cmd = new SqlCommand("CustOrderHist", cn);
```

Next, you specify that it's a stored procedure by setting the command's CommandType property to StoredProcedure.

```
cmd.CommandType = CommandType.StoredProcedure;
```

The `CommandType` enumeration is defined in the `System.Data` namespace. If you don't explicitly assign this property, it will default to `CommandType.Text`, which specifies that the command text is an SQL statement. The third value, `TableDirect`, in the `CommandType` enumeration is used to specify that the command text is a table name or a collection of table names separated by semicolons. Currently only the OLE DB .NET Data Provider supports this command type.

Because the `CustOrderHist` stored procedure requires a parameter, `@CustomerID`, that passes in the customer ID, you need to create and add a parameter to the command's `Parameters` collection.

```
cmd.Parameters.Add("@CustomerID", "ALFKI");
```

Now the `Command` object is ready, you can simply open the connection and execute the command.

```
cn.Open();
SqlDataReader dr = cmd.ExecuteReader();
```

You then traverse through the data reader to get all results. The `ReadStoredProc` method in `SqlDrForm` and `OleDbDrForm` in the downloadable code sample contains the complete code.

Advanced Data Retrieval

In addition to reading data with simple SQL queries and stored procedures, it's often necessary to perform more complex data retrieval operations such as retrieving multiple result sets. This section introduces some of the advanced techniques commonly used to achieve such tasks. The first of them, curiously enough, doesn't use a data reader at all.

Retrieving Data Using Output Parameters

It is common for stored procedures to return data using output parameters. If an application needs to read a single record from a database, a common technique is to return the required fields using output parameters in stored procedures. This approach is more efficient than returning a result set containing a single record in a data reader.

An example of this technique is to read the name and price of a given product. Assuming that you know the product's ID, you could create a stored procedure to return the two fields. The stored procedure looks like the one listed below:

```
CREATE PROCEDURE GetProductData
(
    @ProductID    int,
    @ProductName  nvarchar(40) output,
    @ProductPrice money        output
)
AS
    SELECT @ProductName = ProductName, @ProductPrice = UnitPrice
      FROM Products
     WHERE ProductID = @ProductID
GO
```

This is a Transact SQL (T-SQL) stored procedure. Although other databases such as Oracle use slightly different syntax, the concept is the same. It defines three parameters. The first is the `ProductID` you use for passing in the ID to the stored procedure. We call it an input parameter because it's used to pass in values to the stored procedure. The other two are output parameters used to return values back to the callers of the stored procedure. You identify an output parameter by specifying the keyword `output` after its data type. Input parameters need no extra declarative element, as input is the default parameter direction.

> Remember that in order to run this example on the `SqlDrForm` in the code download, you MUST create this stored procedure first. A SQL form called `GetProductData.sql` is provided in the code download for this chapter, and can be run through Query Analyzer in SQL Server, or entered manually in the Enterprise Manager.

The SQL `SELECT` query assigns the two output parameters, `@ProductName` and `@ProductPrice`, with values stored in the corresponding fields in the `Products` table. When the stored procedure returns, the caller of this stored procedure can retrieve the product name and price from the two fields.

To try this example out, create the stored procedure in the Northwind database by entering the above T-SQL statements. In your ADO.NET application, you create a connection and a command object as you do with a normal stored procedure discussed in the *Retrieving Data with Stored Procedures* section.

```
SqlConnection cn = new SqlConnection(DbConnectionString);
cn.Open();

SqlCommand cmd = new SqlCommand("GetProductData", cn);
cmd.CommandType = CommandType.StoredProcedure;
```

Next, add the three parameters to the command's `Parameters` collection. As `ProductID` is an input parameter, you simply specify the parameter name and value.

```
SqlParameter param = cmd.Parameters.Add("@ProductID", ProductID);
```

Adding an output parameter is slightly different. You use the version of the `Parameter` collection's `Add` method that accepts three parameters: parameter name, data type, and optionally data length in bytes.

```
param = cmd.Parameters.Add("@ProductName", SqlDbType.NVarChar, 40);
```

Most SQL data types have fixed length. For instance, `int` is a 32-bit integer occupying 4 bytes, and `datatime` is 8 bytes long. `String` data types, on the other hand, often have variable length. In this example, the `@ProductName` parameter is a string that accepts up to 40 characters. You will also need to explicitly specify the type of the parameter as an output parameter.

```
param.Direction = ParameterDirection.Output;
```

Adding in the last parameter, `@ProductPrice`, is similar as illustrated below:

```
param = cmd.Parameters.Add("@ProductPrice", SqlDbType.Money);
param.Direction = ParameterDirection.Output;
```

Now you have specified all parameters for the command, you can execute the stored procedure by calling the command's `ExecuteNonQuery` method.

```
cmd.ExecuteNonQuery();
```

After the method returns, you can retrieve the product name and price from the two output parameters:

```
string   ProductName = cmd.Parameters["@ProductName"].Value.ToString();
Decimal ProductPrice =
           Convert.ToDecimal(cmd.Parameters["@ProductPrice"].Value);
```

While this example doesn't use a data reader, it's complementary to the other techniques that work with data readers. Just think of it as a more flexible version of the `ExecuteScalar` method, which only returns one value.

In fact, you can use output parameters in stored procedures that also return a result set. The first `SELECT` statement will assign the output parameters with field values, while the second will return a result set. You can populate a data reader using the `ExecuteReader` method as usual.

```
SqlDataReader dr = cmd.ExecuteReader();
listBox1.Items.Clear();
while (dr.Read())
{
  listBox1.Items.Add(dr.GetInt32(0).ToString() + '\t' +
                   dr.GetString(1) + '\t' + dr.GetString(2));
}
dr.Close();
```

To work with such a mixed command, you must access result set data using the data reader first. Once you are done with the data reader, close it before attempting to read the command output parameters. If the data reader is open and you try to read the command parameters, it will throw a `System.NullReferenceException` exception.

Please note that if you don't intend to use the category list, you should call the `ExecuteNonQuery` method. Doing so prevents a potentially large result set from being returned, and therefore we don't incur the overhead of the unwanted data.

The downloadable sample project contains a complete code listing in the `ReadOutputParams` method, in `SqlDrForm`.

Retrieving Multiple Unrelated Result Sets

Sometimes an application needs to retrieve records from different tables. For instance, you may want to allow users to select a customer and a product to report on how many times the selected customer has ordered the product. Therefore you may create a web page to display a list of customers and a list of products, so that the user can select each of them and produce a report. You could create two SQL SELECT queries:

```
SELECT ProductID, ProductName FROM Products WHERE CategoryID = @CategoryID
SELECT CustomerID, CompanyName FROM Customers WHERE Country = @Country
```

You could then create a Command object and run each query, one after the other:

```
const string SelectProductQuery =
    "SELECT ProductID, ProductName FROM Products " +
    " WHERE CategoryID = @CategoryID";
const string SelectCustomerQuery =
    "SELECT CustomerID, CompanyName FROM Customers " +
    " WHERE Country = @Country";
cn.Open();

// Run each query separately
// 1. Get products in the specified category
SqlCommand cmd = new SqlCommand(SelectProductQuery, cn);
cmd.Parameters.Add("@CategoryID", CategoryID);
SqlDataReader dr = cmd.ExecuteReader();
while (dr.Read())
{
   listBox1.Items.Add(dr.GetInt32(0).ToString() + '\t' + dr.GetString(1));
}
dr.Close();

// 2. Get customers in the selected country
cmd.CommandText = SelectCustomerQuery;
cmd.Parameters.Add("@Country", Country);
dr = cmd.ExecuteReader();
while (dr.Read())
{
   listBox1.Items.Add(dr.GetString(0) + '\t' + dr.GetString(1));
}
```

Executing each of the above two queries is simple, and is covered in the previous sections. The only thing you should be aware of is that after you have used the data reader to read through the product records, you must close it before reusing it for the second query.

Nothing is too complex here. However, this method incurs two trips to the database, one to read the selected products and the other to read the selected customers. While one single trip is not going to slow your application down a great deal, calling this bit of code thousands of times is likely to have an impact on the performance of your applications. It's therefore a better idea if we can just go to the database once, retrieve all qualified records, and then work with the results locally.

The ADO.NET `Command` object supports the execution of multiple queries. You just need to concatenate those queries and separate them with semicolons.

```
SELECT ProductID, ProductName FROM Products WHERE CategoryID = @CategoryID;
SELECT CustomerID, CompanyName FROM Customers WHERE Country = @Country
```

The resulting data reader will then contain multiple result sets, one for each query. When the command returns a data reader, the current result set is the first. You can move to the second result set using the data reader's `NextResult` method. This method returns `true` if there indeed exists a second result set. If there is no more result sets, this method returns `false`.

```
dr = cmd.ExecuteReader();
while (dr.Read())
{
    // Do something with records in the first result set
}

if (dr.NextResult())
{
    while (dr.Read())
    {
        // Do something with records in the second result set
    }
}
```

If the data reader contains more result sets, you can call the `NextResult` method repeatedly until it returns `false`. At that point, you have gone through all result sets.

```
while (dr.NextResult())
{
    while (dr.Read())
    {
        // Do something with records in the result set
    }
}
```

The code snippet below shows an example of reading multiple result sets.

```
// Run all queries once
const string SelectQuery =
                SelectProductQuery + ";" + SelectCustomerQuery;

SqlCommand cmd = new SqlCommand(SelectQuery, cn);
cmd.Parameters.Add("@Country", Country);
cmd.Parameters.Add("@CategoryID", CategoryID);

SqlDataReader dr = cmd.ExecuteReader();

// Show all categories
while (dr.Read())
{
```

```
        listBox1.Items.Add(dr.GetInt32(0).ToString() + '\t' + dr.GetString(1));
    }


    // Show products in the specified category
    if (dr.NextResult())
    {
        while (dr.Read())
        {
            listBox1.Items.Add(dr.GetString(0) + '\t' + dr.GetString(1));
        }
    }
}
```

In this example, each SELECT query contains a parameter. As you can see, you handle the parameters just as you do with a single query. The order in which the parameters are added does not matter to the SQL Server .NET Data Provider. For other .NET data providers, you still have to ensure that parameters are added in the order they appear in the combined query.

You can find the complete code listing for both approaches in the ReadMultipleResults method, in SqlDrForm in the downloadable code samples.

Retrieving Related Result Sets

One limitation of reading multiple result sets using a data reader is to do with its forward-only characteristics. Just as you can't move backwards within a result set, you can't move backwards in the result set chain either. There is no method that lets you move to the previous result set. If you need to collate the records in different result sets, you will be better off using multiple data readers.

For this reason, reading multiple result sets using a data reader is more suitable for reading data from unrelated sources. If you need to read related data, such as all categories and products in each category, you can use an SQL JOIN query to organize the results according to their relationships.

```
SELECT Categories.CategoryID, Categories.CategoryName,
       Products.ProductID, Products.ProductName
   FROM Categories
       INNER JOIN Products ON Categories.CategoryID = Products.CategoryID
ORDER BY Categories.CategoryID, Products.ProductID
```

This query returns each category and associated product records. The list below shows a shortened sample output.

CategoryID	CategoryName	ProductID	ProductName
1	Beverages	1	Chai
1	Beverages	2	Chang
2	Condiments	3	Aniseed Syrup
2	Condiments	4	Chef Anton's Cajun Seasoning
3	Confections	16	Pavlova
3	Confections	19	Teatime Chocolate Biscuits

If you execute this query using a `Command` object, the resulting data reader will have a single result set containing all category and product records. You effectively combine the data from different tables to form a single result set. Each row in the result set contains the four fields. You can then go through each row and process the data as required. The implementation of reading `JOIN` queries is identical to that of reading single queries.

Retrieving Hierarchical Result Sets

As you have seen in the previous two sections, data readers provide flexible capability to read both related and unrelated result sets. There is one minor problem though. When you use an SQL `JOIN` query to retrieve related data from different tables, the result set contains duplicated data that is unnecessary. For instance, in the category and product query used in the last section, you read the category ID and name in every row. You can do without such duplication, because you really only need one instance of each unique category ID and name for all products belonging to that category.

Returning such duplicated data is mostly harmless, as you can simply discard the unwanted data. However, this practice when used with large numbers of records can result in increasing network traffic between the database server and the application. This reduces the performance of your application because it is slower than it should be.

Microsoft first introduced the feature of hierarchical `Recordset` in ADO with Microsoft Data Shaping OLE DB Provider. A hierarchical `Recordset` contains only one unique instance of each parent record. The records are returned in the hierarchical format as illustrated below.

CategoryID	CategoryName	ProductID	ProductName
1	Beverages		
		1	Chai
		2	Chang
2	Condiments		
		3	Aniseed Syrup
		4	Chef Anton's Cajun Seasoning
3	Confections		
		16	Pavlova
		19	Teatime Chocolate Biscuits
...			

A hierarchical record set not only reduces network traffic, but also allows you to write cleaner navigation code. This ability carries over to ADO.NET, but unfortunately is only available with the OLE DB .NET Data Provider.

> **You can only return data in a hierarchical result set using the OLE DB .NET Data Provider. The SQL Server and ODBC .NET Data Providers don't support this feature.**

To use hierarchical result sets, you must use the Microsoft Data Shaping Provider and pass it the SHAPE commands. This provider sits on top of a database-specific OLE DB provider. It translates the SHAPE command into normal SQL SELECT queries, executes the queries using the database OLE DB provider, and builds a hierarchical result set from the result sets returned from the database OLE DB provider.

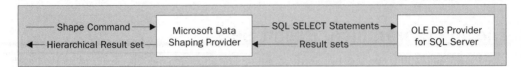

A connection string for the Microsoft Data Shaping OLE DB Provider must specify both the data shaping and the database provider.

```
Provider=MSDataShape;Data Provider=SQLOLEDB;Data Source=(local);
Initial Catalog=Northwind;User ID=donaldx;Password=unbreakable
```

Compare this with a normal OLE DB .NET Data Provider connection string:

```
Provider=SQLOLEDB;Data Source=(local);
Initial Catalog=Northwind;User ID=donaldx;Password=unbreakable
```

You can see that instead of assigning the Provider property with the database-specific OLE DB provider, you assign it the Microsoft Data Shaping OLE DB Provider. You then assign the database-specific OLE DB provider to the data provider property. Other parts of the connection string remain unchanged.

The central part of data shaping is the SHAPE command. A SHAPE command example is demonstrated below:

```
SHAPE
{
    SELECT CategoryID, CategoryName FROM Categories
}
APPEND
(
    {
        SELECT CategoryID, ProductID, ProductName FROM Products
    }
    RELATE CategoryID TO CategoryID
)
```

In the example, the keyword SHAPE denotes the start of a SHAPE command. The parent command is enclosed in a pair of curly brackets, {}. Here the parent command is a SQL SELECT statement that generates the parent result set containing all categories. The keyword APPEND starts a child command, which can be either a SQL SELECT statement or a SHAPE command. In this case, the child command will generate a result set containing all products.

The keyword RELATE starts the specification of the relationship between the parent and child commands. This relationship contains a set of related field pairs in the parent and child command. In this example, there is only one pair. The name of the field in the parent command is on the left-hand side of the keyword TO, while the name of the field in the child record is on the right-hand side. Note that the fields used to specify the parent-child relationship must be present in the parent and child commands.

Microsoft Data Shaping Provider has a shortcoming though. It always retrieves all child records, even if they don't have a matching parent record. For instance, if you use a WHERE clause in the parent SQL SELECT statement to return only the category with an ID of 1, Microsoft Data Shaping Provider still returns all product records, including those that are not in that category. The provider simply discards such child records when it returns the result back to the client application.

From an application developer's point of view, those orphan child records are never returned, but you should be aware of the fact that they are indeed retrieved. Such a design limitation often slows down the data retrieval process considerably; therefore you should perform some benchmarking to see if the performance is acceptable. For more details, please see MSDN Knowledge Base article *PRB: SHAPE Provider Pulls Down All Records in Child Table (Q196968)* at:

http://support.microsoft.com/default.aspx?scid=kb;EN-US;q196968

This is only a very brief introduction to the SHAPE command. To find out more about the SHAPE command and its formal syntax, please read Chapter 9: *Data Shaping* in the *ADO Programmer's Guide*, available via the following link:

http://msdn.microsoft.com/library/en-us/ado270/htm/mdmschierarchicalcursorsdatashaping.asp.

For now, let's see how we execute a SHAPE command and populate a data reader with a hierarchical result set.

```
const string DbShapeConnectionString =
    "Provider=MSDataShape; Data Provider=SQLOLEDB; Data Source=(local);" +
    "Initial Catalog=Northwind;User ID=sa;password=";

const string ShapeCommand =
    "SHAPE " +
    "{" +
    "    SELECT CategoryID, CategoryName FROM Categories" +
    "}" +
    "APPEND" +
    "(" +
    "    {" +
    "        SELECT CategoryID, ProductID, ProductName FROM Products" +
    "    }" +
    "    RELATE CategoryID TO CategoryID" +
    ")";

OleDbConnection cn = new OleDbConnection(DbShapeConnectionString);
cn.Open();

OleDbCommand cmd = new OleDbCommand(ShapeCommand, cn);
OleDbDataReader dr = cmd.ExecuteReader();
```

As you can see, apart from using a different connection string and a SHAPE command, you essentially apply the same technique as you used for executing a normal command. To traverse the returned hierarchical result set, you always move through the parent result set.

```
while (dr.Read())
{
    listBox1.Items.Add(dr.GetInt32(0).ToString() + '\t' + dr.GetString(1));
    OleDbDataReader ChildDr = (OleDbDataReader)dr.GetValue(2);
    while (ChildDr.Read())
    {
        listBox1.Items.Add('\t' + ChildDr.GetInt32(1).ToString() +
                            '\t' + ChildDr.GetString(2));
    }
}
```

The parent result set contains all fields in the parent command. Therefore you can read their values just like you do with a normal result set. In addition, each row in the parent result also contains a child result set in its last field. The child result set contains all child records related to the parent record. For instance, if the parent category is Beverages with an ID of 1, the child result set contains all products with a CategoryID that equals 1.

To retrieve the child result set, you call the data reader's GetValue method and cast the value to an OleDbDataReader. Once you have the data reader containing the child result set, you can read its rows. You need not explicitly close the data reader containing a child result set. When you close the parent data reader, all child result sets are closed and discarded.

The downloadable sample project for this chapter contains a Windows Form, OleDbDrForm. You can see a complete example of reading a hierarchical result set in the ReadChapter method.

Retrieving Binary Data

You often find applications storing some binary data in a database. For instance, you may want to store a thumbnail picture for each product so that you can display it along with the product description later on. Note that because many database implementations don't provide very optimized binary data access, it is in general better practice to store graphics in external files and only store a link to the file in the database. This is especially true if the graphics are large. However, as the need to use graphics in mainstream applications is growing, we can expect database vendors to improve binary data access significantly.

Retrieving binary data using a data reader requires us to use slightly different approaches. First, you must instruct the DataReader object to load data in sequence by passing in the CommandBehavior.SequentialAccess enumeration value to the ExecuteReader method.

```
SqlDataReader dr = cmd.ExecuteReader(CommandBehavior.SequentialAccess);
```

Next, you should extract columns in the order they are retrieved. Let's say that you read extended publisher information from the pub_info table in the sample pub database; your query would look like this.

```
SELECT pub_id, pr_info, logo FROM pub_info WHERE pub_id = '0736'
```

You should extract the pub_id field value first, followed by pr_info and then the logo. Note that you don't have to do so if you don't need to read all of the fields. For instance, if you want to skip the pr_info field, you can read the pub_id and then the logo. However, after you have read the logo, you can't go back and read pr_info. Otherwise, it will throw a System.InvalidOperationException.

Lastly, you need to read binary data in chunks. The conventional technique is to repeatedly call the GetBytes method to read a block of data from the binary field into a buffer. You can then either combine the blocks in-memory or write them to an I/O device such as a disk file. The code snippet below reads the logo, which is a binary field, into a memory block.

```
System.IO.MemoryStream stream = new System.IO.MemoryStream();
System.IO.BinaryWriter writer = new System.IO.BinaryWriter(stream);
int     BufferSize = 1024;
byte[]  Buffer     = new Byte[BufferSize];
long    Offset     = 0;
long    BytesRead  = 0;

do
{
  BytesRead = dr.GetBytes(2, Offset, Buffer, 0, BufferSize);
  writer.Write(Buffer, 0, (int)BytesRead);
  writer.Flush();
  Offset += BytesRead;
}
while (BytesRead == BufferSize);
```

It reads the logo into a memory buffer, Buffer, one kilobyte at a time, and writes the buffer to a memory stream using a binary writer. .NET provides a BinaryWriter class that you can instantiate to copy binary data between devices, including memory or other I/O devices. In this example, it writes a memory buffer, Buffer, to another memory block, stream.

The GetBytes method requires some explanation. Its syntax is:

```
long GetBytes(
    int FieldIndex,
    long FieldOffset,
    byte[] Buffer,
    int BufferOffset,
    int NumOfBytes
)
```

Parameter	Description
FieldIndex	The index of the binary field in the record. In this case, the logo is the third field in the records returned by the SELECT query. So you pass its index (2) to the GetBytes method.
FieldOffset	The starting position in the field to read. When you call this method for the first time in this example, the FieldOffset is 0 meaning that you read from the first byte. The next call will pass in 1024, which is the 1,025th byte because you read 1,024 bytes at a time.

Table continued on following page

Parameter	Description
Buffer	The memory block to hold the bytes read from the field.
BufferOffset	The starting position in the buffer where the read data should be placed. In most cases, such as this example, you fill the buffer from the beginning. Therefore it is always 0 in this example.
NumOfBytes	The maximum number of bytes to read. In this example, the buffer is 1,024 bytes long so it can hold up to 1,024 bytes read from the field.

The GetBytes method returns the number of bytes that are actually read. If the size of the logo is 2,000 bytes, the first call to this method will return 1,024. The second call will return 2,000 − 1,024 = 976 as this method never reads past the end of the field. This is actually a good indicator for the read status. If the current GetBytes call hasn't reached the end of the field, the return value will always be the same as NumOfBytes which is the same as the size of the buffer, BufferSize. Otherwise, the return value is less than the buffer size. You may argue that if, say, the size of the logo is 2,048 bytes, the second call to the GetBytes method will return 1,024, the same as the buffer size. Strictly speaking, however, it has not reached the end of the field. The end of the field is 1 byte past the last byte in the field. You will only get to the end in the third call, which will return 0 because there aren't any more bytes to read.

This method has a minor flaw, albeit a syntactical one. While the maximum number of bytes to read, NumOfBytes, is a 32-bit integer, the returned value, which is the number of bytes it actually read, is a 64-bit integer. It's not a big deal, but you need to be aware of this problem and code your program accordingly. The above example defines BufferSize as an int and BytesRead as a long, but then compares them. This forces an implicit promotion of BufferSize to a long.

After it reads a chunk of data, the writer writes it to a memory stream. The offset is then increased so that the next call to the GetBytes method will start reading from the first unread byte in the field. This process repeats until the whole field is read.

The downloadable sample project has a ReadBinary method in the SqlDrForm. It includes the code snippet presented above and displays the logo in a PictureBox control.

Retrieving Schema Information

While data readers are most suitable for reading data from databases, they also provide a limited means of reading table schema information. For instance, if your business directory application (for instance, a customized yellow pages) allows your users to customize the search result format, you will probably build the query dynamically to return only the fields required by the user. It's possible that you don't know at design time which fields will be returned at run time. Therefore you will need to dynamically work out the types of the returned fields on the fly.

To read the schema information for columns, you create a Command object and assign its CommandText property a SQL SELECT query that returns the columns required. For instance, if you need to find out schema information for the CategoryID and CategoryName columns in the Categories table, you could use:

```
SqlCommand cmd = new SqlCommand(
    "SELECT CategoryID, CategoryName FROM Categories", ConnectionObject);
```

Next, you obtain a data reader by calling the command's `ExecuteReader` method:

```
SqlDataReader dr = cmd.ExecuteReader();
```

By default, executing a command doesn't automatically retrieve schema information. Therefore you must call the data reader's `GetSchemaTable` method, which returns a `DataTable` object populated with schema information for the columns in the `SELECT` query:

```
DataTable SchemaTable = dr.GetSchemaTable();
```

It's worth noting that the above code is not very efficient. First you have to execute a query before being able to retrieve schema information. This seems a bit redundant because, in many cases, all we really want is the schema information. The actual records are not of great interest. Unfortunately this is a design decision Microsoft has made and there is not much we can do to change this mechanism.

However, we can do something to minimize the impact of this design at our end. The most straightforward solution is to specify that the data reader should return schema information only. That is, we don't want it to return any records. You do this by passing in the `CommandBehavior.SchemaOnly` enum value to the command's `ExecuteReader` method:

```
SqlDataReader dr = cmd.ExecuteReader(CommandBehavior.SchemaOnly);
```

Alternatively, you can modify the query so that it doesn't return any records. Data readers will pull column schema information from the database regardless of whether or not the command returns any records. Assuming that you don't need the category records in this case, you can modify the query by adding a `WHERE` clause to it:

```
SELECT CategoryID, CategoryName FROM Categories WHERE CategoryID = 0
```

It ensures that no records will be returned, as the category IDs are all positive integers in the `Categories` table. This technique is most significant when the number of category records is large.

Back to the table containing column schema information, you can now extract column properties from it. In this table, each row in that table represents a column returned by the SQL `SELECT` query, and each field in a row represents a property of the column. You can therefore extract a column from the table's `Rows` collection:

```
DataRow SchemaColumn = SchemaTable.Rows[0];
```

Here the index 0 denotes the first row in the schema table, which represents the first column in the `SELECT` query. So the above row represents the `CategoryID` column. Because the `Rows` collection, which is of type `DataRowCollection`, doesn't support named element index, you can't retrieve a column by its name. For instance, the statement below will generate a syntax error.

```
DataRow SchemaColumn = SchemaTable.Rows["CategoryID"];
```

Once you have the row representing the schema information for a column, you can extract any properties of that column. Because each column in the schema table represents a column schema property, you can extract the property name from the schema table's `Columns` collection. On the other hand, the `Columns` collection, an instance of the `DataColumnCollection` class, supports both ordinal and named element indexing. Therefore you can extract a property name using either of the following two methods:

```
PropertyName = SchemaTable.Columns[ColumnName]
PropertyName = SchemaTable.Columns[ColumnIndex]
```

The value of the property can then be extracted from the corresponding field:

```
PropertyValue = SchemaColumn[PropertyName]
```

Confused? An example will clear it up. In ADO.NET, each column has a `ColumnName` and a `DataType` property. The code snippet below will retrieve those two properties for the `CategoryID` column:

```
DataRow CatIDSchema        = SchemaTable.Rows[0];
DataColumn ColumnNameProp  = SchemaTable.Columns["ColumnName"];
string ColumnNamePropName  = ColumnNameProp.ColumnName;
string ColumnNamePropValue = CatIDSchema[ColumnNameProp].ToString();
DataColumn DataTypeProp    = SchemaTable.Columns["DataType"];
string DataTypePropName    = DataTypeProp.ColumnName;
string DataTypePropValue   = CatIDSchema[DataTypeProp].ToString();
```

The last four string variables will now contain the value listed in the table below:

Variable	Value
ColumnNamePropName	ColumnName
ColumnNamePropValue	CategoryID
DataTypePropName	DataType
DataTypePropValue	System.Int32

You can also loop through the rows in the table to get a list of properties and their values for each column. For instance, the code snippet below shows a list of property name-value pairs in the format of `PropertyName = PropertyValue`.

```
DataRowCollection SchemaColumns = SchemaTable.Rows;
DataColumnCollection ColumnProps = SchemaTable.Columns;
foreach(DataRow SchemaColumn in SchemaColumns)
{
    foreach(DataColumn SchemaColumnProp in Props)
    {
        listBox1.Items.Add(SchemaColumnProp.ColumnName + " = " +
            SchemaColumn[SchemaColumnProp].ToString());
    }
}
```

Here is a sample output for the `CategoryID` column:

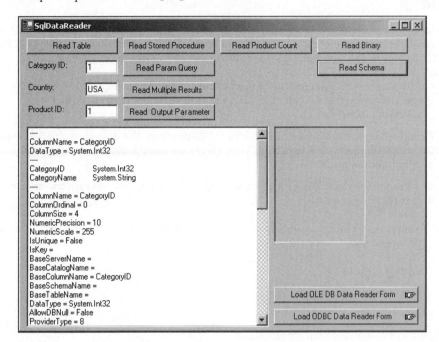

If you examine the above list closely, you'll notice several unexpected results. For instance, the `IsUnique` property is `false` and the `IsKey` property is empty. Surely there is something wrong, as the `CategoryID` is the primary key of the `Categories` table. This demonstrates a limitation of retrieving schema information using data readers – you just don't get a perfectly accurate result. Having said that, I've found that the `ColumnName` and `DataType` properties always contain the correct values.

In practice, the most common use of retrieving schema information with data readers is to find out the data types of columns returned by queries. The aforementioned business directory application is a good example. In such cases, using a data reader to return both the search result and column data type would be very useful.

Note that you can retrieve schema information for columns from different tables. All you need to do is to build an SQL `SELECT` query containing all required columns. For instance, you can retrieve schema information from both the `Categories` and `Products` tables using a `JOIN` query.

```
SELECT Categories.CategoryID, Categories.CategoryName,
       Products.CategoryID, Products.ProductID, Products.ProductName
   FROM Categories
       INNER JOIN Products ON Categories.CategoryID = Products.CategoryID
   WHERE Categories.CategoryID = 0
```

The downloadable sample project contains `ReadSchema` methods in both `SqlDrForm` and `OleDbDrForm`. They contain a complete code listing containing all code described in this section for the SQL Server and OLE DB data providers.

Summary

In this chapter, you have learned to read data from databases using .NET data readers. Data readers provide an object-oriented mechanism for efficient forward-only and read-only data access. Regardless what .NET data providers you use, your code should always follow a similar pattern, and:

❑ Create a `Connection` object to connect to a database. This `Connection` object has a connection string that specifies the database, authentication method, and other connection properties.

❑ Create a `Command` object and attach it to the connection. The `Command` object always contains the statement that will be executed. To retrieve data using a data reader, the command text usually returns a result set.

❑ Execute the `Command` using the `ExecuteReader` method. You can then traverse the returned data reader to extract data.

ADO.NET supports several command types. You can use data readers to retrieve data using any of the following types of command text:

❑ Plain SQL queries

❑ Parameterized SQL queries

❑ Stored procedures

❑ OLE DB hierarchical `SHAPE` commands

You can also retrieve basic data column schema information using data readers. This provides a simple way to facilitate dynamic query processing.

While data readers are well suited for fast, one-pass data retrieval, almost all applications call for other data manipulation functions. They need to provide users with the ability to add new records, modify existing records, and delete unwanted records. Those update operations require functionality beyond that provided by the data readers. In the next chapter, you will learn to perform such operations using data adapters.

162

6

DataAdapters

In the previous chapter, you learned how to use DataReaders to read data from a database. DataReaders are optimized to provide read-only, forward-only access to data read from the database, which means that they are ideal for reading data in a result set in sequential order. However, most applications call for more functionality, such as the ability to search the result set randomly in either forward or backward direction. Furthermore they also need to able to modify the data.

ADO.NET defines a powerful and flexible DataSet class for more advanced data manipulation tasks. Unlike data readers that are connected to the underlying database while its data is being read, a DataSet does not maintain the connection. In fact, we always load data from the underlying database into a DataSet in the application memory using a data provider-specific adapter. A DataSet doesn't have any knowledge of the database. A DataSet is like a mini-database living in the memory, which is disconnected from the database. We can define data constraints and table relationships, create a DataSet and manually populate it with data without connecting to a data store, search for a record in one or more table, create new records, and modify or delete existing records.

Yet, despite all this power, a DataSet still needs help to really become useful for any real-world applications. On its own, a DataSet only lives as long as the host application is loaded in memory. Once the application unloads, the DataSet's memory is wiped out and any DataSet objects will vanish like other objects. This means that if we need to keep the data contained in a DataSet beyond the lifespan of the current instance of the application, we need to find some way of storing the data in persistent storage for later use.

An application will also need to retrieve this saved data at a later time. After all, the whole purpose of storing application data is so that it can be used as needed. A .NET **Data Provider** implements a DataAdapter class that offers the capability to populate a DataSet with data in the underlying data store and to update the latter with changes made to the DataSet.

Each of the currently available Microsoft .NET data providers – SQL Server .NET Data Provider, OLE DB .NET Data Provider, and ODBC .NET Data Provider – defines its own `DataAdapter`. This chapter shows how to use the following features of the `DataAdapter` class:

❑   How `DataAdapters` fit in the .NET Data Provider object model

❑   How to use `DataAdapters` to read data from databases

❑   How to manage database connections

❑   How to read data from multiple database tables

❑   How to read data with multiple queries or adapters

❑   How to update databases with `DataAdapters`

❑   How to manage insertion into tables with identity columns

❑   How to use connections to ensure data integrity

❑   How to manage concurrency issues

We'll begin with an overview of ADO.NET `DataAdapters` and their roles in the ADO.NET architecture.

DataAdapter Overview

A `DataAdapter` acts as a channel between a memory-bound `DataSet` object and a persistent data store. In most cases, a data store is a relational database such as SQL Server or Oracle. However, it could be just about anything containing useful data, such as an XML file, an Excel spreadsheet, or even a plain text file. A `DataAdapter` can be used to load data from the data store into the `DataSet`, and to update the data store with changes made to the `DataSet`.

By definition, a `DataAdapter` should have knowledge about all parties involved – the data store, the `DataSet`, and, of course, the data. However, encapsulating and implementing such knowledge in a single class inevitably results in a class that knows too much and has too many responsibilities. For example, such a class will need to know how to connect to a data store, how to manage the connection, where to look for requested data, how to populate a `DataSet` with requested data, and how to synchronize the data between the `DataSet` and the data store.

Of course, this doesn't happen in ADO.NET because each .NET Data Provider already offers two provider-specific classes – a `Connection` class that knows all about connection-related tasks and a `Command` class that knows all about reading and writing data in a data store. This means that a `DataAdapter` object can delegate such tasks to instances of those classes. It will still manage the communication between the `DataSet` and the two data provider-specific objects. (If you are familiar with design patterns, you'll be interested to know that a `DataAdapter` implements the Adapter pattern.) The `DataAdapter` ensures that all three other objects will work together, while keeping them apart, so that they don't have to know each other.

The last point is very important in ADO.NET architecture. The `DataSet` class is independent of the data providers, while the `Connection` and `Command` classes are provider-specific. If the `DataSet` class must know the provider-specific classes, it may have trouble working with any unknown data providers. On the other hand, a `DataAdapter` knows the `Connection` and `Command` classes because they all belong to the same data provider. The following diagram illustrates the relationship among the `DataSet` class and various .NET Data Providers:

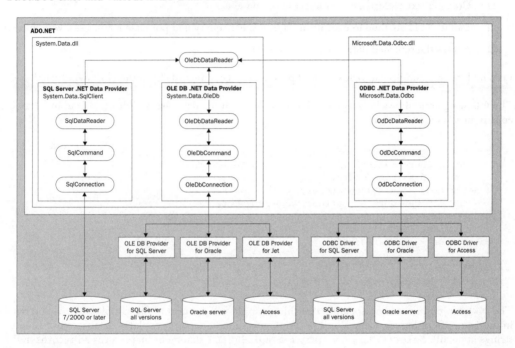

This chapter demonstrates the common techniques used to read and write data using `DataAdapters`. As in the last chapter, most of the examples use the SQL Server .NET Data Provider. You can read all examples in the sample project contained in the code download.

You can use virtually the same code with any of the other Microsoft .NET Data Providers simply by replacing the SQL Server-specific classes with those defined in the data provider you use. As all three Microsoft .NET Data Providers follow the same naming convention, the converting code between different data providers is a straightforward global find-and-replace process. For example, we can convert the SQL Server .NET Data Provider-specific code to OLE DB .NET Data Provider code by importing the `System.Data.OleDbClient` namespace and replacing `SqlConnection`, `SqlCommand`, and `SqlDataAdapter` with `OleDbConnection`, `OleDbCommand`, and `OleDbDataAdapter` respectively. If the code uses other classes, such as `SqlParameter`, you can convert them accordingly.

Reading Data

Reading data from a database using a DataAdapter is pretty simple, especially when the query returns a single result set. The minimum steps we would need to go through are:

- ❏ Create a DataAdapter to connect to the database
- ❏ Call its Fill method to execute an SQL SELECT query and populate a DataSet with the result
- ❏ Access the returned data from the DataSet

Let's look at an example that reads a list of product category records from the Northwind database.

The following code shows how to read all categories from the database and display them in a DataGrid control in a Windows Form:

```
const string DbConnectionString =
    "Data Source=(local);Initial Catalog=Northwind;" +
    "User ID=sa;password=";
const string SelectCategoryQuery =
    "SELECT CategoryID, CategoryName FROM Categories";
SqlDataAdapter da = new SqlDataAdapter(SelectCategoryQuery,
    DbConnectionString);
DataSet ds = new DataSet();

da.Fill(ds);
dataGrid1.DataSource = ds.Tables[0];
```

The DbConnectionString specifies that this example will connect to the sample Northwind database in the local SQL Server, using Windows Authentication (Chapter 5 explains database connection strings in detail). SelectCategoryQuery is a SQL SELECT statement that returns all records in the Categories table. For each Category, only the ID and Name fields are returned. In the real world, you can include more fields as you wish.

The third statement creates a SqlDataAdapter object. It accepts a SQL statement and a connection string, which specify the expected data in the Northwind database. It is one of the four overloaded constructors supported by the SQL Server .NET Data Provider and has the following syntax:

```
SqlDataAdapter(string SelectCommandText, string ConnectionString)
```

We pass a SQL SELECT statement as the SelectCommandText argument. We can also use the name of a stored procedure, which will be explained later in this chapter. The second argument, ConnectionString, is used to assign the data adapter a connection string, with which a connection can be established. The other three constructors will be explained shortly.

The next statement creates a new DataSet object that will be used to store the data read by the data adapter. You call the data adapter's Fill method and pass it the DataSet. The Fill method in this example creates a new data table in the DataSet, and populates the table with all the category records loaded from the database. It has several overloaded versions, some of which will be discussed in this chapter. You can look up all the Fill method definitions in the MSDN documentation for the respective DataAdapter classes. The simplest version has the following syntax:

```
int Fill(DataSet ds)
```

This version accepts a `DataSet` object and populates it with the records returned from the `SELECT` command. If the `DataSet` contains no table, the data adapter creates a table, and then loads the records into it. It returns the number of rows loaded into the `DataSet`.

Finally, to display the records, you can bind a `DataGrid` control to this table, which (in this example) is the only table in the `DataSet`.

The code looks deceptively simple. If we ignore the definitions of the two constants containing the database connection string and the SQL `SELECT` query, there are only four lines of code. It certainly does the job we want it to do, but there is actually a lot happening in the background. Most of the background activities occur in the constructor and the `Fill` method. Let's take a good look at what is actually happening.

First of all, it appears that the data adapter automatically connects to the database because it is created with a connection string. However, it doesn't do this itself. Instead, the data adapter constructor creates a `SqlConnection` object and a `SqlCommand` object. The `Connection` object is initialized with the connection string being passed to the data adapter's constructor. The `Command` object contains the SQL `SELECT` query and is attached to the `Connection`. At this time, the `Connection` is not open. You can access the `Command` and `Connection` objects through the data adapter's `SelectCommand` property. For example, you can add the following statement right after the data adapter is created to see the `Connection` and `Command` information:

```
SqlDataAdapter da = new SqlDataAdapter(SelectCategoryQuery,
    DbConnectionString);

SqlCommand SelCmd = da.SelectCommand;
SqlConnection TempConn = SelCmd.Connection;

Debug.WriteLine("ConnectionString = " + TempConn.ConnectionString);
Debug.WriteLine("Connection state = " + TempConn.State.ToString());
Debug.WriteLine(SelCmd.CommandText);
```

The `Debug` class is defined in the `System.Diagnostics` namespace. Its `WriteLine` method writes a line of text in the **Output** window of the Visual Studio .NET IDE. When you run the code in debug mode, the three `WriteLine` method calls will print the `ConnectionString`, the `Connection` state (closed), and the SQL `SELECT` statement in the **Output** window.

The data adapter constructor performs the preliminary tasks required for the data adapter to work. At this stage, no real work has been done yet. The connection remains closed and no data access has taken place. The real work starts when you call the data adapter's `Fill()` method.

The `Fill()` method opens the connection and executes the command using the `Command` object. When it receives the result set, it creates a new `DataTable` object in the `DataSet` and fills the table with the returned category records. After it finishes processing the result set, the `Fill()` method closes the connection automatically. However, both the `Connection` and the `Command` objects stay in the data adapter, and will only be destroyed when the data adapter itself is destroyed. You can check out the SQL `SELECT` command through the `SelectCommand` property, as we did previously.

The `ReadDataForm.ReadData1()` method in the sample project contains the complete code. Please note that both the `ConnectionString` and the `SelectCommandText` are defined as form-level constants in order to reduce the duplication among different methods.

Managing Connections

It's usually adequate to implicitly open and close the database connection in the `Fill()` method. In many cases, you simply want to connect to a database and read some records into a `DataSet`. Users can work on the data without holding on to the connection. When they wish to read in more records or are ready to update the database, you can connect to the database again to perform the required operations.

On the other hand, you might want to keep the connection open beyond the current `Fill()` method. For instance, you may need to fill the `DataSet` with records from different tables, and using separate `SELECT` commands. In this case, repetitively opening and closing database connections for each `Fill()` method call introduces unnecessary overhead to the process. It would be nice to keep the connection open and use it for all calls to the `Fill()` method, and disconnect once you have done everything.

Managing Implicit Connections

One way to keep the connection open even after the `Fill()` method is to explicitly open the implicitly created connection. The following code snippet demonstrates this technique:

```
SqlDataAdapter da = new SqlDataAdapter(SelectQuery, DbConnectionString);

SqlCommand SelCmd = da.SelectCommand;
SqlConnection  TempConn = SelCmd.Connection;
DataSet ds = new DataSet();

// Explicitly open the connection
TempConn.Open();
Debug.WriteLine("Connection state = " + TempConn.State.ToString(),
    "Before Fill");
da.Fill(ds);

// Verify that the connection is still open
Debug.WriteLine("Connection state = " + TempConn.State.ToString(),
    "After Fill ");

// Explicitly close the connection
TempConn.Close();
```

After getting hold of the `Connection` object automatically created by the data adapter, you can open it by explicitly calling its `Open()` method. The `Fill()` method will detect that the connection is already open before it is invoked. It will therefore not close the connection implicitly. Of course, you are then responsible for closing it yourself.

The principle here is whoever opens the connection is responsible for closing it. It is a good design for the `Fill` method to respect the current connection state. It provides you, as the programmer, with full control of the connection when you want it, while still maintaining the ability to perform its own task properly by opening and closing a connection if necessary.

This example only calls the `Fill()` method once. You will see how to call the `Fill()` method multiple times later in this chapter. You can find the complete code for this example in the `ReadDataForm.ReadDataWithImplicitConnection()` method in the sample project.

Managing Explicit Connections

To expand on the scenario of making multiple calls to the `Fill()` method of a `DataAdapter` object, you may want to make calls to the `Fill()` methods of multiple data adapters. For example, you may define one data adapter for reading and updating category records and another for reading and updating customer records. In such cases, it's desirable to use one connection for both data adapters.

Data adapters have another constructor that accepts a `Connection` object as an argument:

```
SqlDataAdapter(string SelectCommandText, SqlConnection ConnectionObject)
```

The first argument is either a SQL SELECT statement or a stored procedure. The second is an `SqlConnection` object. If you have an existing `Connection` object, you can pass it in so that the data adapter will use this `Connection` object rather than implicitly creating one of its own. For example:

```
SqlConnection cn = new SqlConnection(DbConnectionString);
SqlDataAdapter da = new SqlDataAdapter(SelectCategoryQuery, cn);
DataSet ds = new DataSet();

da.Fill(ds);
dataGrid1.DataSource = ds.Tables[0];
```

Apart from explicitly creating a `Connection` object and passing it to the data adapter constructor, this example looks identical to the one used previously. Behind the scenes, the process is also similar. The data adapter constructor still sets the `SelectCommand` property implicitly. This time, instead of creating a new connection, it attaches the `Command` object to the received `Connection` object.

The `Fill()` method also behaves the same as before. It checks to see whether the connection is open. If it is not, it opens the connection, executes the `SelectCommand`, and closes the connection before it returns. You can explicitly open the connection anywhere after the `Connection` object has been created, and close it when it's no longer required. In this latter case, the `Fill()` method doesn't close the connection implicitly. You can find the complete code for this example in the `ReadDataForm.ReadDataWithExplicitConnection()` method in the sample project.

Again, this example only invokes the `Fill()` method in a single data adapter. Before moving on to show you how to call the `Fill()` method multiple times, I'd like to complete the discussion on data adapter creation.

Creating Data Adapters Using Commands

So far we have created data adapters using two overloaded constructors that both accept a SQL SELECT statement. The difference between them is whether or not you explicitly create a `Connection` object yourself for the adapter to use. Given that both constructors create an internal command from the SQL SELECT statement, it's not surprising to see you can also create a `Command` yourself and hand it to the data adapter.

```
SqlDataAdapter(SqlCommand CommandObject)
```

Because `Command` objects are always attached to a connection, this constructor does not accept a `Connection` object. Instead, it uses the connection for the `Command` object. Apart from this small difference, everything else works in identical fashion. Here is a short example:

```
SqlConnection cn = new SqlConnection(DbConnectionString);
SqlCommand cmd = new SqlCommand(SelectCategoryQuery, cn);
SqlDataAdapter da  = new SqlDataAdapter(cmd);
DataSet ds = new DataSet();

da.Fill(ds);
dataGrid1.DataSource = ds.Tables[0];
```

This code creates a `Command` object and attaches it to an existing connection. You can find the complete code for this example in the `ReadDataForm.ReadDataWithCommand()` method in the sample project. The `Command` class's constructor used here accepts a SQL statement as its command text. The `Command` class also has several overloaded constructors to provide you with the flexibility to instantiate differently. You should read ADO.NET documentation for details of `Command` classes and their constructors.

As you probably noticed, you don't have to explicitly open the connection by calling its `Open()` method. The data adapter checks the connection state to decide whether or not it needs to open the connection in the `Fill()` method. If the connection is not open when the `Fill()` method is called, the data adapter will open it implicitly and close it after the data has been loaded in the `DataSet`. Again, if you open the connection before calling the adapter's `Fill()` method, you are responsible for closing it when you no longer need it.

The last data adapter constructor is a constructor that has no parameters, which is often called the default constructor:

```
SqlDataAdapter da = new SqlDataAdapter();
```

If you create a `DataAdapter` object using this default constructor, you need to assign a `Command` object to its `SelectCommand` property.

Using Commands with Parameters

As you have learned in the *Retrieving Data with Parameterized Queries* section in last chapter, you can define and use parameters for `Command` objects. When working with data adapters, you can also use commands with parameters to read data. Using commands to execute parameterized queries or stored procedures in data adapters is very similar to using commands with data readers. Let's take a look at exactly how to read data using parameters:

```
const string SelectProductQuery =
    "SELECT ProductID, ProductName FROM Products" +
    " WHERE CategoryID = @CategoryID";

SqlConnection cn = new SqlConnection(DbConnectionString);
SqlCommand cmd = new SqlCommand(SelectProductQuery, cn);
cmd.Parameters.Add("@CategoryID", 1);
```

```
SqlDataAdapter da = new SqlDataAdapter(cmd);
DataSet ds = new DataSet();

da.Fill(ds);
```

This example is very similar to the previous example. First, it creates a connection. Next it creates a `Command` object and attaches it to the `Connection`. Because the `SELECT` query now contains a parameter, we need to create a parameter for the command. This example assigns a hard-coded category ID value, 1, to the `@CategoryID` parameter. You can use any expression containing the category ID value in place of the hard-coded value.

The rest should be rather familiar by now. It creates a data adapter and initializes it with the `Command` object constructed previously. Finally, it creates a `DataSet` object and fills it using the `Fill()` method of the data adapter. You can find the complete code for this example in the `ReadDataForm.ReadDataWithParamCommand()` method in the sample project.

Using Commands with Stored Procedures

You can also use commands to execute stored procedures. If a stored procedure doesn't define any parameters, you can execute it just as you do with non-parameterized `SELECT` queries. The only thing you must remember to do when executing stored procedures is to specify `StoredProcedure` as the `SelectCommand`'s command type. For instance, the Northwind database has a stored procedure, `Ten Most Expensive Products`, hat returns the top ten most expensive products. You can call this stored procedure using the following sample code:

```
SqlDataAdapter da = new SqlDataAdapter("Ten Most Expensive Products",
    DbConnectionString);
da.SelectCommand.CommandType = CommandType.StoredProcedure;

DataSet ds = new DataSet();
da.Fill(ds);
```

Obviously, you can create a data adapter using any of the overloaded constructors. For instance, you can explicitly create a `Command` object, and then create a data adapter using the `Command` object:

```
SqlConnection cn = new SqlConnection(DbConnectionString);
SqlCommand cmd = new SqlCommand("Ten Most Expensive Products", cn);
cmd.CommandType = CommandType.StoredProcedure;
SqlDataAdapter da = new SqlDataAdapter(cmd);

DataSet ds = new DataSet();
da.Fill(ds);
```

If a stored procedure requires you to pass in one or more parameters, you will need to create the required parameters and add them to the `Command` object. The snippet below shows how you call the `CustOrderHist` stored procedure in the Northwind database. This stored procedure accepts a customer ID and returns a list of products, and their quantities, that the customer has ordered in the past:

```
SqlConnection cn = new SqlConnection(DbConnectionString);
SqlCommand cmd = new SqlCommand("CustOrderHist", cn);
```

173

```
cmd.CommandType = CommandType.StoredProcedure;
cmd.Parameters.Add("@CustomerID", "ALFKI");

SqlDataAdapter da = new SqlDataAdapter(cmd);
DataSet ds  = new DataSet();

da.Fill(ds);
dataGrid1.DataSource = ds.Tables[0];
```

You can find the complete code for many of these examples in the
`ReadDataForm.ReadDataWithStoredProc()` method in the sample project. In later sections, I will
show you how you can use stored procedures to insert, update, and delete records from the database.

Reading Multiple Tables

Reading data from multiple tables doesn't necessarily require calling the `Fill()` method multiple
times, nor does it require you to use multiple data adapters. In general, there are four different methods
to read records from multiple tables. In this section, we will look at each of them.

Reading Using a SQL JOIN Query

If you read records from related tables, you can use a `JOIN` query to retrieve all records at once. For
instance, the Northwind database has two tables, `Categories` and `Products`. Each product belongs to
a category, identified in the `CategoryID` column in the `Products` table. This represents a classic
parent-child relationship. If you need to read all categories with their child products, you can use a SQL
`JOIN` query:

```
SELECT Categories.CategoryID, Categories.CategoryName,
    Products.ProductID, Products.ProductName
FROM Products INNER JOIN
    Categories ON Products.CategoryID = Categories.CategoryID
ORDER BY Categories.CategoryID, Products.ProductID
```

You use a data adapter to read from both the `Categories` and `Products` tables in exactly the same
way as you read from a single table, except that the SQL `SELECT` command is different:

```
const string SelectCategoryProductQuery =
    "SELECT Categories.CategoryID, Categories.CategoryName, " +
    "Products.ProductID, Products.ProductName " +
    "FROM Products " +
    "INNER JOIN Categories " +
    "ON Products.CategoryID = Categories.CategoryID " +
    "ORDER BY Categories.CategoryID, Products.ProductID";

SqlDataAdapter da = new SqlDataAdapter(SelectCategoryProductQuery,
    DbConnectionString);
DataSet ds = new DataSet();

da.Fill(ds);
dataGrid1.DataSource = ds.Tables[0];
```

The data adapter still creates a single table in the `DataSet` object. This table contains the result of the `JOIN` query, and each row contains all four fields from two different tables in the database. You can find the complete code for this example in the `ReadMultipleTableForm.ReadDataWithJoinQuery()` method in the sample project.

Reading Using Multiple SQL SELECT Statements

If the records you wish to read come from unrelated tables, you can't use a SQL `JOIN` query. For instance, if you want to read both category and customer records, you will find that there is no direct relationship between the two tables. However, you can still read them all using only one `Fill()` method call. The trick is to combine two SQL `SELECT` statements into one and separate them with a semicolon. This is the same technique used by data readers to return multiple result sets as demonstrated in the last chapter:

```
SELECT CategoryID, CategoryName FROM Categories;
SELECT CustomerID, CompanyName FROM Customers
```

Except that you now are using a `SelectCommand` text that consists of multiple SQL `SELECT` statements, you construct your code in exactly the same way as in the last section. The following code snippet shows an example:

```
const string SelectCategoryCustomerQuery =
    "SELECT CategoryID, CategoryName FROM Categories;" +
    "SELECT CustomerID, CompanyName FROM Customers";

SqlDataAdapter da = new SqlDataAdapter(SelectCategoryCustomerQuery,
    DbConnectionString);
DataSet ds = new DataSet();

da.Fill(ds);
dataGrid1.DataSource = ds;
```

When the `Fill()` method populates the `DataSet` with data returned by the combined `SelectCommand`, it creates two tables. The first table contains all the category records, which are the result of the first `SELECT` statement. The second table, not surprisingly, contains all the customer records returned from the second `SELECT` statement. You can find the complete code for this example in the `ReadMultipleTableForm.ReadDataWithMultipleSelect()` method in the sample project.

In previous examples, we bind the `DataGrid` control with the contents of the first table in the `DataSet`. When you do the same here, only category records will be displayed in the grid. This example binds the grid to the `DataSet` itself so that you can see the records from each table. Programmatically, you can reference the second table as `ds.Tables[1]` and extract the customer records from it.

175

Naming and Mapping Tables

Before getting on to the third method of reading data from multiple tables, let's take a slight detour to look at the issues of naming tables in `DataSet` objects. One of the "Rules of Thumb" for writing professional quality applications is that you should not use "magic" literal values in your code, especially when those values have significant meaning in your application. The examples above break this rule by hard-coding the table indices. While it's fine for demonstration purposes, you will get into trouble doing this in more complex data sets. Even if you can remember the index for each table in a `DataSet` containing several tables, your code will be hard to read and maintain.

Clearly we can (and should) do better. The `DataSet` class's `Tables` collection actually allows you to reference a table using its name. You can assign each table a name and use it to find the table in the collection. If you don't assign table names, data adapters automatically assign tables with default names. For example, `SqlDataAdapter` assigns the first table in a `DataSet` with name `Table`, the second table with name `Table1`, and so on.

The default table names are like default class and control names assigned by Visual Studio .NET – they both work, but you should always avoid them except for the simplest experimental programs, such as examples in books. For instance, I use the default name, `dataGrid1`, for the `DataGrid` control used to display the records throughout this chapter. However, you won't find such names in real applications I deliver to my customers.

You can name tables when they are created. The `Fill()` method has an overloaded version that accepts a second parameter specifying the name of the table to be populated with records:

```
int Fill(DataSet ds, string TableName)
```

If the named table already exists in the `DataSet`, the `Fill()` method loads the returned records into the table. Otherwise, it creates a new table with the given name, and then populates it with the returned records. You can then access the table using its name:

```
da.Fill(ds, "CategoryTable");
dataGrid1.DataSource = ds.Tables["CategoryTable"];
```

Strictly speaking, this still breaks the rule by using hard-coded names. However, you can define a set of table name constants, each containing the name of a table used in your application. Your application will then be much cleaner.

While naming a table on the fly is simple, it falls short when the data adapter gets data from a combined query. In such cases, the data adapter loads the result set of each `SELECT` statement into a separate table. Unfortunately there is no overloaded `Fill()` method to accept more than one table name. So if you used this technique in the sample code used in the last section, you would end up creating two tables in the `DataSet`. The first has the name `CategoryTable`, and the second has the name `CategoryTable1`. It's still not good enough!

ADO.NET provides a better solution. It defines a `DataTableMapping` class in the `System.Data.Common` namespace, which specifies the mapping of names between a table returned from a `SelectCommand` and a table in the `DataSet`. Each data adapter class contains a collection of `DataTableMapping` objects and exposes them through its `TableMappings` property. By default, this collection contains no `DataTableMapping` objects and it's up to you to add the mapping into the collection.

Adding a table mapping into the `TableMappings` collection is easy – you simply call its `Add()` method and pass in the source and target table names:

```
DataTableMapping DataTableMappingCollection.Add (string SourceTableName,
                                                 string TargetTableName)
```

Just when you thought that you had finally found the perfect solution, you will be hit with surprises. When I learned about the table mapping and tried it in my little learning project, I went for the obvious code:

```
SqlDataAdapter da = new SqlDataAdapter(SelectCategoryCustomerQuery,
    DbConnectionString);

// Create table mappings
da.TableMappings.Add("Categories", "CategoryTable");
da.TableMappings.Add("Customers", "CustomerTable");

DataSet ds = new DataSet();
da.Fill(ds);

// Check the table names
for (int i = 0; i < ds.Tables.Count; ++i)
{
  Debug.WriteLine("Table " + i.ToString() + " Name = " +
      ds.Tables[i].TableName);
}
```

Guess what gets displayed? `Table` and `Table1`; oops, there must be something wrong here! It turns out that the data adapter doesn't think like us – it doesn't pick up the names of the tables from the SELECT statement. Therefore it has no idea that the category records returned from the SQL SELECT statement:

```
SELECT CategoryID, CategoryName FROM Categories
```

are from the `Categories` table. Instead, it just applies the default rule and names it `Table`. Similarly, it names the result set from the SELECT customer query `Table1`. Once you know it, the solution is pretty simple – you just map against those automatically generated table names:

```
da.TableMappings.Add("Table", "CategoryTable");
da.TableMappings.Add("Table1", "CustomerTable");
```

It's not as elegant as you'd have hoped, but at least it gets the job done. You can find the complete code for this example in the `ReadMultipleTableForm.ReadDataWithMappingTables()` method in the sample project.

Mapping Columns

In addition to explicitly naming tables, you can also name columns explicitly. The `DataTableMapping` class contains a `ColumnMappings` collection, to which you can add column mapping information. The following code snippet shows an example:

```
SqlDataAdapter da = new SqlDataAdapter(SelectCategoryQuery,
    DbConnectionString);
da.MissingMappingAction = MissingMappingAction.Error;
DataTableMapping TableMapping =
    da.TableMappings.Add("Table", "CategoryTable");
TableMapping.ColumnMappings.Add("CategoryID", "ID");
TableMapping.ColumnMappings.Add("CategoryName", "Name");

DataSet ds = new DataSet();
da.Fill(ds);
```

You can find the complete code for this example in the
`ReadMultipleTableForm.ReadDataWithMappingColumns()` method in the sample project.

With table and column mappings, you can create `DataSet` objects using application specific naming
conventions. Client objects need to know only the table and column names defined in `DataSet` objects.
They need not know the names of the tables and columns in the underlying database. This technique
effectively decouples the application-level objects from databases, therefore allowing you to change
database objects without affecting the application objects, other than the ones that manage the
communication between `DataSet` objects and the database.

The MissingMappingAction Property

A question that arises from the discussion of table and column mappings is what happens if there are no
mappings between a result set and a table in the `DataSet`. Obviously data adapters have so far handled
this without any trouble, given that there are no table and column mappings until you explicitly create them.

Data adapters have a `MissingMappingAction` property that specifies the behavior of the data adapter
when it finds no table mapping information. This property can have any one of the values in the
`MissingMappingAction` enumeration defined in the `System.Data` namespace. The possible values
are `Error`, `Ignore`, or `PassThrough`.

By default, the `MissingMappingAction` property value is `PassThrough`. If there is no mapping table
for a result set, the data adapter creates a table and loads the result data into this table. If there are no
mapping columns, the data adapter appends unmapped columns from the result set to the existing table.
This works for us well so far, as the data adapter simply creates tables and columns silently.

In applications where you want to explicitly define the table and its columns, you can specify a different
behavior for data adapters by assigning different values to their `MissingMappingAction` properties.

```
da.MissingMappingAction = MissingMappingAction.Error;
da.MissingMappingAction = MissingMappingAction.Ignore;
```

If you assign the `MissingMappingAction` property as `Error`, the data adapter will throw a
`System.InvalidOperationException` if it can't find a mapping table or mapping columns for a
result set. In such cases, even code as simple as the following will fail:

```
SqlDataAdapter da = new SqlDataAdapter(SelectCategoryQuery,
    DbConnectionString);
da.MissingMappingAction = MissingMappingAction.Error;
```

```
DataSet ds = new DataSet();
da.Fill(ds);
```

Recall that as the data adapter names the result set with the default name `Table`, it will look for a mapping table in the `DataSet` for this result set. Since the above code snippet doesn't create such a mapping, the data adapter will throw the exception. Please note that you must create both table and column mappings, otherwise the data adapter will throw the exception.

The last value, `MissingMappingAction.Ignore`, forces the data adapter to ignore any records that have no table or column mappings. These records will not be loaded into the `DataSet`.

Reading Using Multiple Select Commands

Now back to our main task. The third method of reading data from multiple tables is to execute a sequence of `SelectCommands`, each of which returns records from one table. Here we will explicitly manage our connection, so that we can use just one open connection to perform two reads.

```
SqlConnection cn = new SqlConnection(DbConnectionString);
SqlDataAdapter da = new SqlDataAdapter(SelectCategoryQuery, cn);
DataSet ds = new DataSet();

// Open the connection explicitly so that we can use it
// for multiple fills.
cn.Open();

// Get all category records
da.Fill(ds);

// Get all customer records
da.SelectCommand.CommandText = SelectCustomerQuery;
da.Fill(ds);

// Remember to close the connection explicitly.
cn.Close();

// Check the table names
for (int i = 0; i < ds.Tables.Count; ++i)
{
  Debug.WriteLine("Table " + i.ToString() + " Name = " +
      ds.Tables[i].TableName);
}

dataGrid1.DataSource = ds.Tables[0];
```

This example creates a data adapter and initializes it with the select category SQL statement. It explicitly opens the connection and calls the `Fill()` method to load the category records in to the `DataSet`. Because it doesn't specify a table name, the data adapter creates a table named `Table` and loads all the records into it.

179

Next, it assigns the `SelectCommand` text with the select customer SQL statement. The next call to the `Fill()` method uses the existing open connection to load all the customer records. But where does it load the records? Because the data adapter has no knowledge of the source table in the database, it loads the records into the default table, which is the same table where all the category records are already stored. The `for` loop confirms this when it prints only one table name. The `DataGrid` control displays both category and customer records.

An interesting fact is that the `Fill()` method doesn't just load customer records into the existing table. It also creates two new columns in the table for the customer records, because it can't find any column mapping information. This is the default behavior when the data adapter doesn't know how to map the result set to the `DataSet` tables. As usual, this default behavior somehow achieves its task of loading records, but the result is far from desirable.

The better solution is to explicitly name the tables:

```
// Get all category records
da.Fill(ds, "CategoryTable");

// Get all customer records
da.SelectCommand.CommandText = SelectCustomerQuery;
da.Fill(ds, "CustomerTable");
```

The data adapter now creates two tables, `CategoryTable` and `CustomerTable`, and populates them with the category and customer records respectively. You can find the complete code for this example in the `ReadMultipleTableForm.ReadDataWithMultipleCommands()` method in the sample project.

Reading Using Multiple Data Adapters

Modifying the `SelectCommand` property of a data adapter so that we can use it to load different data from a database is not always a good solution. Data adapters are often responsible for not only pulling the data out of the underlying databases, but also pushing the changes made by applications down to the databases. In addition to having a select command, a data adapter also has `INSERT`, `DELETE`, and `UPDATE` commands, which will be explained later in this chapter. Just as we design a class to represent one thing and one thing only, we should keep a data adapter to work with one data source only. It's therefore a good practice to keep all four commands in sync.

It is very likely that an application will want to separate the management of category and customer records. From the business perspective, maintaining those two types of records may be the responsibility of two different departments. Technically, it's also desirable to use two data adapters, one for category records and the other for customer records.

Reading data using multiple adapters is a simple process. The following code snippet shows an example:

```
SqlConnection cn = new SqlConnection(DbConnectionString);
SqlDataAdapter CategoryDA = new SqlDataAdapter(SelectCategoryQuery, cn);
SqlDataAdapter CustomerDA = new SqlDataAdapter(SelectCustomerQuery, cn);
DataSet ds = new DataSet();

// Open the connection explicitly so that we can use it
// for multiple adapters.
```

```
    cn.Open();

    // Get all category records
    CategoryDA.Fill(ds, "CategoryTable");

    // Get all customer records
    CustomerDA.Fill(ds, "CustomerTable");

    // Remember to close the connection explicitly.
    cn.Close();
```

This example creates two data adapters, one for categories and the other for customers. It attaches both data adapters to the same connection. As in the last example, it opens the connection and keeps it open when calling the Fill() methods of both adapters. By specifying table names for the Fill() methods, it ensures that the category and customer records are loaded into separate tables in the DataSet. Finally, it closes the connection when it no longer needs to be connected to the database. You can find the complete code for this example in the ReadMultipleTableForm.ReadDataWithMultipleAdapters() method in the sample project.

Defining Primary Key

When a data adapter populates a table with data from the database, it loads, by default, basic schema information such as the column name and data type. This is adequate when you only need to read records sequentially, that is moving from the beginning of a table to the end, or from the end back to the beginning. If you need to find records randomly, you will need to uniquely identify each row in a table.

Relational database design theory requires that each row in a table must contain a key that uniquely identifies the row. We normally refer this key as the **primary key**. As primary key values are frequently used to retrieve records from a table, it's desirable to define the primary key containing only simple values. In practice, primary keys are generally integers or short strings. In some cases, a primary key may contain more than one column. This is generally acceptable as long as the columns contain only integers or short strings. If they may contain other data types or long strings, it's preferable to create a separate column as the primary key.

Since a table in a well-designed database always defines a primary key, you can instruct the data adapter to load the primary key information from the database. To do so, you can change the default behavior of a data adapter by specifying a MissingSchemaAction. Similar to the table-mapping feature discussed previously, data adapters also allow you to specify the desired action regarding the mapping of database schema to the DataSet table. A data adapter has a MissingSchemaAction property that has any one of the following values defined in the System.Data.MissingSchemaAction enumeration:

Value	Description
Add	Add the database schema information into the DataSet table. This is the default value.
AddWithKey	Add the database schema information including primary key into the DataSet table.

Table continued on following page

Value	Description
Error	Throw an exception. You use this if you are populating a table that has already been created with correct column definitions.
Ignore	Ignore the columns that have not been defined in the DataSet table you are populating.

To load primary key information from the database, you assign the data adapter's `MissingSchemaAction` property to `AddWithKey`. Once you have loaded in the primary key information, you can find a row in the table. The `Rows` collection, which is an instance of the `System.Data.DataRowCollection` class, defines a `Find` method that allows you to find a row with a primary key. The following code snippet shows an example:

```
SqlDataAdapter da = new SqlDataAdapter(
"SELECT CustomerID, CompanyName FROM Customers", DbConnectionString);
DataSet ds = new DataSet();

da.MissingSchemaAction = MissingSchemaAction.AddWithKey;
da.Fill(ds, "CustomerTable");

DataTable CustomerTable = ds.Tables["CustomerTable"];
DataRow  row = CustomerTable.Rows.Find("AAAAA");
Debug.WriteLine("CompanyName = " + row["CompanyName"].ToString());
```

Because the `CustomerID` column in the `Customers` table is the primary key, the data adapter will define the corresponding column, `CustomerID`, as the primary key in the `CustomerTable` in the `DataSet`. You can then call the table's `Rows` collection `Find()` method and pass in a `CustomerID` value. It returns a `DataRow` object with the matching `CustomerID`. If there is no record in the table with matching `CustomerID` value, the `Find()` method returns NULL. You can access any field values in the row.

Alternatively, you can explicitly define the primary key for a table. In some cases, a single column makes up the primary key. In others, the primary key may be a composite key containing several columns. The `DataTable` class has a `PrimaryKey` property that contains a collection of columns making up the primary key. You define it by initiating it with all columns that makes up the primary key:

```
CustomerTable.PrimaryKey = new DataColumn[]
    {CustomerTable.Columns["CustomerID"] };
```

In this example, the primary key of `CustomerTable` contains only one column, `CustomerID`. To specify a primary key that contains multiple columns, you list all the columns in the `DataColumn` collection's initialization list. For instance, assuming that the primary key of the `ProductTable` consists of `CategoryID` and `ProductID`, you would define the primary key as:

```
ProductTable.PrimaryKey = New DataColumn()
{
    tbl.Columns("CategoryID"), tbl.Columns("ProductID")
}
```

As I have mentioned above, it's a good idea to keep the primary key small. If you find that you have to use a combination of columns to form a primary key, consider creating a single column containing small, but unique values.

We have covered just about all the common usages of data adapters for loading data into `DataSet` objects. You can allow the data adapters to implicitly create and open connections, and subsequently close the connections once they have loaded the `Datasets`. If you need the connections for multiple `Fill` operations, you can also explicitly manage them yourself.

There are different techniques for reading data from multiple tables. You can assign the data adapter's `SelectCommand` either a SQL `JOIN` query or multiple `SELECT` queries. You can build more than one `SelectCommand` and use them to fill a `DataSet`, or you can use multiple data adapters to fill a single `DataSet`.

In addition, you have also learned to explicitly name the tables in `DataSets`, and to map the result sets returned by any `SelectCommand` objects to predefined table names. You can use any combinations of the above techniques that are desired in your applications to provide flexible data access functionality. It's now time to take a well-deserved break and get ready to move on to the next area – updating data in `DataSets` using data adapters.

Updating Data

Once the data in the `DataSet` has been modified, it's time to push the changes down to the corresponding tables in the database. There are several ways of updating the database from the data contained in the `DataSet`. You can create a `Command` object to execute SQL `UPDATE` queries, or you can reconnect the `DataSet` to the database using a data adapter. Let's look at how each of those approaches works.

Using Commands to Update Data

As discussed earlier, every .NET Data Provider defines a `Command` class. So far, you have learned to use `Command` objects to execute SQL `SELECT` statements or stored procedures that return result sets. You can also use `Command` objects to execute other SQL statements to add new records, and modify or delete existing records in a database.

In situations where we have direct reference to new or changed data, using a command to save it to the underlying database is an efficient approach. For instance, if you allow your users to create a new customer record on an ASP.NET page, you know exactly what the values of different fields are through the form posted back to you. In such cases, you can create a `Command` object and pass it a SQL `INSERT` statement with the values obtained from the form. When you execute the `Command`, the changes will be saved to the database straightaway. In most applications, you can also use a `Command` object to execute a stored procedure to perform update operations.

The advantage of this approach is that you cut out the middleman, which in this context is an intermediate `DataSet` object. You don't have to build a `DataSet` to store the changed data and then push it into the database using a data adapter. In other situations when you already have the changes in a `DataSet`, updating it using a data adapter would be a better choice.

In a nutshell, using a Command object to update a database is a very simple process. We need to:

❑ Create a database connection.

❑ Create a Command object and specify an SQL INSERT, UPDATE, DELETE query or a stored procedure.

❑ Attach the Command object to the database connection.

❑ Invoke the ExecuteNonQuery() method of the Command object to execute the UPDATE query. The name of this method is slightly confusing though. It doesn't mean that it will not execute a query, but rather you tells it that the query about to be run will not return any result set. Please note that here a result set refers to a collection of rows. The query itself may return statistics about the update operation, such as the number of records affected by the query.

❑ Close the connection.

Let's look at each of the insert, update, and delete operations in turn.

Updating Records

The following skeleton code shows a simple database update operation:

```
const string UpdateQuery =
    "UPDATE Categories SET Description = 'Milk, Ice Cream, Cheeses'" +
    " WHERE CategoryName = 'Dairy Products'";

// Create a database connection
SqlConnection cn = new SqlConnection(DbConnectionString);

// Create a command object with a UPDATE query
// and link it to the connection
SqlCommand cmd = new SqlCommand(UpdateQuery, cn);

// Invoke the command object's ExecuteNonQuery method
cn.Open();
int RecordsAffected = cmd.ExecuteNonQuery();
MessageBox.Show("RecordsAffected = " + RecordsAffected.ToString());
cn.Close();
```

The code itself is simple enough, as it follows the process outlined above. One useful feature people often ignore is the return value of the ExecuteNonQuery() method. This method returns the number of records affected by the command. For instance, if the command is a SQL UPDATE statement, ExecuteNonQuery() returns the number of records updated. Similarly, ExecuteNonQuery() returns the number of records inserted into database when executing an INSERT command. If you expect a command to update a record, but receive 0 as the return value from ExecuteNonQuery(), you know the update has failed. You can find the complete code for this example in the UpdateCommandForm.UpdateUsingCommand() method in the sample project.

If a query contains parameters, you will need to define and add the relevant parameters to the command. For instance, assuming that the above update query accepts two parameters, @CatName and @CatDescription, you will create and add two parameters to the command. The following code snippet demonstrates an example:

```
const string UpdateQuery =
    "UPDATE Categories SET Description = @CatDescription" +
    " WHERE CategoryName = @CatName";

// Create a database connection
SqlConnection cn = new SqlConnection(DbConnectionString);

// Create a command object with a UPDATE query and add parameters
SqlCommand cmd = new SqlCommand(UpdateQuery, cn);
cmd.Parameters.Add("@CatName", "Dairy Products");
cmd.Parameters.Add("@CatDescription", "Milk, Ice Cream, Cheeses");

// Invoke the command object's ExecuteNonQuery method
cn.Open();
int RecordsAffected = cmd.ExecuteNonQuery();
MessageBox.Show("RecordsAffected = " + RecordsAffected.ToString());
cn.Close();
```

Instead of embedding the category name and description in the query, UpdateQuery now defines them as parameters. In UpdateQuery, @CatName, and @CatDescription indicate where the two parameters will be placed. Two Parameter objects are created and added to the Command's Parameters collection. Each Parameter object contains the value for the corresponding parameter. You can find the complete code for this example in the UpdateCommandForm.UpdateUsingParamCommand() method in the sample project.

Adding Records

From a programmer's perspective, adding new records to a database is no different from modifing existing records. You create a Command for an SQL INSERT command or a stored procedure, adding parameters if required, and execute it. For example, to create a new customer record in the Customers table, you can use the following example:

```
const string InsertQuery =
    "INSERT Customers (CustomerID, CompanyName) " +
    "VALUES ('AAAAA', 'New Customer')";

// Create a database connection
SqlConnection cn = new SqlConnection(DbConnectionString);

// Create a command object with an INSERT query
// and link it to the connection
SqlCommand cmd = new SqlCommand(InsertQuery, cn);

// Invoke the command object's ExecuteNonQuery method
cn.Open();
int RecordsAffected = cmd.ExecuteNonQuery();
MessageBox.Show("RecordsAffected = " + RecordsAffected.ToString());
cn.Close();
```

185

You can find the complete code for this example in the `UpdateCommandForm.InsertUsingCommand()` method in the sample project. Remember that if you run this code more than once (it is accessed via the **Insert Using Command** button on the `UpdateCommandForm`) it will throw an exception as it will be being asked to create the same customer twice.

Apart from using a SQL `INSERT` command, this example looks identical to the example that updates a category record. So why have I given this subject a section of its own?

The reason is more to do with the common practice that defines a primary key for each table in relational databases. In some cases, a table contains one column that uniquely identifies its records. For instance, a social security number (SSN) uniquely identifies a person. Therefore in a database table storing all staff members working for a company, employee SSN is a good candidate for the primary key. The `Customers` table in the Northwind database is an example, where the `CustomerID` is always unique. As you can see from the above example, creating new record is pretty simple. Obviously you will have to assign the `CustomerID` field a value that hasn't already been used by any existing records. There are many techniques that can ensure this. For instance, you can execute a `SELECT` query to see if a value has already been used.

In other cases, such a unique identifier doesn't always map to a single attribute. For instance, if you store all your customers in a table, you may not always be able to find a column for a primary key. You may not always know the customer's SSN, and customer names are not always unique. In such cases, you may want to programmatically generate a primary key for each record.

Many databases provide facilities to generate unique values to be used as primary keys. For instance, SQL Server allows you to define a column as identity. Each time a new record is inserted into a table with an identity column, SQL Server automatically generates a unique number for the identity column. Oracle also defines sequences, which provide you with a unique value each time you query the sequence.

In many cases, when you insert a new record to a table, you want to obtain its primary key value so that you can distinguish this newly created record from existing records. For instance, if your web page displays a list of customers, you may want to highlight the new customer you've just created. The best way to uniquely identify a customer record is to use its primary key value. However, if this primary key value is generated by the database, you need to somehow obtain it after inserting a new record.

Different databases use different mechanisms for you to extract the primary key of a newly created record. For instance, SQL Server stores the last automatically generated identity value in a variable, `@@IDENTITY`. Therefore you can read this variable immediately after inserting a new record to obtain the identity value. Here is a Transact SQL example:

```
INSERT TableName (Field2, Field3) VALUES (Field2Value, Field3Value)
PRINT @@IDENTITY
```

A commonly used technique is to wrap the SQL `INSERT` statement in a stored procedure. After the `INSERT` statement is executed, the stored procedure reads `@@IDENTITY` and returns its value. Your program can then use this returned identity value to identify the newly created record.

The `Categories` table in the Northwind database is an example of a table containing an identity column as its primary key. Each category record has a `CategoryID`, which is an identity column. To create a new category record, you can use the following `INSERT` command:

```
INSERT Categories (CategoryName, Description)
VALUES ('Frozen Food', 'Freshly frozen food')
```

The `Picture` column is ignored here for simplicity. Note that you must not specify a value for the identity column, `CategoryID` in this table, or SQL Server will report an error. When you execute this query, SQL Server automatically assigns it a unique integer. You can then retrieve the `CategoryID` value by reading the `@@IDENTITY` variable.

This code snippet creates a stored procedure to insert a category record and return its identity value:

```
CREATE PROCEDURE spAddCategory
(
  @CategoryName nvarchar(15),
  @Description  ntext
)
AS
  INSERT Categories (CategoryName, Description)
  VALUES (@CategoryName, @Description)
  RETURN @@IDENTITY
```

You can create a new stored procedure in the SQL Server Enterprise Manager and enter the above code, enter and run the code in the SQL Server Query Analyzer, or, if you are using MSDE, enter the code into SQL Window in Visual Studio, which you can call on by clicking on one of the tables in the MSDE databases. The code is in the download, in the file `spAddCategory.sql`. To call this stored procedure in your ADO.NET program, you first create a `Connection` and a `Command` as usual:

```
SqlConnection cn = new SqlConnection(DbConnectionString);
SqlCommand cmd = new SqlCommand("spAddCategory", cn);
cmd.CommandType = CommandType.StoredProcedure;
```

Here you pass the name of the stored procedure to the `Command` class's constructor and then specify the `CommandType` as `StoredProcedure`. The next step is to create two input parameters:

```
cmd.Parameters.Add("@CategoryName", "Frozen Food");
cmd.Parameters.Add("@Description", "Freshly frozen food");
```

Standard stuff so far. Now how do you retrieve the return value of the stored procedure? In ADO.NET, you create another parameter for retrieving the return value of the stored procedure, and add it to the `Command` object:

```
SqlParameter param = cmd.Parameters.Add("@CategoryID", SqlDbType.Int);
param.Direction = ParameterDirection.ReturnValue;
```

Instead of providing a value for it, you specify the type of the returned value. As this is for retrieving the return value, you can name the parameter anything you like. You will use this name later to extract this parameter from the `Parameters` collection. In SQL Server, identity columns are all of type integer; therefore you specify this type using the `SqlDbType.Int` enumeration value. You also need to indicate that this parameter is used for retrieving the return value of the stored procedure by assigning its `Direction` property with the `ParameterDirection.ReturnValue` enumeration value.

You can then execute this stored procedure as you usually do:

```
cn.Open();
int RecordsAffected = cmd.ExecuteNonQuery();
MessageBox.Show("RecordsAffected = " + RecordsAffected.ToString());
```

The `ExecuteNonQuery()` method here returns the number of records, 1 in this case, inserted into the database. Next, you can retrieve the return value of the stored procedure from the parameter `@CategoryID`:

```
int CategoryID =
    System.Convert.ToInt32(cmd.Parameters["@CategoryID"].Value);
MessageBox.Show("Category ID = " + CategoryID.ToString());
```

This converts the return value to the .NET CLR 32-bit integer, which maps to C# `int`. The program here displays the return value, but you can do anything with it as required in your applications. Finally you close the `Connection`:

```
cn.Close();
```

As you can see, inserting a record in to a table with an identity column is slightly more involved. The extra work helps you to retrieve the identity value for the newly created record. If you don't need to know this value, you don't need to create the parameter for the return value. You can find the complete code for this example in the `UpdateCommandForm.InsertUsingStoredProc()` method in the sample project.

Deleting Records

The last data operation is to delete records from a database. It is quite similar to using commands to update records, if not simpler. You simply specify a SQL `DELETE` command or a stored procedure when creating the `Command` object and call its `ExecuteNonQuery()` method to execute the command. I won't repeat the process here, as we have already discussed it. Here is a sample code snippet that deletes a category record (be sure to replace the `CategoryID` value with the one returned from the previous `INSERT` example):

```
// Create a database connection
SqlConnection cn  = new SqlConnection(DbConnectionString);

// Create a command object with an UPDATE query
// and link it to the connection
SqlCommand    cmd = new SqlCommand(
                        "DELETE Categories WHERE CategoryID = 9", cn);

// Invoke the command object's ExecuteNonQuery method
cn.Open();
int RecordsAffected = cmd.ExecuteNonQuery();
MessageBox.Show("RecordsAffected = " + RecordsAffected.ToString());
cn.Close();
```

As there is a relationship between the `Categories` and `Products` tables, you can delete a category record that is referenced by product records. If you wish, for practice, you can delete the category record created in the previous section, which creates category records with no related products.

Using Data Adapters to Update Data

If you need to add, update, or delete records in a `DataSet`, you can loop through the relevant tables and perform the appropriate operations using `Command` objects as demonstrated in the previous sections.

In ADO.NET, you can use the same `DataAdapter` object used to retrieve the data to link up the `DataSet` to the database and to update the database with the changes made in the `DataSet`:

```
cn.Open()
adapter.Update(ds, "CustomerTable")
cn.Close()
```

Simple, isn't it? However, you will probably ask, "How in the world does ADO.NET know which table and records to update, and how to update them?" The answer is not straightforward. Let me answer the first question first.

Row State and Field Value Versions

ADO.NET finds out which records to update by examining all the records in the specified table in the `DataSet CustomerTable` in this example. Each row in a `DataSet` table has a `RowState` property that indicates the current state of the row. It may be one of the following five values defined in the `DataRowState` enumeration:

Value	Description
Added	The row has been added to the table.
Deleted	The row has been deleted from the table. Note that it's just been marked as deleted and has not been physically removed. This allows ADO.NET to later delete the corresponding row in the database. The *Deleting Records* section earlier in this chapter explains this in more detail. This also allows us to rollback the DELETE operation should it becomes necessary, for instance, when any of other records fail to update.
Detached	The row is not in a table. This happens when you have created a new `DataRow` object for a `DataSet` table but has not added it to the table's `Rows` collection, or you have removed the row from the table using the `Remove()` method.
Modified	The row has been modified. For instance, you have assigned a new value to one of the fields in the row.
Unchanged	The row has not been changed. When you first populate the `DataSet` using a data adapter, the status of all rows is set to `Unchanged`.

In addition, each record field may have one of the following three value versions:

Version	Description
Original	The most recent value loaded from database.
Current	The current value of the field. When the record is loaded from database, this version is identical to the original version.
Proposed	The value to be assigned to the field. This version exists only when you have created a new row, but have not yet added to the table.

Field value versions are defined in the System.Data.DataRowVersion enumeration. You can examine those values by specifying the version for a field:

```
row["CustomerID", DataRowVersion.Original]
row["CustomerID", DataRowVersion.Current]
row["CustomerID", DataRowVersion.Proposed]
```

This enumeration contains a fourth value, Default, which represents the default version used by the field:

```
row["CustomerID", DataRowVersion.Default]
```

This returns an identical result to the following expression, which doesn't specify any version:

```
row["CustomerID"]
```

All fields in a row have at least one version depending on the current state of the parent row. Therefore you can always retrieve a field value by not specifying a version. For instance, row["CustomerID"] is certain to return a value. However, we can't guarantee that a value will be returned for all of the versions above. If you try to access a specific version that doesn't exist, ADO.NET will throw a System.Data.VersionNotFoundException exception. While you may catch such an exception to decide what to do if the required version doesn't exist, you should usually prevent such an exception by checking whether that version exists using the HasVersion method of the DataRow class:

```
if (row.HasVersion(DataRowVersion.Current))
    Debug.Write(row["CustomerID", DataRowVersion.Current].ToString());
```

The following code snippet shows an example that has all existing versions for all fields in a given row, which is included in the UpdateUsingAdapterForm in the sample project:

```
private void DebugWriteRow(DataTable table, DataRow row)
{
    foreach(DataColumn col in table.Columns)
    {
        Debug.Write(col.ColumnName + " = " + row[col].ToString());
        if (row.HasVersion(DataRowVersion.Current))
        {
```

```
        Debug.Write("\tCurrent = " +
            row[col, DataRowVersion.Current].ToString());
      }
      if (row.HasVersion(DataRowVersion.Original))
      {
        Debug.Write("\tOriginal = " +
            row[col, DataRowVersion.Original].ToString());
      }
      if (row.HasVersion(DataRowVersion.Proposed))
      {
        Debug.Write("\tProposed = " +
            row[col, DataRowVersion.Proposed].ToString());
      }
      Debug.Write("\t");
    }
    Debug.WriteLine("\t" + row.RowState);
}
```

Whenever you fill the `DataSet` with records from a database, ADO.NET loads the field value stored in the database into both the `Original` and `Current` versions for each field. The `RowState` is set to `Unchanged` for all rows.

Modifying Records in DataSet

When you create a new row to the table, the `RowState` is set to `Detached`. Each field has a `Proposed` version containing `System.Data.DBNull`. Neither the `Original` version nor the `Current` version is created. You can assign a value to each field. The `Proposed` version will contain the assigned value. When you add the row into the table's `Rows` collection, the `RowState` is changed to `Added`. `Proposed` values will be moved to the `Current` version. The `Proposed` version will then be discarded. The code snippet below shows an example:

```
DataRow row = CustomerTable.NewRow();
row["CustomerID"]  = "AAAAA";
row["CompanyName"] = "New Customer";
DebugWriteRow(CustomerTable, row);

CustomerTable.Rows.Add(row);
DebugWriteRow(CustomerTable, row);
```

The `NewRow()` method of the `DataTable` class creates a new `DataRow` object, which contains fields corresponding to the table's columns. The first `DebugWriteRow()` call will show that the `RowState` property of the `DataRow` object is `Detached`, and the `Proposed` version of each field contains the new values. This row is added to the table with the `Add()` method of the `Rows` collection. The second call will show that the `RowState` property of the row is `Added`, and the `Current` version of the each field contains the new value.

You can change the value of a field in an existing row, for example:

```
DataRow row = CustomerTable.Rows.Find("AAAAA");
row["CompanyName"] = "VIP Customer";
```

The CompanyName field's Current value will be set to the new value. The RowState will be set to Modified. The Original value stays unchanged, representing the value in the underlying database.

You can call the AcceptChanges method of a row to change the Original values of all fields to the Current value. This method also sets the RowState to Unchanged for that row. Alternatively, you can call the AcceptChanges method on a table to accept changes to all rows in the table.

You can discard any changes made to a row by calling the RejectChanges() method of either the Row object or its parent Table object. Calling the row's RejectChanges method changes its RowState back to Unchanged. If you call the RejectChanges method of a table, changes to all rows will be lost and the RowState of all rows will be reset to Unchanged. Calling the table's RejectChanges() method will also remove all added rows from the table.

To delete a row, you call its Delete() method:

```
DataRow row = CustomerTable.Rows.Find("AAAAA");
row.Delete();
```

This method marks the record as deleted by changing its RowState property to Deleted. The row itself remains in the table's Rows collection. Alternatively, you can remove a row from the Rows collection using the Rows collection's Remove() method. In the previous code snippet, you can replace the call to DataRow class's Delete() method with the following call to Rows.Remove() method:

```
CustomerTable.Rows.Remove(row)
```

This changes the DataRow object's RowState property to Detached. Either way, only the DataSet is affected, the corresponding record in the database has not been deleted. However, there is a very important difference between those two.

When you call the DataRow.Delete() method, the row is marked as Deleted. Yet the row remains in the Rows collection. You can undelete it by calling the RejectChanges() method of either the DataRow object or its parent DataTable object. The RejectChanges() method changes its RowState back to Unchanged.

If a record is marked as Deleted, you can later attach a DataAdapter to the DataSet and invoke the Update method on the DataAdapter. The DataAdapter object will delete the corresponding record from the database. The Update method also permanently removes the row from the DataSet.

On the other hand, once you have called the Rows.Remove() method, the row is removed from the DataSet and its RowState is changed to Detached. Importantly, the corresponding row will not be removed from the database when you invoke the Update method of an associated DataAdapter object. Therefore this method is more useful when you only need to manipulate data in memory. If you intend to later delete a record from the database, you should use the DataRow.Delete() method to delete the row.

RowState and Update Operations

You now know that rows in a table may be in a different state, depending on what operations you have performed on them. Data adapters also check the `RowState` to decide which rows should be added, updated, or deleted in the underlying database. Each data adapter has three properties – `InsertCommand`, `UpdateCommand`, and `DeleteCommand` – that specify the operations the data adapter will perform when the `RowState` is `Added`, `Modified`, and `Deleted`, respectively.

> Out of the five possible values of **RowState**, only the above three signify that the row should be updated to the database. Recall that calling **AcceptChanges()** on a row or its parent table sets its state to **Unchanged**; you should *not* call this method if you intend to update the row. The **Update()** method of data adapters will perform the required database operations and call **AcceptChanges()** on the table automatically.

The next question is how ADO.NET knows how to update the record earmarked as needing to be updated. The answer can't be simpler – it doesn't know. You, as a programmer, must tell the adapter how to add, update, and delete those rows in one of the following two ways.

Using a Command Builder

The first approach is to use a handy feature of ADO.NET – the **command builder**. If a table in the `DataSet` is initially populated from a single table from the database, ADO.NET can figure out how to update the records by reading the table schema from the database. However, ADO.NET doesn't automatically do it for you. So, if you need to update records as we do here, you must instruct ADO.NET to create the three update commands, `InsertCommand`, `UpdateCommand`, and `DeleteCommand`, by creating a `CommandBuilder` object for the `DataAdapter` object. This is very easy to do:

```
SqlCommandBuilder cb = new SqlCommandBuilder(adapter);
```

All you need to do is to create a `SqlCommandBuilder` object and pass in the `DataAdapter` object to its constructor. The `SqlCommandBuilder`'s constructor will create a `SqlCommand` object with appropriate SQL INSERT, UPDATE, and DELETE statements based on the adapter's `SelectCommand`. It will then assign those `Command` objects to the `DataAdapter`'s `InsertCommand`, `UpdateCommand`, and `DeleteCommand` properties, respectively. You can then invoke the adapter's `Update()` method to update the database. For example:

```
private void ChangeCustomerDataset()
{
   SqlConnection  cn = new SqlConnection(DbConnectionString);
   SqlDataAdapter da = new SqlDataAdapter(SelectCustomerQuery, cn);
   DataSet        ds = new DataSet();

   // Explicitly open the connection and use it for
   // all read and update operations
   cn.Open();

   // Populate CustomerTable in the DataSet with records
   // in the Customers table and load the primary key information
```

```
    da.MissingSchemaAction = MissingSchemaAction.AddWithKey;
    da.Fill(ds, "CustomerTable");

    DataTable CustomerTable = ds.Tables["CustomerTable"];
    dataGrid1.DataSource = CustomerTable;

    // Create a few customer records in the DataSet
    for (int i = 1; i <= 3; ++i)
    {
      DataRow row = CustomerTable.NewRow();
      row["CustomerID"]  = "A0" + i.ToString();
      row["CompanyName"] = "Customer " + i.ToString();
      CustomerTable.Rows.Add(row);
    }
    // Build update commands using CommandBuilder
    SqlCommandBuilder cb = new SqlCommandBuilder(da);

    // Peek at the generated update command
    MessageBox.Show(cb.GetUpdateCommand().CommandText);

    // Add records to the database
    da.Update(ds, "CustomerTable");

    // Delete a row and modify another
    DataRow row01 = CustomerTable.Rows.Find("A01");
    row01.Delete();

    DataRow row02 = CustomerTable.Rows.Find("A02");
    row02["CompanyName"] = "Customer 02";

    // Push the changes to the database
    da.Update(ds, "CustomerTable");

    // Don't forget to close the connection
    cn.Close();
}
```

This method is defined in `UpdateUsingAdapterForm` in the sample project. It first loads all the customer records from the database into the `DataSet`. It creates a `Connection` object to establish a connection to the database. It also loads primary key information from the database, so that it can find some records in the table. Next, it adds three new customer records to the table in the `DataSet`. It then creates a `CommandBuilder` object to generate the `UpdateCommands` for the data adapter. Note that it uses the same adapter object as used to populate the table. In applications that load data from the database and update the changes in different places, you can create a new data adapter with the same `SelectCommand`, and generate the `UpdateCommands` for it:

```
public DataSet GetRecords()
{
  SqlDataAdapter da = new SqlDataAdapter(SelectCommand, ConnectionString);
  DataSet ds = new DataSet();
  da.Fill(ds, "CustomerTable");
  return ds;
}
```

```
public void UpdateRecords(DataSet ds)
{
  SqlDataAdapter da = new SqlDataAdapter(SelectCommand, ConnectionString);
  SqlCommandBuilder cb = new SqlCommandBuilder(da);
  da.Update(ds, "CustomerTable");
}
```

Once the records have been added to the database, this method modifies one arbitrary customer record and deletes another in the DataSet. It then calls the adapter's Update() method to push the changes to the database.

You can peek at the automatically generated update command by calling the CommandBuilder object's GetUpdateCommand function:

```
MessageBox.Show(cb.GetUpdateCommand().CommandText);
```

Similarly, you can look at the insert and delete commands using the CommandBuilder object's GetInsertCommand and GetDeleteCommand functions, respectively.

Creating Update Commands Manually

While the CommandBuilder classes is handy and saves you a lot of coding, it has its drawbacks:

❑ If the SelectCommand is a stored procedure, the command builder will not be able to build insert, update, or delete commands.

❑ It is limited to updating records in a single database table only. If you have a query that pulls records from two tables or more, the CommandBuilder won't build the UpdateCommand for you.

❑ The SelectCommand of the DataAdapter object must return a column containing values that uniquely identify the returned records.

❑ It must execute the SelectCommand to retrieve metadata about the table in order to generate the update commands.

❑ If the SelectCommand has changed, you must call the RefreshSchema method of the DataAdapter object to update the metadata used for the insert, update, and delete commands

To overcome those limitations, you can build the UpdateCommands manually. In the above example, assuming that you have already created a customer record with customer ID A02, you can build an UpdateCommand yourself and assign it to the adapter's UpdateCommand:

```
private void ChangeCustomerUsingManualCommand()
{
  SqlConnection  cn = new SqlConnection(DbConnectionString);
  SqlDataAdapter da = new SqlDataAdapter(SelectCustomerQuery, cn);
  DataSet ds = new DataSet();

  // Explicitly open the connection and use it for
  // all read and update operations
  cn.Open();
```

```
// Populate CustomerTable in the DataSet with records
// in the Customers table and load the primary key information
da.MissingSchemaAction = MissingSchemaAction.AddWithKey;
da.Fill(ds, "CustomerTable");

DataTable CustomerTable = ds.Tables["CustomerTable"];
dataGrid1.DataSource = CustomerTable;

// Change a row
DataRow row = CustomerTable.Rows.Find("A02");
row["CompanyName"] = "Best Customer";

// Manually create a update command
SqlCommand cmd = new SqlCommand(
    "UPDATE Customers SET CompanyName = @CustomerName" +
    " WHERE CustomerID = @CustomerID", cn);

// Create parameters
SqlParameter param = cmd.Parameters.Add("@CustomerID", SqlDbType.NChar,
    5);
param.SourceColumn = "CustomerID";
param.SourceVersion = DataRowVersion.Original;

param = cmd.Parameters.Add("@CustomerName", SqlDbType.NVarChar, 40);
param.SourceColumn = "CompanyName";
param.SourceVersion = DataRowVersion.Current;

// Assign the command to the adapter
da.UpdateCommand = cmd;

// Update records
da.Update(ds, "CustomerTable");
cn.Close();
}
```

This method is defined in `UpdateUsingAdapterForm` in the sample project. You create a `Command` object and pass to its constructor the SQL `UPDATE` statement or the stored procedure that performs the update. Because, at this time, you don't know the exact record to be updated, you specify that the customer `ID` and `Name` will be provided later by parameterizing the `UPDATE` statement. You indicate the parameters by prefixing them with the @ symbol. In this example, `@CustomerID` and `@CustomerName` represent the two parameters, which you will define explicitly. Please note that you must include every column in the table that you want to update. If you changed values for some fields, but don't include the relevant columns in the `UPDATE` statement, the changes you made will not be made to the database.

Next, you add two parameters to the Command. The first is @CustomerID and it is a string of type NChar in the SQL Server. For string fields, it's best to specify their length, so that values containing more characters than defined in the table will be truncated automatically for you and therefore avoid triggering database data overflow errors. In the Customers table, the CustomerID column contains at most five characters; therefore the @CustomerID parameter is created with size 5. The Add() method of the Command.Parameters property returns the newly added Parameter object. You then specify that it should be bound to the CustomerID column in the DataSet table. Because the CustomerID is the unique key to a customer record in the database, you must ensure that it contains the value as stored in the database. As we mentioned above, the Original version of a field in the DataSet contains the value loaded from the database. Therefore you want to bind the @CustomerID parameter to the original customer ID value by assigning the parameter's SourceVersion property with the DataRowVersion.Original enumeration value. Note that in this example, we are not going to change the CustomerID, so you could have also used the Current version. However, it's a good habit to set its Source to the Original version regardless in such situations.

The second parameter, @CustomerName, is then added to the Command object. You bind it to the CompanyName column and the Current version so that it will contain the modified value. Now you have defined the Command object, you can assign it to the DataAdapter's UpdateCommand property. When you invoke the Update() method of the DataAdapter, this command is executed to update the correct customer record in the database.

Updating DataSet with Identity Value

Creating a new customer record and adding it to the database is a simple process, as you have seen in previous sections. You can either let ADO.NET generate an InsertCommand for the data adapter, or you create your own. Either way, the update is a one-way operation. You always update the database with the records in the DataSet. If the underlying data table has an identity column and you want to update the records in the DataSet with the automatically generated identity value, things can get a bit more complex.

In an earlier section, you learned how you can use a stored procedure to add a new category record to the database and extract the automatically generated identity value from the return value. Let's see how you use such a stored procedure with a data adapter (it's included in the UpdateUsingAdapterForm in the sample project):

```csharp
private void AddCategory()
{
  const string SelectCategory =
      "SELECT CategoryID, CategoryName, Description FROM Categories";
  SqlConnection cn = new SqlConnection(DbConnectionString);
  SqlDataAdapter da = new SqlDataAdapter(SelectCategory, cn);
  DataSet ds = new DataSet();

  cn.Open();

  // Load all category records from the database
  da.Fill(ds, "CategoryTable");
  DataTable CategoryTable = ds.Tables["CategoryTable"];
  dataGrid1.DataSource = CategoryTable;
```

```
// Add a new category record to the DataSet
DataRow row = CategoryTable.NewRow();
row["CategoryName"]  = "Frozen Food";
row["Description"] = "Freshly frozen food";
CategoryTable.Rows.Add(row);

// Create a command to execute the spAddCategory stored procedure
SqlCommand cmd = new SqlCommand("spAddCategory", cn);
cmd.CommandType = CommandType.StoredProcedure;

// Add two input parameters
SqlParameter param =
    cmd.Parameters.Add("@CategoryName", SqlDbType.NVarChar, 15);
param.SourceColumn = "CategoryName";
param.SourceVersion = DataRowVersion.Current;

param = cmd.Parameters.Add("@Description", SqlDbType.NText);
param.SourceColumn = "Description";
param.SourceVersion = DataRowVersion.Current;

// Add parameter for the return value and bind it to
// the CategoryID field
param = cmd.Parameters.Add("@CategoryID", SqlDbType.Int);
param.Direction = ParameterDirection.ReturnValue;
param.SourceColumn = "CategoryID";

// Assign InsertCommand and update the database
da.InsertCommand = cmd;
da.Update(ds, "CategoryTable");

cn.Close();

MessageBox.Show("The new category ID is " +
    cmd.Parameters["@CategoryID"].Value.ToString());
}
```

Loading category records and adding a new category to the CategoryTable should be pretty straightforward for you now. This method creates a Command object for the spAddCategory stored procedure. It then adds two parameters for the two input parameters defined in sqAddCategory. Because we want to save their new values to the database, we bind them to the current value of the corresponding columns in the table.

To add a new parameter for the return value, you need to assign its Direction property ParameterDirection.ReturnValue. Because the identity value returned is the ID of the new category, this method binds it to the CategoryID. Note that you don't have to specify the SourceVersion, since ADO.NET will automatically assign the return value to both the Original and Current versions of the CategoryID field. You can specify a particular version, but it won't affect the result. ADO.NET will still assign the value to both versions.

Updating Data Using Transactions

So far, we have seen how to create, update, and delete records using different techniques. All examples have one thing in common – they all update just a single record. If the update operation fails for any reason, the changes are not made to the database. In real-world applications, things can get a bit more complex.

Consider the scenario where you create a purchase order. An order typically consists of a header record and several line items. You may create a header record first, followed by the line items. In general, you expect to create them all. However, if there is a problem in creating an item record, you may not want the header record or other item records to be created at all. In other words, it's an all-or-nothing situation – either all records are created or none of them are.

Such a requirement is best handled by wrapping all the operations into a **transaction**. Many databases such as SQL Server implement a transaction using a two-phased commit. They execute each operation and store the preliminary result in a temporary storage space. If all operations execute successfully, the database management system commits the result. That is, it writes all preliminary results, or proposed changes to the database permanently. On the other hand, if any execution fails, the system rolls back the transaction. That is, it throws away all preliminary results. The database will not be updated.

In the following example, we will create an order and a couple of line items. In the sample Northwind database, an order record in the `Orders` table is the parent record of all order item records in the order. Each order details record in the `Order Details` table relates to these records and also to a product record in the `Products` table. The following figure illustrates their relationships:

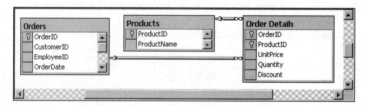

This example will load a `DataSet` with records from all three tables. It will then create a new order record and two items for that order. All three new records will be written to the database in a transaction, ensuring that they will either all be created in the database, or none of them will.

The first task is to load records from the three tables into a `DataSet`. In the *Reading Using Multiple Select Commands* section, you learned that you could concatenate multiple SQL `SELECT` commands and execute them to create three tables in a `DataSet`:

```
const string SelectProductQuery =
    "SELECT ProductID, ProductName, UnitPrice FROM Products";
const string SelectOrderQuery =
    "SELECT OrderID, OrderDate FROM Orders";
const string SelectOrderItemQuery =
    "SELECT OrderID, ProductID, UnitPrice, Quantity " +
```

```
        "FROM [Order Details]";
const string SelectQuery = SelectProductQuery + ";" +
    SelectOrderQuery + ";" + SelectOrderItemQuery;

SqlConnection cn = new SqlConnection(DbConnectionString);
SqlDataAdapter da = new SqlDataAdapter(SelectQuery, cn);

// Load data with primary key info
da.MissingSchemaAction = MissingSchemaAction.AddWithKey;
da.TableMappings.Add("Table", "ProductTable");
da.TableMappings.Add("Table1", "OrderTable");
da.TableMappings.Add("Table2", "OrderItemTable");

DataSet ds = new DataSet();

cn.Open();

// Load all product and order records from the database
da.Fill(ds);
dataGrid1.DataSource = ds;
```

When an item record is created in the DataSet, an arbitrary product is picked and the product's unit price used as the price for the item. Therefore a primary key must be defined for the ProductTable. This can be done by assigning AddWithKey to the data adapter's MissingSchemaAction property. The table mappings assign each table in the DataSet a descriptive name. The Fill() method will then create the three tables and populate them with records from the database.

Once the tables are created, we can define the relationships among them:

```
DataTable ProductTable = ds.Tables["ProductTable"];
DataTable OrderTable = ds.Tables["OrderTable"];
DataTable OrderItemTable = ds.Tables["OrderItemTable"];

ds.Relations.Add("FK_ProductID",
    ProductTable.Columns["ProductID"], OrderItemTable.Columns["ProductID"]);

ds.Relations.Add("FK_OrderID",
    OrderTable.Columns["OrderID"], OrderItemTable.Columns["OrderID"]);
```

The relationship between the ProductTable and OrderItemTable is not strictly necessary in this example. However, if you cache records from database tables in a DataSet, it's always a good idea to maintain the relationship among database tables in the DataSet. Doing so gives you the constraints useful for maintaining data integrity in memory, and reduces the risk of trying to write invalid data to the database.

The relationship between the OrderTable and the OrderItemTable, on the other hand, is useful in this example. When you change the OrderID of a record in the OrderTable, the DataSet will automatically modify the OrderID of child records in the OrderItem table. This feature helps to synchronize the records in related tables, and is especially useful when you create a record in the parent table with an identity column. We'll see more on this shortly.

The next step is to create a new order record and two companion item records:

```
// Create a new order
DataRow OrderRow = OrderTable.NewRow();
OrderRow["OrderID"] = 0;
OrderRow["OrderDate"] = System.DateTime.Now;
OrderTable.Rows.Add(OrderRow);

// Create items for the new order
DataRow ProductRow = ProductTable.Rows.Find(1);
DataRow OrderItemRow = OrderItemTable.NewRow();
OrderItemRow["OrderID"] = 0;
OrderItemRow["ProductID"] = ProductRow["ProductID"];
OrderItemRow["UnitPrice"] = ProductRow["UnitPrice"];
OrderItemRow["Quantity"] = 10;
OrderItemTable.Rows.Add(OrderItemRow);

ProductRow = ProductTable.Rows.Find(2);
OrderItemRow = OrderItemTable.NewRow();
OrderItemRow["OrderID"] = 0;
OrderItemRow["ProductID"] = ProductRow["ProductID"];
OrderItemRow["UnitPrice"] = ProductRow["UnitPrice"];
OrderItemRow["Quantity"] = 15;
OrderItemTable.Rows.Add(OrderItemRow);
```

If you look at the Orders table definition in the SQL Server Enterprise Manager, you will see that the OrderID column is an identity column. Therefore you must not specify an Order ID value when inserting a new record into the table. However, since this column is also the primary key of the table in both the database and the DataSet, ADO.NET will not allow you to leave it unassigned. In addition, you also want to link the two item records to the order record. Therefore you need to assign an Order ID in both the order and item records, so that the DataSet will have those records synchronized.

The two item records are created containing the two arbitrary products, one with ProductID 1 and the other 2. The UnitPrice of each record is assigned with the UnitPrice of the corresponding product record. The Quantity fields are also assigned with arbitrary values.

Once the new records are added to the tables in the DataSet, it's time to write them to the database. As discussed earlier, we should wrap the creation of records in a transaction. You can create a new Transaction object by calling the BeginTransaction method of a Connection object:

```
// Start a transaction to update order header and items
SqlTransaction txn = cn.BeginTransaction();
```

You will usually place the database update operations in a try block so you can catch any exceptions thrown during the update process:

```
try
{
```

This example will use a stored procedure to create an order record in the database. This stored procedure returns the `OrderID` value for the newly created order record. The stored procedure follows:

```
CREATE PROCEDURE spAddOrder
(
  @OrderDate datetime
)
AS
  INSERT Orders (OrderDate)  VALUES (@OrderDate)

    RETURN @@IDENTITY
GO
```

The last section explained how to execute such a stored procedure and update the record in a `DataSet` table with the returned identity value. This example uses the same approach:

```
SqlCommand cmd = new SqlCommand("spAddOrder", cn, txn);
cmd.CommandType = CommandType.StoredProcedure;

SqlParameter param = cmd.Parameters.Add("@OrderDate", SqlDbType.DateTime);
param.SourceColumn = "OrderDate";
param.SourceVersion = DataRowVersion.Current;

param = cmd.Parameters.Add("@OrderID", SqlDbType.Int);
param.Direction = ParameterDirection.ReturnValue;
param.SourceColumn = "OrderID";

// Assign InsertCommand and update the Orders table
da.InsertCommand = cmd;
da.Update(OrderTable);
```

What's new here is that the `Command` object is now attached with the `Transaction` object created earlier. Associating a `Command` to a `Transaction` ensures that this `Command` will be executed within the transaction. When you execute this `Command`, such as through the data adapter's `Update` method in this example, the new record is created, but not actually written to the table yet.

The fact that the new record has been created enables the data adapter to extract the automatically generated order ID and update the new order record in `OrderTable` with this new ID. Because the two new item records are children of this order record as defined in the relation between `OrderTable` and `OrderItemTable`, their `OrderID` fields will also be updated with this new order ID. Therefore you can use their values when creating the item records in the database.

To insert order item records in the database, we will use the following parameterized query:

```
const string InsertOrderItem =
    "INSERT INTO [Order Details] " +
    "(OrderID, ProductID, UnitPrice, Quantity) " +
    "VALUES (@OrderID, @ProductID, @UnitPrice, @Quantity)";
```

You can then create a `Command` object and bind the parameters to the corresponding fields in `OrderItemTable`:

```
cmd = new SqlCommand(InsertOrderItem, cn, txn);
param = cmd.Parameters.Add("@OrderID", SqlDbType.Int);
param.SourceColumn = "OrderID";
param.SourceVersion = DataRowVersion.Current;

param = cmd.Parameters.Add("@ProductID", SqlDbType.Int);
param.SourceColumn = "ProductID";
param.SourceVersion = DataRowVersion.Current;

param = cmd.Parameters.Add("@UnitPrice", SqlDbType.Money);
param.SourceColumn = "UnitPrice";
param.SourceVersion = DataRowVersion.Current;

param = cmd.Parameters.Add("@Quantity", SqlDbType.SmallInt);
param.SourceColumn = "Quantity";
param.SourceVersion = DataRowVersion.Current;

da.InsertCommand = cmd;
da.Update(OrderItemTable);
```

If everything goes according to plan, both order and item records are created successfully. Therefore you can commit the transaction to write them to the database:

```
        txn.Commit();
}
```

If anything goes wrong in the process, for instance, if you lost database connection at some point, you can catch the exception and perform any recovery action as required:

```
catch(Exception x)
{
  txn.Rollback();
  Debug.WriteLine("Caught exception " + x.Message);
}
```

Of course, we will remember to close the connection after we are done in the `finally` block, which will be executed regardless whether the transaction is committed.

```
finally
{
  cn.Close();
}
```

Handling Concurrency Problems

`DataSet` objects are disconnected from a database. While records in a `DataSet` may be loaded from the database, they are really local copies of their original records in the database. While you work with the `DataSet`, other users may change some of the records in the database. Your own copy of the data, therefore, may not match what is in the database. This causes a **concurrency problem**.

So far, we haven't considered any concurrency issues. When we update a record, we simply overwrite the fields in database with values in the `DataSet`. This may not be desired in certain circumstances. For example, you load all orders to a `DataSet` and decide to apply a discount to orders with a total value exceeding $100. However, while you are calculating the discount, a customer may have altered their order and reduced the total order amount to $70. In such case, you may want to withdraw the discount for that order. How do you handle this situation?

By default, when you call the `Update()` method of a data adapter, it checks the original value of each record to be updated against the corresponding record in the database. If any of them don't match, it raises a concurrency violation exception and aborts the update:

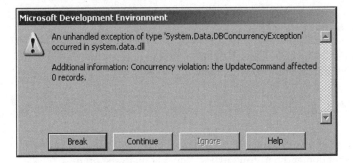

While you can catch such exceptions and act on them to correct the problem, you can prevent such exceptions from being thrown with a little bit of extra work. You have two choices. One is to set the data adapter's `ContinueUpdateOnError` to `True`, which instructs the data adapter to ignore the problematic record and carry on. This is fine as long as you don't need to know which record fails. If you need to take some actions on those records, you should use the second approach.

The `Update()` method of data adapters raises two events, `RowUpdating` and `RowUpdated`, The `RowUpdating` event is fired right before the update takes place, while the `RowUpdated` event is fired right after the update is completed. To perform some proactive operations for potentially problematic records, you can define a handler for the `RowUpdating` event. The next example demonstrates this technique by attempting to change two customer records:

```
SqlConnection  cn = new SqlConnection(DbConnectionString);
SqlDataAdapter da = new SqlDataAdapter(SelectCustomerQuery, cn);
DataSet        ds = new DataSet();

cn.Open();

// Populate CustomerTable in the DataSet with records
// in the Customers table and load the primary key information
```

```
da.MissingSchemaAction = MissingSchemaAction.AddWithKey;
da.Fill(ds, "CustomerTable");

DataTable CustomerTable = ds.Tables["CustomerTable"];
dataGrid1.DataSource = CustomerTable;

// Change two records
DataRow row = CustomerTable.Rows.Find("A02");
row["CompanyName"] = "Customer 02";

row = CustomerTable.Rows.Find("A03");
row["CompanyName"] = "Customer 03";

// Build update commands using CommandBuilder
SqlCommandBuilder cb = new SqlCommandBuilder(da);
```

The complete code is in the `UpdateUsingAdapterForm.ChangeCustomerConcurrency()` method in the sample project.

Nothing is new here. It simply loads all customer records and changes two of them. It then uses a `CommandBuilder` to generate update commands. Before it calls the data adapter's `Update` command, it hooks up a handler to the `RowUpdating` event:

```
da.RowUpdating += new SqlRowUpdatingEventHandler(OnRowUpdating);
```

I will explain the handler, `OnRowUpdating()`, in a moment. Once you have hooked up the handler, you can call the `Update()` method. For each record to be updated, the `RowUpdating` event will fire and offer you a chance to resolve potential concurrency, and other, issues:

```
// Push the changes to the database
da.Update(ds, "CustomerTable");

// Don't forget to close the connection
cn.Close();
```

Now let's take a look at the `RowUpdating()` event handler, which is also defined in the `UpdateUsingAdapterForm` in the sample project:

```
private void OnRowUpdating(object sender, SqlRowUpdatingEventArgs e)
{
  Debug.WriteLine(e.Status.ToString());
  string OriginalCustomerID =
      e.Row["CustomerID", DataRowVersion.Original].ToString();
  string OriginalCompanyName =
      e.Row["CompanyName", DataRowVersion.Original].ToString();
  string SelectCustomerQuery =
      "SELECT CompanyName FROM Customers " +
      "WHERE CustomerID = '" + OriginalCustomerID + "'";

  SqlConnection cn = new SqlConnection(DbConnectionString);
  SqlCommand cmd = new SqlCommand(SelectCustomerQuery, cn);
```

```
    cn.Open();
    string CompanyNameInDb = cmd.ExecuteScalar().ToString();
    cn.Close();

    if (OriginalCompanyName != CompanyNameInDb)
        e.Status = UpdateStatus.SkipCurrentRow;
}
```

The event argument is an instance of the `SqlRowUpdatingEventArgs` class. It has a `Row` property containing the row that is about to be updated. Here it extracts the original version of each field and generates a SQL `SELECT` command to return the `CompanyName` field value for the record in the database. Here it uses the `ExecuteScalar()` method since the query returns only one record containing only one field.

Once it has the `CompanyName` field values in both database and `DataSet`, it compares them to find out whether the name has been changed since it was loaded to the `DataSet`. If so, it sets the event argument's `Status` property to `SkipCurrentRow`, which indicates that the data adapter should skip this row and get on to the next. By default, the `Status` is `Continue`, which indicates that this record should be updated. You can abort the update operation by setting it to one of the other two values:

Value	Description
ErrorsOccured	Abort the update and raise an exception. You can assign the `SqlRowUpdatingEventArgs.Errors` to any exception.
SkipAllRemainingRows	Abort the update, but don't raise an exception.

This example is somewhat simplified, as it just skips any records that have been changed in the database. You can do just about anything deemed as good in your own applications. For example, you can raise your own exception detailing the problem:

```
if (OriginalCompanyName != CompanyNameInDb)
{
  e.Status = UpdateStatus.ErrorsOccurred;
  e.Errors = new Exception(
      "Customer name has been changed since loaded:" +
      "\nLoaded value = " + OriginalCompanyName +
      "\nCurrent value = " + CompanyNameInDb);
}
```

The user can then decide what action must be taken to correct this problem.

While the `RowUpdating` event provides you with the ability to pre-process data for updating, the `RowUpdated` event allows you to post-process data after the update operations have been completed. You can use them in your applications to fine-tune your data update routines.

Summary

In this chapter, we learned to read data from databases and update databases with data in a `DataSet` using .NET data adapters. While the ADO.NET `DataSet` class provides a powerful tool for application developers to read and manipulate disconnected data in memory, it requires communication channels to underlying databases to pass the data to and from them. Data adapters provide a uniform database access mechanism to work with different .NET Data Providers.

Data adapters offer the ability to read data from a database with a variety of methods. You can execute single or multiple SQL `SELECT` queries, and stored procedures that return record sets. They also provide application developers with flexible table and column mappings between `DataSet`s and databases.

When used for updating databases with records in `DataSet`s, data adapters provide automatic `UpdateCommand` generation with the help of `CommandBuilder`s. Where the automatic command generation reaches its limit, you can define more advanced and application-specific commands and use them in data adapters to perform custom update operations. Of course, you always remember to close the connection as soon as you have done with it, don't you?

7

ADO.NET in the Enterprise

This book has so far been all about *how* and *why* to use ADO.NET. This chapter will try and help you decide *where* and *when* to use ADO.NET. Knowing how to create a "Hello World" application will only get you so far. Most programmers admit that just knowing the syntax of a language isn't enough to program: you need to know how to implement the algorithms and techniques to best accomplish your task. This chapter will endeavor to illustrate some best practices with regard to ADO.NET when it comes to creating robust, scalable, enterprise applications.

The same goes for ADO.NET. Just knowing how to populate the tables, columns, and rows in a `DataSet` isn't going to write your enterprise application for you. It will make some things easier, but that isn't the whole picture.

This chapter will take you through some discussion of where ADO.NET fits in the enterprise and in classic n-tier architectures. After that, we'll take a look at data binding in Windows and with ASP.NET, and we'll discuss some of the benefits and drawbacks of data binding. Finally, we'll round out this chapter with a discussion of how to create a COM+ component and how to create your own standardized data access layer.

Where Does ADO.NET Fit?

There are a lot of different things to consider when building an enterprise application. Most people familiar with building applications using **WinDNA (Windows Distributed interNet Application)** architecture are familiar with the concept of 3-tier and *n*-tier applications. If you are not, then please feel free to look at *Professional Windows DNA: Building Distributed Web Applications with VB, COM+, MSMQ, SOAP, and ASP* (ISBN: 1-86100-445-1) from Wrox Press.

The main concern most people have with building *n*-tier applications is the separation of data and business tiers, as well as the separation of the business tier from the presentation tier. For example, many designers feel that there should be a set of components that are essentially wrappers for stored procedures, as well as a set of components to encapsulate business logic components. Others believe that the business components should access the database directly.

No matter what you believe, the single fact remains: you need to figure out how you're going to get data in and out of your database, and you need to decide what aspects of ADO.NET you're going to use for that.

What we'll do is compare a few different approaches for where our data access technology (ADO.NET) stops and where the pure OOP (Object-Orientated Programming) design takes over. Each of these approaches has some benefits and some drawbacks. Hopefully, after we've presented this list, you'll have a good idea of where you'd like ADO.NET to fit in your next enterprise project.

"Nothin' but ADO.NET"

The "Nothin' but ADO.NET" approach is one that is typically favored by those that have the most experience with classic ADO. Generally programmers who are familiar with and prefer the J2EE approach frown upon this attitude. The reason for this is that in the J2EE (Java 2 Enterprise Edition) environment, the concept of "beans" and "entity beans" provides for a much more object-oriented approach toward data access whereas the `DataSet` and `DataTable` are much more traditional, functional treatments of data access.

In the "Nothin' but ADO.NET" approach, essentially the use of ADO.NET permeates all tiers of the application. The data layer, provided by the application, returns objects from the ADO.NET library, such as `DataSets` and `DataReaders`. The business tier performs all of its business logic and intermediary calculations on the ADO.NET objects, and the information returned to the presentation tier is also in the form of ADO.NET objects.

One technique often used in this method is strongly-typed `DataSets`, which are used to enforce a structure on a `DataSet`. Strongly-typed `DataSets` function almost as miniature business components, as they can enforce business, validation, and type rules on the data they contain.

The main advantage of this approach is that it allows for data to get from the database to the presentation tier in pretty short order. By short order, I mean that there isn't all that much processing going on to massage the data for use on the presentation tier. It is essentially retrieved from the database and passed up through the tiers directly to the end user or client. For systems that do a lot of pure retrieval, such as search engines or content delivery sites, this is often one of the fastest approaches allowing for fast data retrieval and large amounts of simultaneous users.

On the other hand, there are a few downsides to this approach (as there are to virtually any architecture). This approach may provide for a fast read-only application, but generally creates too much overhead for an update-heavy application such as a corporate intranet application. Approaches like this are often hard to maintain in the case where a new version of the application requires a change to the back-end data source.

To illustrate a sample flow of information (including information contained in ADO.NET objects), we'll take a look at a UML (Unified Modeling Language) sequence diagram. The diagram I've done might make some UML purists cringe (it has a lot of semantic errors), but it should get the point across. We have several object lifelines that we're depicting here:

❑ **Presentation (HTML)** – This essentially represents the final rendered HTML output and the pure HTML interaction with the server, such as raw form posting and HTTP GETs.

❑ **Presentation Objects** – These are essentially the code-behind classes. This represents the server-side functionality invoked in response to the pure HTML of the raw, rendered presentation tier.

❑ **Business components** – These are, obviously, the business components. This represents the classes that perform business logic, invoke business rules, perform data modification and manipulation according to those rules, and maintain state. This is where a lot of "beans" fall in the J2EE world.

❑ **Data Services** – This represents either a suite of classes designed to wrap individual stored procedures or components designed to further abstract and facilitate data access. There are usually two approaches to a data-services tier: create a class for each stored procedure, or create some classes that make creation and execution of stored procedures easy and standardized. Regardless of the approach used, all of these approaches belong to the data services section of our sequence diagram.

❑ **Database** – This represents the database itself, or rather, the execution of queries and stored procedures by the database.

Let's take a look at the sequence diagram below:

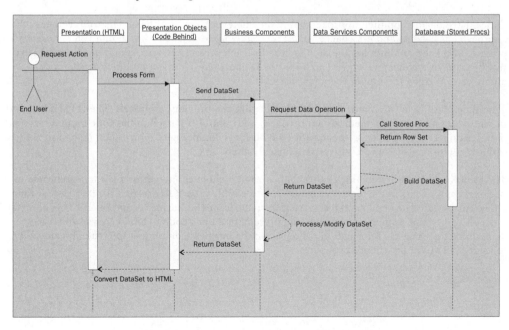

What we're looking at is the flow "down" of user input and the flow back "up" of response from the database. In the "Nothin' but ADO.NET" approach, the data services components return pure ADO.NET objects. Those objects are passed back up to the calling tier or layer, where they are analyzed and further manipulated in the business tier. The business tier then returns the validated and/or modified data up to the presentation tier code-behind classes. Those classes are then responsible for producing rendered HTML. Those of us with experience in ASP.NET know that this is accomplished by data binding (which we'll see later on in this chapter) or by manually creating HTML output and various other methods. This also includes converting the data into a form that can be exposed by a Web Service and "rendered" to the Web Service client.

As we mentioned, data binding is a fairly common practice using this approach. This is mostly because all of the bindable server-side ASP.NET controls make it extremely easy to bind to ADO.NET components. However, as we'll see later in this chapter, it is possible to bind to objects not native to ADO.NET with a little bit of effort on the programmer's part.

Most of you who are reading this book have probably had plenty of experience with this model. This model is the one that most people who have been programming classic ADO are familiar with. As we mentioned, many people familiar with that model find it very easy to migrate to .NET projects using this same model because of its familiarity.

"A Little Bit of Both"

This next approach that we're going to talk about is a nearly 50/50 blend of the two extreme approaches (all ADO.Net or as little ADO.NET as possible). When you talk to some people about where they draw the line between ADO.NET and the rest of their enterprise application, some programmers feel very strongly about it and consider it a personal philosophy.

Others have decided on their approach based on whatever works for them. The truth is that each approach has benefits and drawbacks, and it is entirely up to you as to which one you choose for your project. Also keep in mind that the architecture for each project can and should be designed separately. Just because an architecture worked well for one product doesn't mean that reusing the same architecture is going to help for the next project.

The "little bit of both" architecture starts off much like the previous approach. The HTML forms are processed (or Web Service methods are invoked) and control is passed to the code-behind classes. From there, parameters are passed to the appropriate business components, which then make use of the data services components to accomplish a particular database task.

The return value, if it is something other than a primitive like an integer or a string, is returned to the business components in the form of a `DataSet` (or possibly a `DataReader`). This `DataSet` is then analyzed, modified or manipulated and used to create a stateful business component. This new stateful business component is then passed up to the presentation tier's code-behind classes, which are responsible for using the information contained in the business component to create dynamically rendered HTML in the client's browser.

Let's take a look at a sequence diagram for this particular approach for laying out ADO.NET, business components, and stateful classes:

It looks fairly similar to the first approach. The main difference is that instead of passing the `DataSet` all the way up to the presentation tier, we create a new business component, which could be anything from a collection to a complex component that houses all kinds of detailed information and methods.

The first downside to this approach should be pretty obvious to anyone who has worked with enterprise applications before: statefulness. There is a big danger here of creating components that require their state to be maintained. If you'll take a close look at the diagram above, you'll see that only the actual stateful components are being used as return values. Because they're being used as return values, we can actually just consider these stateful object return values as highly complex return values that don't actually violate the stateless nature of our back-end. This allows us to keep our back-end in services like COM+ and still utilize architecture like this. Java programmers are also familiar with this approach and refer to these temporary business components used as return values as "entity beans".

Secondly, data binding in the presentation tier becomes more difficult with this approach. Without the use of a `DataSet` or a `DataReader`, the default ASP.NET server-side controls are slightly more difficult to automatically bind to. Often programmers resort to using "old fashioned" data binding by iterating through the data and populating the item collections of the "bound" controls. This is tedious and time consuming and error-prone. One solution to this that a lot of programmers prefer is to structure their business objects in such a way that they too can support automatic data binding.

So, the first downside that we mentioned is more like a caution. Any time you start passing around business components rather than primitive types, you need to make sure that you treat them properly and don't run into a trap of assuming states. The upside of this approach is that the information being handed to the presentation tier is entirely detached from ADO.NET. This allows the presentation tier to provide that data to Web Services clients just as easily as it can render it as HTML to a web client. We'll discuss more about the drawbacks of ADO.NET and Web Services later.

All in all, this approach is highly favored by people who have a strong ADO background and are also aware of some of the limitations of ADO.NET and Web Services. It provides good search and retrieval performance and also allows for more complex business processing by allowing programmers to encapsulate more complex and scalable business logic closer to the database without interfering with the presentation layer.

"No ADO.NET for Me, Thanks"

This architecture is one that truly makes the J2EE and Object-Oriented Design purists happy. The use of ADO.NET is limited only to its base functionality, in that it provides an interface to the stored procedures contained within the database. Beyond that, ADO.NET is barely used.

When the form processing begins and the code-behind objects are invoked, entity-type business components are created. These essentially are encapsulations of the form data posted as well as information pertaining to what type of action the user would like to perform, be it a search, a retrieval, an update, or a delete. Those objects are then passed through the business components to the data services components. The business components will massage, validate, or manipulate the data if needed before the database action takes place. Information from other third-party data sources such as Exchange, Commerce Server, or BizTalk Server, among others, might also be incorporated here. For example, the business components might add into the entity-type component information about the current user or the current user's profile such as their address or other billing information. Once the additional information and processing is done on the entity-type objects, those objects are passed in their entirety to the data services components. The data services components then typically know how to pull relevant information from the entity component and turn that into a database call.

One of my favorite implementations of this architecture involves a custom interface created for the entity components. Each entity component has a set of methods that allow the data services components to pull the appropriate information from their public properties to supply the database with enough information to update, delete, insert, or retrieve that entity.

This allows the creation an interface, say `IEntityObject`. A standardized data access layer can then be coded that can take any reference to any object that implements that interface and commit the changes in that object to the database. Presumably the set of methods and properties required by the `IEntityObject` would be sufficient to allow the database component to determine which type of database operation was being performed, and where to find the information required for that operation.

This approach has a huge upside in that it is an extremely elegant approach. It satisfies many staunch Object-Oriented Design purists and looks extremely familiar to those programmers who have been doing extensive programming with J2EE. This approach also lends itself extremely well to large development teams in that it provides a rigid, structured framework to which all programmers on the team must conform. Extensive use of `DataSets` allows individual programmers a lot of flexibility in choosing data structures and data access methods.

The downside to an approach like this is that it does create quite a bit of code. There are a lot of objects and a lot of code to keep track of. This approach is not one that lends itself well to being implemented by a team with poor organization skills.

Let's take a look at the sequence diagram for this type of approach:

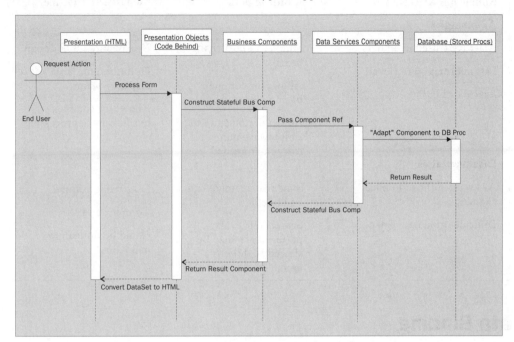

As you can see, as soon as the form has been processed and the code-behind objects have control, a stateful entity object is created and passed down to the business tier. The business tier then has full control over validation and manipulation of that object. At this point, context information is probably going to be added to the entity object, such as information on the user performing the request. This allows for tracing and logging information to automatically be stored etc. The updated entity object is then passed to the data services components. These components have been coded so that they know how to convert the entity instances into their appropriate database commands and they know how to obtain the necessary information to populate the parameters for the stored procedure calls. The results of the stored procedure call are then placed in an entity instance, which is then returned all the way up to the presentation tier. This way, if the entity instance was blank and was to be the target for a retrieve operation, it will have been populated and passed up to the presentation tier where it can be displayed appropriately.

Comparison

The following is a quick summary chart that includes a few of the positive and negative aspects of the various enterprise architectures we've discussed with regard to *where* to place ADO.NET. As we've said, this chapter is about helping you determine the best place and the best implementation of ADO.NET for your next enterprise project.

Nothin' but ADO.NET	A little of both	No ADO.NET for me
Advantages		
ADO.NET used in all tiers	Simpler to post changes to DB	Nearly pure OOP design
Fast information retrieval		Optimized for large and/or disparate teams
Easy data binding	Allows for complex business processing	Allows for complex business logic processing
	Allows architecture to shift toward either extreme if needed	
Disadvantages		
Awkward/difficult to make changes	State management can be difficult	Large code volume
		Complex code
Difficulty in maintenance	Search/retrieval performance may be slowed slightly by architecture overhead	Could be difficult to maintain

Data Binding

Data binding is a facility that allows visual controls, such as a `DataGrid`, a `ComboBox`, a `ListBox`, or a `TreeView`, to be automatically bound to a particular source of data. If you've ever done any Windows programming for VB, or even in MFC (Microsoft Foundation Class Library), and Visual C++ it's likely that you're familiar with the generic concept of data binding.

The .NET Framework has implemented data binding for both Windows *and* ASP.NET programming, an upgrade that has many "classic" ASP programmers drooling with delight. Data binding and various classes within ADO.NET have been designed to work seamlessly together. For example, you'll find that there really aren't many things easier to do than to bind a `DataGrid` to a `DataSet` and sit back and watch the GUI build itself. This brings up one of the points of my previous discussion: where does ADO.NET fit? If you've decided to place the ADO.NET functionality close to the database and use business objects and entity objects in your presentation tier, then you'll find that data binding is more difficult, but certainly not impossible. On the other hand, if you've decided to carry `DataSets` all the way back up from the database through each of your tiers, you'll find that data binding and GUI generation is truly a breeze.

In this section of the chapter we're going to show you just how easy it is to automatically bind data to controls (or controls to data, depending on how you look at it) with ADO.NET and Windows Forms and ASP.NET. One thing that we want to stress is that you can bind to *anything* so long as the source you're binding to conforms to certain rules. For example, most controls that are bindable only require that the object they are bound to implement the `IList` interface. Both `DataSets` and arrays automatically implement this interface, but there is nothing stopping you from creating your own class that implements this interface.

Windows Forms Data Binding

One of the biggest advantages of using Windows Forms is that you automatically gain the benefit of being able to produce a rich client interface. This includes code that instantly responds to clicks, drags, and other user actions without having to make a round-trip to the server.

One task commonly assigned to traditional Windows applications when it comes to dealing with data is browsing. There are just some limitations to examining data in an HTML format that are easily overcome with Windows programming. In our next example, we'll illustrate a little of that. We'll be cheating and taking the `books.xml` file that was borrowed from Microsoft's XML 4.0 SDK for Chapter 4 and reusing it here.

We'll essentially be creating a browser for that XML file. We'll create a listbox that contains a list of all of the books. The rest of the form will be dedicated to displaying the details of each individual book selected. Traditionally, we would have to trap the click event on the listbox, look up the details for that particular item, and then manually change them on the form. Through data binding, all of this is done for us automatically.

Here's a screenshot of the finished product:

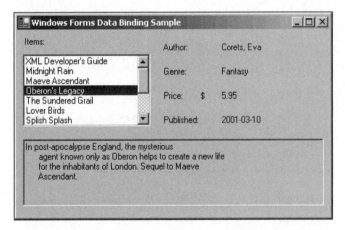

You can't see it from the screenshot, but a single click on any of the items in the listbox on the left will automatically update all of the detail labels and the description textbox. As we said, this is all done through data binding. The data binding in a Windows Forms application is live, unlike the static nature of the read-only binding in ASP.NET. By binding the labels on the right to the individual pieces of information contained in the table, the information displayed by the labels changes each time the binding cursor changes position.

Create a new C# Windows Application project and call it `WinBinding`. I've put all of the code for this chapter in a folder named `FTrackADONET/Chapter07/WinBinding`, underneath the main root directory for all of the code for this book. Set up the form to look like what you see in the screen above. Make sure that you have the following bindable controls on your form:

- ❑ `lbItems` – The main listbox. This will be bound to the table of books itself.

- ❑ `lblAuthor` – This is the label that will contain the author text.

❑ lblGenre – The label that will contain the genre text.

❑ lblPrice – The label that will contain the price text.

❑ lblPublished – The label that will contain the publish date.

❑ txtDescription – The textbox that will contain the description of the book.

Now that your form is set up in the designer we're ready to create some data-binding code. The following is the source code listing for the main form (we just left it Form1.cs):

```
using System;
using System.Drawing;
using System.Collections;
using System.ComponentModel;
using System.Windows.Forms;
using System.Data;

namespace WinBinding
{
  /// <summary>
  /// Summary description for Form1.
  /// </summary>
  public class Form1 : System.Windows.Forms.Form
  {
    private System.Windows.Forms.ListBox lbItems;
    private System.Windows.Forms.Label lblItems;
    /// <summary>
    /// Required designer variable.
    /// </summary>
    private System.ComponentModel.Container components = null;
    private System.Windows.Forms.Label label1;
    private System.Windows.Forms.Label lblAuthor;
    private System.Windows.Forms.Label label2;
    private System.Windows.Forms.Label lblGenre;
    private System.Windows.Forms.Label label3;
    private System.Windows.Forms.Label lblPrice;
    private System.Windows.Forms.Label label4;
    private System.Windows.Forms.Label lblPublished;
    private System.Windows.Forms.TextBox txtDescription;
    private DataSet dsBooks;

    public Form1()
    {
      //
      // Required for Windows Form Designer support
      //
      InitializeComponent();

      //
      // TODO: Add any constructor code after InitializeComponent call
      //
    }
```

```
/// <summary>
/// Clean up any resources being used.
/// </summary>
protected override void Dispose( bool disposing )
{
  if( disposing )
  {
    if (components != null)
    {
      components.Dispose();
    }
  }
  base.Dispose( disposing );
}

#region Windows Form Designer generated code
/// <summary>
/// Required method for Designer support - do not modify
/// the contents of this method with the code editor.
/// </summary>
private void InitializeComponent()
{
  this.lbItems = new System.Windows.Forms.ListBox();
  this.lblItems = new System.Windows.Forms.Label();
  this.label1 = new System.Windows.Forms.Label();
  this.lblAuthor = new System.Windows.Forms.Label();
  this.label2 = new System.Windows.Forms.Label();
  this.lblGenre = new System.Windows.Forms.Label();
  this.label3 = new System.Windows.Forms.Label();
  this.lblPrice = new System.Windows.Forms.Label();
  this.label4 = new System.Windows.Forms.Label();
  this.lblPublished = new System.Windows.Forms.Label();
  this.txtDescription = new System.Windows.Forms.TextBox();
  this.SuspendLayout();
  //
  // lbItems
  //
  this.lbItems.Location = new System.Drawing.Point(8, 32);
  this.lbItems.Name = "lbItems";
  this.lbItems.Size = new System.Drawing.Size(176, 95);
  this.lbItems.TabIndex = 0;
  //
  // lblItems
  //
  this.lblItems.AutoSize = true;
  this.lblItems.Location = new System.Drawing.Point(8, 8);
  this.lblItems.Name = "lblItems";
  this.lblItems.Size = new System.Drawing.Size(35, 13);
  this.lblItems.TabIndex = 1;
  this.lblItems.Text = "Items:";
  //
  // label1
  //
  this.label1.Location = new System.Drawing.Point(200, 16);
```

```
this.label1.Name = "label1";
this.label1.Size = new System.Drawing.Size(64, 23);
this.label1.TabIndex = 3;
this.label1.Text = "Author:";
//
// lblAuthor
//
this.lblAuthor.Location = new System.Drawing.Point(280, 16);
this.lblAuthor.Name = "lblAuthor";
this.lblAuthor.Size = new System.Drawing.Size(144, 23);
this.lblAuthor.TabIndex = 4;
this.lblAuthor.Text = "--";
//
// label2
//
this.label2.Location = new System.Drawing.Point(200, 48);
this.label2.Name = "label2";
this.label2.Size = new System.Drawing.Size(64, 23);
this.label2.TabIndex = 5;
this.label2.Text = "Genre:";
//
// lblGenre
//
this.lblGenre.AutoSize = true;
this.lblGenre.Location = new System.Drawing.Point(280, 48);
this.lblGenre.Name = "lblGenre";
this.lblGenre.Size = new System.Drawing.Size(12, 13);
this.lblGenre.TabIndex = 6;
this.lblGenre.Text = "--";
//
// label3
//
this.label3.Location = new System.Drawing.Point(200, 80);
this.label3.Name = "label3";
this.label3.Size = new System.Drawing.Size(64, 23);
this.label3.TabIndex = 7;
this.label3.Text = "Price:        $";
//
// lblPrice
//
this.lblPrice.AutoSize = true;
this.lblPrice.Location = new System.Drawing.Point(280, 80);
this.lblPrice.Name = "lblPrice";
this.lblPrice.Size = new System.Drawing.Size(12, 13);
this.lblPrice.TabIndex = 8;
this.lblPrice.Text = "--";
//
// label4
//
this.label4.Location = new System.Drawing.Point(200, 112);
this.label4.Name = "label4";
this.label4.Size = new System.Drawing.Size(64, 23);
this.label4.TabIndex = 9;
this.label4.Text = "Published:";
```

```
          //
          // lblPublished
          //
          this.lblPublished.AutoSize = true;
          this.lblPublished.Location = new System.Drawing.Point(280, 112);
          this.lblPublished.Name = "lblPublished";
          this.lblPublished.Size = new System.Drawing.Size(12, 13);
          this.lblPublished.TabIndex = 10;
          this.lblPublished.Text = "--";
          //
          // txtDescription
          //
          this.txtDescription.Location = new System.Drawing.Point(8, 144);
          this.txtDescription.Multiline = true;
          this.txtDescription.Name = "txtDescription";
          this.txtDescription.ReadOnly = true;
          this.txtDescription.Size = new System.Drawing.Size(416, 88);
          this.txtDescription.TabIndex = 11;
          this.txtDescription.Text = "";
          //
          // Form1
          //
          this.AutoScaleBaseSize = new System.Drawing.Size(5, 13);
          this.ClientSize = new System.Drawing.Size(432, 246);
          this.Controls.AddRange(new System.Windows.Forms.Control[] {
              this.txtDescription,
              this.lblPublished,
              this.label4,
              this.lblPrice,
              this.label3,
              this.lblGenre,
              this.label2,
              this.lblAuthor,
              this.label1,
              this.lblItems,
              this.lbItems});
          this.Name = "Form1";
          this.Text = "Windows Forms Data Binding Sample";
          this.Load += new System.EventHandler(this.Form1_Load);
          this.ResumeLayout(false);

      }
      #endregion

      /// <summary>
      /// The main entry point for the application.
      /// </summary>
      [STAThread]
      static void Main()
      {
        Application.Run(new Form1());
      }
```

This is where we're going to do our data binding. We set the `DataSource`, `DisplayMember`, and `ValueMember` of the listbox control, and it will then contain the list of books in the `DataSet`.

```
private void Form1_Load(object sender, System.EventArgs e)
{
  dsBooks = new DataSet();
  dsBooks.ReadXml(@"..\..\books.xml");
  lbItems.DataSource = dsBooks.Tables[0];
  lbItems.DisplayMember = "title";
  lbItems.ValueMember = "id";
  lbItems.Refresh();
```

Here we can create data bindings to virtually any property on any control. This allows us, for our example, to bind the `"text"` property of our label controls to various columns within our books table. This can be carried further and other properties such as size, and Boolean flags can also be bound to live, dynamic data.

```
  // we can bind virtually any property on any control, not just the
  // visible properties.
  lblAuthor.DataBindings.Add( "text", dsBooks.Tables[0], "author");
  lblGenre.DataBindings.Add( "text", dsBooks.Tables[0], "genre");
  lblPrice.DataBindings.Add( "text", dsBooks.Tables[0], "price");
  lblPublished.DataBindings.Add( "text", dsBooks.Tables[0],
      "publish_date");
  txtDescription.DataBindings.Add( "text", dsBooks.Tables[0],
      "description");

  }
  }
}
```

ASP.NET Data Binding

For our ASP.NET data binding example, we're going to illustrate binding to custom classes rather than binding directly to a `DataSet`. Again, keep in mind that all we have to do is bind to something that implements the `IList` interface to bind to something like the `ListBox` control. This example is going to do just that. We'll bind to a sample list of customers that are actually all instances of a `Customer` class that we're going to write. Just to keep things interesting, we'll create a button that, when clicked, displays the selected item's text and value. Here's an example of what our little web form data-binding example looks like in action:

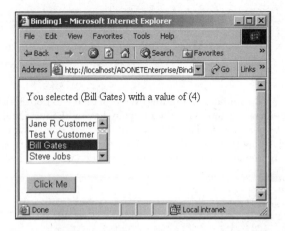

To get things started, we'll create a new C# Web Application called ADONETEnterprise. You can build this yourself, but the code for this example is available in the code download as FTrackADONET\Chapter07\ADONETEnterprise, and all you have to do to run it is to create a virtual directory leading to this path.

In building this code, we've added a new web form to that application called Binding1.aspx, which we will set as the start page. Drag a ListBox control onto the form and call it lbCustomers. Then drag a button onto the form and change the text to something other than Button1. We chose Click Me. Not only are we going to create an event handler for the click event and for the form's Load event, we're going to create a custom class.

Add the following bit of source code to the code-behind file for Binding1.aspx (Binding1.aspx.cs):

```
using System;
using System.Collections;
using System.ComponentModel;
using System.Data;
using System.Drawing;
using System.Web;
using System.Web.SessionState;
using System.Web.UI;
using System.Web.UI.WebControls;
using System.Web.UI.HtmlControls;

namespace chapter7
{
  /// <summary>
  /// Summary description for Binding1.
  /// </summary>
  public class Binding1 : System.Web.UI.Page
  {
    protected System.Web.UI.WebControls.Button Button1;
    protected System.Web.UI.WebControls.ListBox lbCustomers;
```

```
private void Page_Load(object sender, System.EventArgs e)
{
   // Put user code to initialize the page here
   if (!Page.IsPostBack)
   {
```

Here we're going to set up the initial data binding. We don't have to do it if the page has already posted to itself again (that's taken care of automatically for us by having the form maintain state). We create an `ArrayList` of our `Customer` objects. This `ArrayList` is what we're going to bind to. You can see that the `DataValueField` is going to map to the `CustId` property on the `Customer` instance, while the `DataTextField` is going to map to the `Name` property on the `Customer` instance.

```
      ArrayList custArray = new ArrayList();
      custArray.Add( new Customer(1, "John Q Customer") );
      custArray.Add( new Customer(2, "Jane R Customer") );
      custArray.Add( new Customer(3, "Test Y Customer") );
      custArray.Add( new Customer(4, "Bill Gates") );
      custArray.Add( new Customer(5, "Steve Jobs") );

      lbCustomers.DataSource = custArray;
      lbCustomers.DataValueField = "CustId";
      lbCustomers.DataTextField = "Name";
      lbCustomers.DataBind();
   }
}
#region Web Form Designer generated code
override protected void OnInit(EventArgs e)
{
  //
  // CODEGEN: This call is required by the ASP.NET Web Form Designer.
  //
  InitializeComponent();
  base.OnInit(e);
}


/// <summary>
/// Required method for Designer support - do not modify
/// the contents of this method with the code editor.
/// </summary>
private void InitializeComponent()
{
  this.Button1.Click += new System.EventHandler(this.Button1_Click);
  this.Load += new System.EventHandler(this.Page_Load);

}
#endregion

private void Button1_Click(object sender, System.EventArgs e)
{
  ListItem li = lbCustomers.SelectedItem;
  if (li != null)
  {
```

```
        Response.Write("You selected (" + li.Text + ") with a value of ("+
            li.Value + ")");
        }
    }
}

public class Customer
{
    private int custId;
    private string name;

    public Customer()
    {
        custId = -1;
        name = "(No Customer)";
    }

    public Customer(int _custId, string _name)
    {
        custId = _custId;
        name = _name;
    }

    public int CustId
    {
        get
        {
            return custId;
        }
        set
        {
            custId = value;
        }
    }

    public string Name
    {
        get
        {
            return name;
        }
        set
        {
            name = value;
        }
    }
}
}
```

Now we have the basic definition of the individual items that we want to show up in our listbox (Customers).

The ServicedComponent

It would be difficult to have a discussion about enterprise applications and services without actually talking about the `System.EnterpriseServices` namespace, which includes the class `ServicedComponent`. This is the class that all classes that are to be hosted within COM+ inherit from.

There are dozens of books available on COM+, and we don't have the space to go into an incredibly lengthy discussion about COM+. Essentially, COM+ is the successor of MTS (Microsoft Transaction Server). COM+ provides for transactional capabilities for components and component method calls, rather than the database transactions you may be familiar with (commit/rollback). This allows components to actually roll back method calls they may have made if an error were to occur.

In addition to providing the transactional functionality introduced with Microsoft Transaction Server, COM+ provides other enterprise features such as JIT (just-in-time) activation and object pooling. Just-in-time activation provides a scalable way to avoid consuming too many resources for a large application. It allows an object to be *mostly* disposed of in memory if it is not currently being used, even though there may be references to that object in open applications. Object pooling allows multiple instances of the same object to be created and stored in a pool. When a client requests an instance of the object, it is given a reference to an object from the pool. This cuts down on instantiation time and also provides for additional scalability for large-scale applications.

What we're going to show is an implementation of the `ServicedComponent` base class. It will be fairly simplistic. To truly harness the power of all of the features available in COM+, you should consult a book dedicated to that subject. One excellent resource that also contains examples in .NET is Juval Lowy and John Osborn's book *COM and .NET Component Services*. Another book that you might find useful is *C# COM+ Programming* by Derek Beyer.

Before we get started on programming our sample COM+ component, let's take a look at a quick reference on the `ServicedComponent` class.

Method	Description
Activate	This method is called by COM+ when the object is either created or allocated to a client from the object pool. This method can be overridden to add custom initialization code to the component.
CanBePooled	This method is invoked by COM+ to determine whether an object can be placed back in the object pool. If this method returns `false`, then the object will not be placed back in the pool.
Construct	This method is called by COM+ right after the component's constructor is called. It is called to make use of the "construction string", which is a property that can be set by the COM+ explorer. It allows for additional information to be passed to the component at instantiation time.
Deactivate	This method is called by COM+ when the object is about to be de-activated. This method should be overridden to provide custom finalization/destruction code when the component is being pooled or if JIT (Just-in-Time) activation is enabled.

One of the most important things to remember about COM+ component programming is that you can't think about instantiation and finalization in the same way as you think about them for traditional components. Depending on how the component and COM+ is configured, your object could be instantiated long before the `Activate` method is ever called.

To set up our example of COM+ in action we're going to create a new project called `ComPlusTest`. This project is a C# class library.

This code is available in the folder `FTrackADONET\Chapter07\ComPlusTest`, or you could build it yourself by following the instructions below.

The first thing we need to do when we're building a COM+ component is to add a reference to the `System.EnterpriseServices` assembly. We'll change the definition of the default class that Visual Studio .NET gave us to create a COM+ component that will retrieve some book information:

```
using System;
using System.Data;
```

In order to be able to reference the `ServicedComponent` class and many of the attributes in the `System.EnterpriseServices` namespace we should include a `using` clause at the top, which we should add to the project as a reference by right-clicking on the project name and selecting **Add Reference,** and then following the instructions:

```
using System.EnterpriseServices;

namespace ComPlusTest
{
    /// <summary>
    /// Summary description for Class1.
    /// </summary>
```

The following two attributes indicate that this component will use just-in-time activation and that it will participate on object pooling. These attributes are used to configure the COM+ component properties when this component is automatically registered with the COM+ system.

```
[JustInTimeActivation(true)]
[ObjectPooling(true, 1, 10)]
public class TestComponent: ServicedComponent
{
    private DataSet booksData;
```

Remembering from our quick reference, the `Activate` method is called whenever the object is instantiated or when it is taken out of the pool for a client. We'll use this to load our internal `DataSet` with information. Normally, for a data component that loads data from a database (where the connection resource is expensive to maintain), you would not want to do this; you would place the call to open and close the connection in the method that retrieves the data.

Here the path from the code download (copied into `C:`) is the path used to locate `books.xml`; be sure to alter this depending on your own location for this file.

```
protected override void Activate()
{
  // insert code here to  perform any special
  // initialization needed when the object is activated.
  booksData = new DataSet();
  booksData.ReadXml(@"C:\FTrackADONET\Chapter07\ComPlusTest\books.xml");
  booksData.Tables[0].PrimaryKey = new DataColumn[] {
      booksData.Tables[0].Columns["id"] };
}
```

The `Deactivate` method is to be used as a last-minute cleanup routine to release resources just before the object is actually deactivated.

```
protected override void Deactivate()
{
  // insert any clean-up code here to release any held
  // resources.
  booksData.Dispose();
}

protected override bool CanBePooled()
{
  // return true or false here to allow object back into pool
  return true;
}

protected override void Construct(string constructionString)
{
  // insert code here to perform custom activity based on information
  // contained in construction string.
}
```

Here's our simple example of a data access method that retrieves information from a data store and returns it to the calling client:

```
  // now add the actual data access methods
  public string GetBookTitle(string bookId)
  {
    DataRow found = booksData.Tables[0].Rows.Find(bookId);
    return found["title"].ToString();
  }
 }
}
```

This is a good start, but we're not quite done yet. First of all, how are we going to get this component into COM+? If we try to create a new package and add the component from within the COM+ explorer it will fail. The reason for this is that the COM+ explorer only knows how to deal with type libraries and doesn't have the faintest idea how to deal with .NET assemblies and assembly manifests.

Thankfully there are two things we can do to get the component into COM+. The first is to use the REGSVCS.EXE utility that is supplied with the .NET Framework that manages registering .NET assemblies in the COM+ registry. The other alternative (which our code sample utilizes) is to supply some code attributes for the assembly and the class in question. When a .NET client invokes a class that has the appropriate COM+ attributes, a package and component in COM+ will automatically be created. If you try this demo out you'll notice that the first time you run it there will be a long delay before the client completes its call into the COM+ component.

We've already seen a couple of the attributes for COM+ above: the ones that turned on just-in-time activation and object pooling. There are also a couple of attributes that we have to add to the assembly in order to facilitate automatic COM+ configuration.

We've added the following couple of lines to the AssemblyInfo.cs. We make sure that System.EnterpriseServices is referenced with a using statement, and we also insert the following lines of code:

```
[assembly: ApplicationName("COMPlus Test")]
[assembly: Description("This is a COMPlus Example")]
```

We also have to set a public-private key pair in order to complete the strong name for the assembly. You can't register a component in COM+ without a strong name. We do that using the AssemblyKeyFile attribute:

```
[assembly:
AssemblyKeyFile(@"C:\FTrackADONET\Chapter07\ComPlusTest\complustest.snk")]
```

The complustest.snk file that we are pointing to in this attribute we created by issuing the following command line from a Visual Studio .NET command prompt (a command prompt with the .NET Framework binaries in the path):

```
C:\FTrackADONET\Chapter07\ComPlusTest>sn -k complustest.snk
```

Compile and build that project. Now we'll work on the test client. Again, you may build this yourself, following the instructions below, or alternatively, you may download this code from www.wrox.com. To build it, add a new C# Console Application to the project called ComPlusClient. The first thing you have to do is add a reference to the System.EnterpriseServices assembly. We have to add a reference to this assembly because the component we're referencing *also* has a reference to that. Then we add a reference to the *project* that we built for the COM+ component (ComPlusTest).

Here's the code listing for our console application. It looks fairly simple, but there's a lot going on "under the covers" that both .NET and COM+ are taking care of for us:

```
using System;

namespace ComPlusClient
{
    /// <summary>
    /// Summary description for Class1.
    /// </summary>
    class Class1
```

229

```
  {
    /// <summary>
    /// The main entry point for the application.
    /// </summary>
    [STAThread]
    static void Main(string[] args)
    {
      ComPlusTest.TestComponent tc = new ComPlusTest.TestComponent();
      string bookTitle = tc.GetBookTitle("bk108");
      Console.WriteLine("The book title is {0}", bookTitle);
    }
  }
}
```

When we build this client and run it, it will probably sit and munch on our hard drives for about 30 seconds before it finally comes back with some output. The reason for this is that behind the scenes the COM+ component is being registered with COM+ and a new COM+ application is being created. Once the new application is created and the component is registered within that application, then the method call is actually allowed to go through, and we get some output that looks like this:

Creating a Standardized Data Access Layer

For most enterprise applications, data access is one of the tasks that is most able to be generalized. For example, in most enterprise applications, when data access is boiled down to the lowest level, it is all about executing stored procedures and retrieving data. Especially for large teams, generalizing or standardizing the way in which a particular application accesses data can be extremely useful. Not only can it decrease overall development time, but having a single point of entry for all data access means that once that point of entry has been tested and debugged, tracking down data access failures should be significantly easier than if all the programmers on the team were using their own method to access data.

The other side of the story is that if you generalize too much, you lose the advantages that you gain from knowing exactly how your data is going to be treated. One approach that I've found works quite well is to have a couple of tools that automate the mundane tasks of building connections and commands, since those two seem to be the most often used object types within ADO.NET.

Before we get into the code listing for our sample standardized data access layer, I'll go through the standard disclaimer. This code is by no means fit for commercial use. It is a simple demonstration to show you a starting point. There are places in this code where you can add your own command-caching techniques and add in your own error handlers and tracing routines, and expand it to cover more situations.

The Factory Model

A common programming model or design pattern is that of the "Factory". A factory is essentially a class whose sole responsibility is the creation of initialized instances of other classes in a clearly defined, controlled fashion. In our case, we're going to create a factory class for database connections and for commands. The commands that our factory will produce will only be partially fit for use; the code calling the factory will have to finish the initialization.

The purpose for the factory is to ensure that all of our helper tools will function properly whether we're using Oracle, OLE DB, ODBC, or SQL Server. At the time of the writing of this book, the Oracle managed provider from Microsoft is still under beta, so we have commented out the code related to Oracle, even though it works in the current beta. What we essentially do is pass an enumeration for the type of client we want to use, and the factory then creates an instance specific to that type of RDBMS. So, for a SQL Server connection, the connection factory will create an instance of the `SqlConnection` class and for an OLE DB connection, the connection factory will create an instance of the `OleDbConnection` class.

The user of the tools (us) can choose either to use other tools that will in turn make use of the factories, or to use the factories directly themselves. We'll see in our sample that we can use the tools to create a `DataReader` for whatever client type we're using, or we can use the `CommandFactory` class, so we can use that command to build a `DataAdapter` and populate a `DataSet` for binding to a `DataGrid`.

Our generalized data access layer that we're developing will not be utilizing COM+. This is just for clarity, and you should easily be able to adapt it to COM+ with the information you've seen in this chapter on COM+ components. The following is a list of the classes and enumerations that we're going to build:

- ❑ `ConnectionFactory` – A class that abstracts the instantiation of connection objects. This allows us to generalize it and have the same method calls regardless of what connection type (Oracle, OLE DB, SQL) we plan on using.

- ❑ `CommandFactory` – The command factory will make use of the connection factory to create a new connection. That new connection is then used with the `CreateCommand` method to instantiate and return a new command to the caller.

- ❑ `CommandTool` – A "helper" class that automates many common tasks, such as executing stored procedures for scalar and `DataReader` values.

This code is available in the folder `FTrackADONET\Chapter07\DataLayer`, downloadable from the Wrox site.

ConnectionFactory

Let's take a look at the code listing for the `ConnectionFactory` class (`ConnectionFactory.cs` in the C# Class Library project called `DataLayer`):

```
using System;
using System.Data;
using System.Data.SqlClient;
using System.Data.OleDb;
// using System.Data.OracleClient;
```

```
namespace DataLayer
{
  /// <summary>
  /// Summary description for ConnectionFactory.
  /// </summary>
  public class ConnectionFactory
  {
    public static IDbConnection CreateConnection(string dsn)
    {
      return InitializeNewConnection( dsn, ConnectionType.Sql );
    }

    public static IDbConnection CreateConnection(string dsn, ConnectionType
        cType)
    {
      return InitializeNewConnection( dsn, cType );
    }

    private static IDbConnection InitializeNewConnection(string dsn,
        ConnectionType cType)
    {
      IDbConnection conn;

      if (cType == ConnectionType.Sql)
        conn = new SqlConnection();
      // else if (cType == ConnectionType.Oracle)
      //    conn = new OracleConnection();
      else
        conn = new OleDbConnection();

      conn.ConnectionString = dsn;
      return conn;
    }
  }

  public enum ConnectionType
  {
    Sql = 1,
    Oracle = 2,
    OleDb = 3
  }
}
```

Obviously there is some room for improvement here. You can add tracing information and statistics logs so that you can keep track of how many connections you're creating, how long its taking to instantiate them and so on. You could also log how many of each type of connection you're creating.

CommandFactory

Now that we've got a utility class for generically creating connections for us, we need to create one that will generically create commands for us. For our purposes, this class will only create commands that deal with stored procedures, but you can easily upgrade it to deal with more varying types of database commands. Here's the code listing for the CommandFactory:

```
using System;
using System.Data;
using System.Data.SqlClient;

namespace DataLayer
{
  public sealed class CommandFactory
  {
    public static IDbCommand CreateCommand(string spName, string dsn,
        ConnectionType cType)
    {
      IDbConnection newConnection = ConnectionFactory.CreateConnection( dsn,
          cType );
      return CreateNewCommand(spName, newConnection );
    }

    public static IDbCommand CreateCommand(string spName, IDbConnection
        curConnection)
    {
      return CreateNewCommand(spName, curConnection);
    }

    private static IDbCommand CreateNewCommand(string spName, IDbConnection
        curConnection)
    {
      IDbCommand newCommand = curConnection.CreateCommand();
      newCommand.CommandText = spName;
      newCommand.CommandType = CommandType.StoredProcedure;

      return newCommand;
    }
  }
}
```

As you can see, in the first overload of the CreateCommand method, the connection factory is used to create a new connection before the command is created. The other public overload of CreateCommand assumes that a connection has already been created. All of this is available to provide the programmer direct and easy access to command instantiation, as well as to provide the command-building tool with easy access to command instantiation.

Another benefit of creating a factory through which all commands are created is that you have a single point of entry to any and all instances of commands. This allows you to log information about those commands, and detailed statistics can be accumulated. Also, if you're feeling ambitious, you can always code your own stored procedure caching mechanism so that you maintain a singleton instance of a given stored procedure for each named stored procedure invoked. The first invocation could create a new instance, while all others could simply go through the previously instantiated procedure instance. As we said, the code we have provided should be considered a starting point and a learning tool. We fully expect you to find many, many ways to improve the code we've listed here.

CommandTool

Now that we've got factories that we have created, which automate the task of dispensing connections and commands, configured the way we want them to be configured, we can go about the business of providing a class that can automate and ease of the mundane, repetitive tasks involved in calling stored procedures in databases. The following is the code listing for the `CommandTool` class:

```
using System;
using System.Data;

namespace DataLayer
{
    /// <summary>
    /// Summary description for CommandTool.
    /// </summary>
    public sealed class CommandTool
    {
```

This first utility function will execute a stored procedure and return the value. It uses the "RETURN_VALUE" parameter name to indicate the return value. Obviously, this only works if the return value of the stored procedure is actually returned in a parameter named that.

```
public Object ExecuteNonQuery( IDbCommand cmd )
{
    try
    {
        cmd.Connection.Open();
        cmd.ExecuteNonQuery();
    }
    catch (Exception e)
    {
        throw e;
    }
    finally
    {
        cmd.Connection.Close();
    }

    if (cmd.Parameters.Contains("RETURN_VALUE"))
        return cmd.Parameters["RETURN_VALUE"];
    else
        return null;
}
```

This next one will execute a stored procedure returning an instantiated `DataReader` object as a result. It does this by using the command's `ExecuteReader` method.

```
public IDataReader ExecuteReader( IDbCommand cmd )
{
    IDataReader dr;
    try
    {
```

```
      cmd.Connection.Open();
      dr = cmd.ExecuteReader();
   }
   catch (Exception e)
   {
      throw e;
   }
   return dr;
}
```

Here we have the first of the methods that don't assume a previously instantiated command. This method will take the name of the stored procedure, a string indicating the connection string for the connection instance, the type of the connection, and an array of IDataParameter instances to populate the Parameters collection of the stored procedure. It will use the CommandFactory class to create a new command (which in turn uses the connection factory to create a connection).

```
public Object ExecuteNonQuery( string spName, string dsn, ConnectionType
   cType, IDataParameter[] procParams )
{
   IDbCommand newCmd = CommandFactory.CreateCommand( spName, dsn,
      cType );
   foreach (IDataParameter procParam in procParams)
   {
      newCmd.Parameters.Add( procParam );
   }
   try
   {
      newCmd.Connection.Open();
      newCmd.ExecuteNonQuery();
   }
   catch (Exception e)
   {
      throw e;
   }
   finally
   {
      newCmd.Connection.Close();
   }

   if (newCmd.Parameters.Contains("RETURN_VALUE"))
      return newCmd.Parameters["RETURN_VALUE"];
   else
      return null;
}
```

This method is similar to the previous ExecuteReader method. The difference is that this method does not take a command as an argument, but rather all of the evidence required to use the command factory to build a command, then populate the parameters collection and call ExecuteReader on the command instance.

```
    public IDataReader ExecuteReader( string spName, string dsn,
        ConnectionType cType, IDataParameter[] procParams )
{
  IDbCommand newCmd = CommandFactory.CreateCommand( spName, dsn,
      cType );
  IDataReader dr;
  foreach (IDataParameter procParam in procParams)
  {
    newCmd.Parameters.Add( procParam );
  }
  try
  {
    newCmd.Connection.Open();
    dr = newCmd.ExecuteReader();
  }
  catch (Exception e)
  {
    throw e;
  }

  return dr;
}
  }
}
```

Obviously this command tool is incomplete. There are quite a few more situations that the tool has not taken into consideration, and there are quite a few optimizations that could be made to it. However, we think that the process of modifying code like this and enhancing it on your own is as good a learning process as reading this book itself.

After we compile and build this project (results in the DataLayer assembly), we can then work on a client to test out the functionality that we've built into this. Our test client is going to be a simple Windows Forms application.

To create the test client application we'll create a new C# Windows Forms application called DataLayerClient. Alternatively, you can download the code for this application – it is in the folder FTrackADONET\Chapter07\DataLayerClient. Add a reference to the DataLayer project. To get started, drag a ComboBox onto the form and call it cbOrderIds. Then, drag a button onto the form near the ComboBox. Finally, add a DataGrid to the form underneath those two controls and call it dgOrderItems.

Here's the code listing for the main form:

```
using System;
using System.Drawing;
using System.Collections;
using System.ComponentModel;
using System.Windows.Forms;
using System.Data;
using System.Data.SqlClient;
```

```
namespace DataLayerClient
{
  /// <summary>
  /// Summary description for Form1.
  /// </summary>
  public class Form1 : System.Windows.Forms.Form
  {
    private System.Windows.Forms.ComboBox cbOrderIds;
    private System.Windows.Forms.Button button1;
    private System.Windows.Forms.DataGrid dgOrderItems;
    /// <summary>
    /// Required designer variable.
    /// </summary>
    private System.ComponentModel.Container components = null;

    public Form1()
    {
      //
      // Required for Windows Form Designer support
      //
      InitializeComponent();

      //
      // TODO: Add any constructor code after InitializeComponent call
      //
    }

    /// <summary>
    /// Clean up any resources being used.
    /// </summary>
    protected override void Dispose( bool disposing )
    {
      if( disposing )
      {
        if (components != null)
        {
          components.Dispose();
        }
      }
      base.Dispose( disposing );
    }

    #region Windows Form Designer generated code
    /// <summary>
    /// Required method for Designer support - do not modify
    /// the contents of this method with the code editor.
    /// </summary>
    private void InitializeComponent()
    {
      this.cbOrderIds = new System.Windows.Forms.ComboBox();
      this.button1 = new System.Windows.Forms.Button();
      this.dgOrderItems = new System.Windows.Forms.DataGrid();
      ((System.ComponentModel.ISupportInitialize)(this.dgOrderItems))
          .BeginInit();
      this.SuspendLayout();
```

```
        //
        // cbOrderIds
        //
        this.cbOrderIds.DropDownStyle =
            System.Windows.Forms.ComboBoxStyle.DropDownList;
      this.cbOrderIds.Location = new System.Drawing.Point(16, 32);
      this.cbOrderIds.Name = "cbOrderIds";
      this.cbOrderIds.Size = new System.Drawing.Size(121, 21);
      this.cbOrderIds.TabIndex = 0;
        //
        // button1
        //
      this.button1.Location = new System.Drawing.Point(160, 32);
      this.button1.Name = "button1";
      this.button1.Size = new System.Drawing.Size(96, 23);
      this.button1.TabIndex = 1;
      this.button1.Text = "Order Details";
      this.button1.Click += new System.EventHandler(this.button1_Click);
        //
        // dgOrderItems
        //
      this.dgOrderItems.DataMember = "";
      this.dgOrderItems.HeaderForeColor =
            System.Drawing.SystemColors.ControlText;
      this.dgOrderItems.Location = new System.Drawing.Point(16, 64);
      this.dgOrderItems.Name = "dgOrderItems";
      this.dgOrderItems.Size = new System.Drawing.Size(648, 368);
      this.dgOrderItems.TabIndex = 2;
        //
        // Form1
        //
      this.AutoScaleBaseSize = new System.Drawing.Size(5, 13);
      this.ClientSize = new System.Drawing.Size(672, 446);
      this.Controls.AddRange(new System.Windows.Forms.Control[] {
            this.dgOrderItems,
            this.button1,
            this.cbOrderIds});
      this.Name = "Form1";
      this.Text = "Form1";
      this.Load += new System.EventHandler(this.Form1_Load);
      ((System.ComponentModel.ISupportInitialize)(this.dgOrderItems))
            .EndInit();
      this.ResumeLayout(false);

    }
    #endregion

    /// <summary>
    /// The main entry point for the application.
    /// </summary>
    [STAThread]
    static void Main()
    {
      Application.Run(new Form1());
    }
```

When the form first loads, we're going to use our data layer utilities to obtain a new `SqlDataReader` based on the parameters we supply, and then iterate through that data reader. We'll do this to populate the drop-down listbox that contains the order IDs for the first customer in the Northwind database that ships with SQL Server 2000 and MSDE:

```
private void Form1_Load(object sender, System.EventArgs e)
{
  DataSet custOrders = new DataSet();
  DataLayer.CommandTool ct = new DataLayer.CommandTool();
  string sqlConnString = "Initial Catalog=Northwind; User Id=sa;
      Password=; Server=localhost;";

  SqlParameter[] procParams =
  {
    new SqlParameter("@CustomerId", SqlDbType.VarChar, 5)
  };
  procParams[0].Value = "ALFKI";
  SqlDataReader dr = (SqlDataReader)ct.ExecuteReader(
      "CustOrdersOrders", sqlConnString, DataLayer.ConnectionType.Sql,
      procParams );
  while (dr.Read())
  {
    cbOrderIds.Items.Add( System.Convert.ToString(dr.GetInt32(0)) );
  }
}

private void dgCustOrders_Navigate(object sender,
    System.Windows.Forms.NavigateEventArgs ne)
{

}
```

When we click the button after selecting an order ID from the drop-down listbox, we will then use our data layer utilities to get a result set containing all of the particular items that belonged to that particular order ID. We'll do this by using our tools to create a new command instance for the `"CustOrdersDetail"` stored procedure. We'll then create a new data adapter, and use that to fill a `DataSet` that we'll bind to the `DataGrid` on our form.

```
private void button1_Click(object sender, System.EventArgs e)
{
  string sqlConnString = "Initial Catalog=Northwind; User Id=sa;
      Password=; Server=localhost;";
  SqlCommand newCmd = (SqlCommand)
      DataLayer.CommandFactory.CreateCommand( "CustOrdersDetail",
      sqlConnString, DataLayer.ConnectionType.Sql );
  newCmd.Parameters.Add( new SqlParameter("@OrderId", SqlDbType.Int,
      4) );
  newCmd.Parameters[0].Value = System.Convert.ToInt32(
      cbOrderIds.SelectedItem );
  SqlDataAdapter da = new SqlDataAdapter( newCmd );
  DataSet orderItems = new DataSet();
  da.Fill(orderItems, "OrderItems");
```

```
        dgOrderItems.DataSource = orderItems.Tables["OrderItems"];
        dgOrderItems.Refresh();
    }
  }
}
```

Finally, after we've built and executed this test client, we'll get an interface that looks something like this:

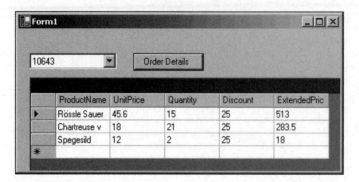

This section of the chapter illustrated how we can utilize some of the ADO.NET skills that we've learned throughout this book to create a set of tools that we can use to make our lives as ADO.NET programmers a bit easier, and allow us to add some very robust code to our data access methods.

Summary

Throughout this book we've discussed the various different ways that you can use ADO.NET and its components. We've covered the syntax and the *how* and even the *why*, but this chapter provided us with a good explanation of *where* to use ADO.NET. We discussed some of the more common strategies for deploying ADO.NET technologies in the enterprise. We rounded out this chapter with discussions on using COM+ and creating a useful set of standardized tools for automating some of the most common and most repetitive ADO.NET programming tasks. After having read this chapter and the book up to this point, you should have a very good idea of not only how ADO.NET works, but also where and when it can and should be used.

FAST TRACK

ADO.NET

8

Web Services and ADO.NET

Given the amount of publicity and hype that has surrounded **Web Services** in the past year, it's probably safe to assume that this is not the first time you have heard about them. In fact, Web Services have, quite possibly, been the single most advertised feature of the .NET platform. In this chapter we'll explore the basics of .NET Web Services and pay particular attention to data-centric Web Services.

We will start by examining the underlying protocols of Web Services, along with some other rudimentary information about them. We will then focus on the transfer of data to and from Web Services, and wrap up the chapter with a discussion of other important issues pertaining to Web Services and in particular, data-centric Web Services.

Introduction to Web Services

From a conceptual standpoint, Web Services are nothing new. They are a natural evolution from the search for interoperability between various platforms, which has been a hot topic for a very long time. The proliferation of the Internet and the rise of distributed/decentralized computing have made it even more important for different types of systems to communicate effectively with each other. Component-based object models such as Remote Method Invocation (RMI), Common Object Request Broker Architecture (CORBA), and Distributed Component Object Model (DCOM) were all designed to address some of the problems with distributed object models, but, in one way or another, they all fell short, mostly due to the lack of standards and vendor-neutral industry support. Furthermore, the proprietary nature of most of these standards along with existing security infrastructure made them impractical for mass use over the Internet.

The acceptance of XML as a platform-neutral data representation and exchange language was unprecedented and has allowed a large number of industry heavyweights such as IBM, Microsoft, and HP to agree on a set of standards for Web Services. This alone has been a great step to ensure the success of Web Services in the enterprise. Web Services are a new model for component-based services that are self-describing, self-contained and can be published, located, and consumed entirely over the Internet using standard protocols such as HTTP and the XML-based SOAP protocol. We will briefly examine these standards in the next few sections. The following figure is a graphical representation of the Web Services architecture over the Internet:

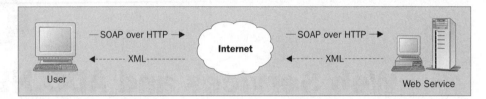

Just a note: you might want to consider .NET Remoting over Web Services when you are going from Windows to Windows applications. Web Services are great for Windows to non-Windows for interoperability. When it comes to Windows to Windows communication, .NET Remoting is faster than Web Services and can go through the firewall through HTTP just like Web Services. From an architectural point of view, Web Services are for broad availability. DCOM needed extra ports in order to be used via the Internet. We won't be covering Remoting in this book, but more information can be found in the *Visual Basic .NET Remoting Handbook* (ISBN: 1-86100-740-X) from Wrox Press. For a comparison of Web Services and Remoting, and when you should use each, see *Professional Visual Basic .NET Transactions* (ISBN: 1-86100-595-4) also from Wrox Press.

Web Service Standards and Protocols

Visual Studio .NET and the .NET Framework have done a great job of abstracting away much of the infrastructure and technical intricacies of Web Services. This allows users to leverage the power of Web Services with much the same amount of effort required to create and/or consume regular Windows components. Nevertheless, it is still important to understand the protocols and standards on which Web Services are built and operate. Such an understanding is absolutely crucial to the ability to create advanced functionality with Web Services – especially when it comes to planning for interoperability with non-.NET platforms.

Since covering the details of any of those protocols would go well beyond the scope of this chapter (and book), we are going to have to limit our discussion to only the basic concepts. There are countless books and other publications that focus exclusively on Web Services and provide a much more in-depth coverage of Web Services protocols, including *Beginning .NET Web Services with C#* from Wrox Press (ISBN: 1-86100-757-4). With that said, let's dive into the world of Web Services by examining one of the key standards – SOAP.

SOAP

SOAP (Simple Object Access Protocol) is an XML-based messaging protocol designed to enable software components and services-based applications to communicate using the standard Internet protocol, HTTP.

SOAP provides specifications for invoking and consuming methods on servers, services, components, and objects. It also codifies the existing practice of using XML and HTTP as a method invocation mechanism. SOAP was created to address and alleviate many problems that arose with the use of various RPC mechanisms over the Internet.

The SOAP protocol runs on top of HTTP, which is a ubiquitous internet protocol. This means that many of the technical issues – such as security – associated with the use of RPC are no longer a problem. SOAP relies on HTTP 1.0 or greater and can take advantage of the HTTP extension framework with relative ease. However SOAP is not completely dependent on HTTP over TCP/IP, as it is transport-protocol independent. As of mid-2002, the World Wide Web Consortium (W3C) has accepted the SOAP 1.1 specification, and a working draft of SOAP 1.2 specification is awaiting formal acceptance. For the most part, the differences between versions 1.1 and 1.2 are not significant and almost anything that has been written to work on the SOAP 1.1 standard is guaranteed to work on SOAP 1.2.

Armed with this background information on SOAP, we'll go ahead and take a closer look at SOAP from a technical angle.

A SOAP message is an XML document and usually consists of four main parts:

- ❑ **SOAP Envelope** – The Envelope is the top element of a SOAP message and is the basic wrapper for the content of the message. This element must be present in order to send a SOAP message. It uses the namespace identifier http://schemas.xmlsoap.org/soap/envelope.

- ❑ **SOAP Header** – The Header is a generic mechanism for adding features to a SOAP message in a decentralized manner without prior agreement between the communicating parties. SOAP defines a few attributes that can be used to indicate who should deal with a feature and whether it is optional or mandatory.

- ❑ **SOAP Body** – The Body element contains the actual message that you want to send. It is a mandatory element.

- ❑ **SOAP Fault** – SOAP Faults are really a subset of the Body element. They indicate an error message and can be thought of as SOAP exceptions. Usually, the Fault element appears in a SOAP response message to indicate that there was something wrong with the SOAP request.

To better understand the anatomy of a SOAP message, let's take a look at a short example. The following code is an actual SOAP request for a Web Service that returns a stock quote:

```
<?xml version="1.0" encoding="utf-8"?>
<soap:Envelope xmlns:soap="http://schemas.xmlsoap.org/soap/envelope/">
  <soap:Header>
  </soap:Header>
  <soap:Body>
    <GetStockQuote xmlns="http://tempuri.org/">
      <stockSymbol>IBM</stockSymbol>
    </GetStockQuote>
  </soap:Body>
</soap:Envelope>
```

As you can see a SOAP message is itself an XML document. The entire message is within the `soap:Envelope` element. A request is being made to a service named `GetStockQuote`, which returns the appropriate quote information for `IBM`. The `Header` element is empty, as it is an optional element. The `Header` element provides a mechanism to extend the functionality of a SOAP message. For instance, one of the more common uses of the `Header` element entails authentication. In such a case, there will be an authentication framework, which will use SOAP as a lower-level transport and will place digest or other key-based information within a `Header` element.

We have seen a simple SOAP request, so it makes sense to look at the SOAP response that the request could generate:

```xml
<?xml version="1.0" encoding="utf-8"?>
<soap:Envelope xmlns:soap="http://schemas.xmlsoap.org/soap/envelope/">
  <soap:Header>
  </soap:Header>
  <soap:Body>
    <StockQuote>
      <stockSymbol>IBM</stockSymbol>
      <stockPrice>105.23</stockPrice>
      <stockPriceChange>2.4</stockPriceChange>
      <stockVolume>15234572</stockVolume>
    </StockQuote>
  </soap:Body>
</soap:Envelope>
```

As you can see, the SOAP response message is fairly similar to the request message, except that it now has a few new fields to describe the quote information. If there was something wrong with the request such as an invalid field name, a SOAP `Fault` element would be added within the `Body` element to signify the error that had occurred.

That's SOAP in a nutshell. I exaggerate, of course. In fact, we have barely scratched the surface of SOAP and there are many other important topics to discuss. The .NET Framework contains functionality that can be used to extend SOAP, all of which allows a greater degree of customization. For instance, you can use SOAP extensions to extend the base handling of SOAP messages, such as making modifications to the content of a SOAP message – say for encryption purposes.

We don't have the time to cover them in this chapter, as we have much to discuss about the use of data-driven Web Services.

WSDL

The **Web Services Definition Language (WSDL)** provides a standard format for representing Web Services. WSDL is an XML-based contract language jointly developed by Microsoft and IBM that extends earlier contract languages from Microsoft and IBM Service Description Language (SDL), SOAP Contract Language (SCL), and Network Accessible Services Specification Language (NASSL).

A WSDL document contains information about exactly what it is that the Web Service does, as well as a service contract, which describes the type of message that will be accepted by the Web Service and the type of response that will be generated. In many ways WSDL is analogous to IDL files used to describe the COM interfaces, but, unlike IDL files, WSDL files are much less cryptic since they're basically XML Schema documents.

Every WSDL document contains a root `definitions` element, within which there are five types of child elements:

❏ **Types** – Contains the schema definitions of the messages using XML Schema

❏ **Message** – Contains information about the operations the Web Service provides

❏ **PortType** – Defines a set of interfaces that the Web Service can expose. An interface is associated with one or more `messages`.

❏ **Binding** – Associates the `portType` definition with a protocol.

❏ **Service** – Contains one or more `port` elements, each associated with a `binding`. Each `binding` references a `portType`, thereby describing where the Web Service is located.

If you're using Visual Studio .NET to create a Web Service, a WSDL document is generated automatically. For the most part it will be sufficient. However, if you are designing your Web Services to be used along with other services that run on non-.NET platforms, then you may have to dive into the WSDL document and make a few changes and additions.

The types in the `System.Web.Services.Description` namespace in the .NET Framework Class Library provide a great deal of control over a WSDL document by allowing object-based access to virtually all the elements of a WSDL Document.

UDDI

IBM, Microsoft, and Ariba originally developed the **Universal Discovery Description and Integration (UDDI)** specification to manage distributed Web-based information registries of Web Services. An industry-wide consortium (uddi.org) now manages the specification.

UDDI provides a publicly accessible set of implementations of the specification that allows businesses to register information about the Web Services they offer so that other businesses can find them – UDDI in essence, is the yellow pages of Web Services. UDDI's massive industry support is yet another reason why Web Services are well poised for wide acceptance and adoption in the IT community. Based exclusively on XML, SOAP, and HTTP, UDDI facilitates the creation, description, discovery, and integration of Web Services by defining standards for Business-to-Business (B2B) and Business-to-Consumer (B2C) interoperability.

A common UDDI registration includes:

❏ **White Pages** – As the name implies, this section contains business name, text description, and contact information

❏ **Yellow Pages** – Basic description of product services, industry codes (if any), and location

❏ **Green Pages** – Description of services offered as well as instructions for connecting to and using these services

DISCO

DISCO (short for Discovery) is the last of the Web Services standards that we'll cover that is proprietary to Microsoft. DISCO is the mechanism used to locate and use a Web Service. An XML file with `.disco` extension is created when publishing the Web Service within Visual Studio .NET.

You might be thinking: didn't I just say that it's the job of UDDI to act as a yellow pages repository for information about a Web Service? Well, UDDI is a central repository and relies on organization-specific information to locate a Web Service, but the browse and find approach of DISCO makes it easier for developers to locate a Web Service on a particular machine. This feature also makes DISCO ideal for development environments in which there is a need to quickly expose and consume Web Services for testing purposes among other things.

DISCO files have `.vsdisco` extension within Visual Studio .NET. The .NET Framework SDK also includes a command-line utility (`disco.exe`) that generates DISCO documents for existing XML Web Services.

Creating and Using a Web Service

Now that we've had a brief introduction to the inner-workings of Web Services and have a basic understanding of the standards and protocols involved in creating a Web Service, let's go ahead and create a simple Web Service in Visual Studio .NET. Since nothing says simple and introductory more than the classic "Hello World" example, we will create a Web Service that just returns the string "Hello World" upon invocation. To do so, start by opening Visual Studio .NET and creating a new ASP.NET Web Service project under Visual C# Projects:

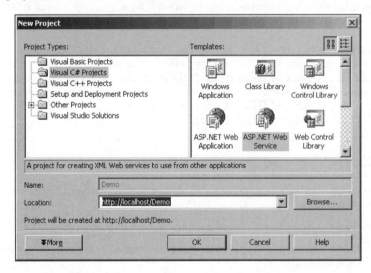

Name the project anything you want, I've called it Demo. The Web service is going to be hosted on IIS, so you'll need to have IIS installed and running on your machine.

Visual Studio .NET creates a default Web Service called `Service1`. Switch to the code view by pressing *F7*. Handily, there is already a commented code segment in the generated code that just returns the "Hello World" string. Visual Studio .NET includes that when you select a new **ASP.NET Web Service** project as a placeholder where you can start writing your own functions. Uncomment that code. In addition, all the necessary namespaces have already been imported:

```
using System;
using System.Collections;
using System.ComponentModel;
using System.Data;
using System.Diagnostics;
using System.Web;
using System.Web.Services;

namespace Demo
{
  /// <summary>
  /// Summary description for Service1.
  /// </summary>
  public class Service1 : System.Web.Services.WebService
```

The `WebService` class defines the optional base class for XML Web Services. It provides direct access to common ASP.NET objects, such as application and session state.

```
  {
    public Service1()
    {
      //CODEGEN: This call is required by the ASP.NET Web Services Designer
      InitializeComponent();
    }

    #region Component Designer generated code
      ...
    #endregion

    // WEB SERVICE EXAMPLE
    // The HelloWorld() example service returns the string Hello World
    // To build, uncomment the following lines then save and build the
    // project
    // To test this Web service, press F5

    [WebMethod]
    public string HelloWorld()
    {
      return "Hello World";
    }
  }
}
```

Press *F5* to run this Web Service. A web page is automatically created (with the name of the Web Service as its title) along with some preliminary documentation about the Web Service. There is also a link to the Service Description of the Web Service. This service contract is basically the WSDL contract for the Web Service. Feel free to click on that if you want to have a better understanding of how WSDL works. Then, click on the HelloWorld link to invoke our actual Web service, which we can see in the screenshot below:

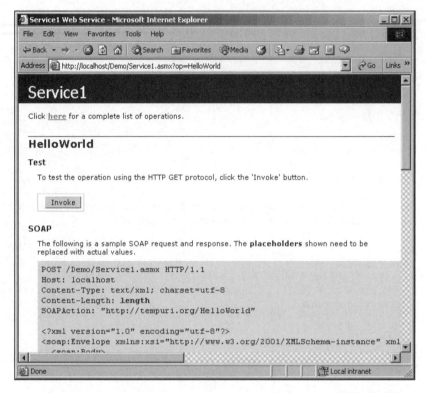

The underlying SOAP code is displayed as well as the HTTP binding code that is used in the Web Service. Keep in mind that you didn't actually have to worry about any of this plumbing, as it was all done automatically by VS.NET.

Click the Invoke button to invoke the Web Service:

```
<?xml version="1.0" encoding="utf-8" ?>
<string xmlns="http://tempuri.org/">Hello World</string>
```

A simple XML document is returned with the result of our Web Service. tempuri.org is just the default namespace generated by Visual Studio .NET since we didn't specify any namespaces for our Web Service.

The WebMethod Attribute

A Web Service class can contain one or more functions. Some of these functions could be public and others could be private functions. WebMethod is a custom attribute that we can apply to public functions to allow access to the function from remote web clients. Private functions are not callable from remote Web clients. Public functions within the Web Service that are not marked with the WebMethod attribute cannot be called from remote web clients. You can also have more than one Web Method in the Web Service class.

A list of all the Web Methods is made available when you access the .asmx file. The WebMethod attribute contains a number of properties that can be used for more customization and control. The following table lists the main properties of the WebMethod attribute:

Property	Description
BufferResponse	Determines whether the response is buffered in memory before sending it to the client. Setting this property to true will buffer the response. Setting this property to false will send the response back to the client as the response is generated.
CacheDuration	Sets the duration in seconds for which the response should be stored in the cache. By default the value is 0 and so the response is not cached. If the value is set greater than 0, the response will be stored in cache for the duration specified. A subsequent request within the cache duration will get the response from the cache.
Description	Provides a descriptive statement about the WebMethod for the consumers of the service. The statement will be displayed next to the WebMethod in the service description or in the service help page.
EnableSession	Determines whether Session state is enabled for the Web Service. Setting the value to true enables the Session state and setting the value to false disables the Session state. By default the Session state is disabled.
MessageName	The name used for the Web Service method in the data passed to and returned from a Web Service method. This is useful when there are two or more Web Methods with the same name.
TransactionOptions	Indicates the transaction support of the Web Method. It can be one of five modes: Disabled, NotSupported, Supported, Required, and RequiresNew.

Using a Web Service

We've seen that creating a Web Service with VS.NET is extremely easy. In fact just about the only thing that differentiates a regular method from a Web Service method is the [WebMethod] attribute before the method declaration that we just talked about. Let's now talk about how we can create a client application to consume a Web Service.

So far we have accessed the Web service using the browser by calling the .asmx file. However, in reality we would like the Web Service to be accessible from a Web Form, a Windows client application, or another Web Service.

To access the Web Service from a client such as Windows application or a Web Form, we need to create a proxy class for the Web Service. The proxy class is going to act as an intermediary agent that will take care of a few technical administrative tasks that need to be done when interacting with a Web Service. For instance, the proxy object will take care of all the XML serialization that needs to take place in order for data to be encoded in SOAP messages.

> *You might be wondering: "how come you don't need a proxy when you call it directly from the browser, but you need it for applications? What is the fundamental difference? Is the browser (IE) another form of application?"*

> *This is because when it is accessed through the browser, there's no need for specified marshaling. The data is just spat out as raw XML, whereas when we invoke a Web Service from a rich client, we often need the data back from the Web Service in an RPC fashion. The proxy class takes care of all that plumbing for us.*

The following figure demonstrates the logical position of the proxy object in a typical Web Service application architecture:

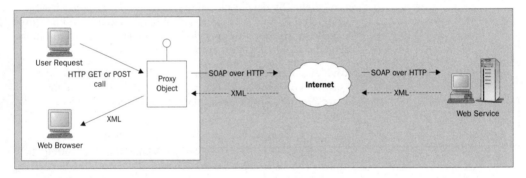

If you're using Visual Studio .NET, a proxy client is generated when a web reference is added to the Web Service. In the address bar you can just type in the path of the Web Service, which for our example is http://localhost/Demo/Service1.asmx:

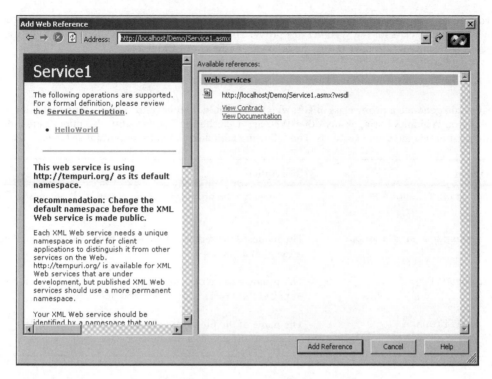

The right-hand pane has links to the WSDL (the contract) and the documentation page. By clicking the **Add Reference** button a proxy object is created with the appropriate SOAP contract in it. You can then reference the Web Service just as you would any other class within your application.

Let's do just that. Open FTrackADONET\Chapter08\DemoService\Form1.cs, which is shown below. This is, quite simply a regular C# Windows Form project and is an example of just how easily a Web Service can be invoked once a web reference has been added to the project.

This is the piece of the code that we are interested in:

```
private void button1_Click(object sender, System.EventArgs e)
{
    localhost.Service1 ws = new localhost.Service1();
    MessageBox.Show(ws.HelloWorld());
}
```

When the button is clicked, a message box with the string **Hello World** appears:

If you are not using Visual Studio .NET, there is a command line utility `wsdl.exe` that you can use to generate a proxy class for the Web Service proxy. To create a proxy class for the Web Service we created earlier, we would have to run the following at the command line:

```
wsdl /language:cs http://localhost/Demo/Service1.asmx?wsdl
```

That would generate a proxy class in C#, which you would then have to compile into a DLL for use in a Web Form, Windows Form, or any other Web Service. The `wsdl.exe` utility also offers a great deal of customization via the use of switches. The following table lists the more important switches:

Option	Description
`/language:language`	The language the proxy class is generated in. It defaults to C#.
`/namespace:anyNamespace`	The namespace used to generate the proxy class. The default is the global namespace.
`/protocol:protocol`	The protocol to invoke the Web Service method. It can be `HttpGet`, `HttpPost`, or `SOAP`. The default is `SOAP`.
`/out:filename`	The name of the file to contain the generated proxy. It defaults to the name of the Web Service itself.

DataSets and Web Services

In most cases we would want to return some data from a Web Service that would be more useful than the "Hello World" string. So for the rest of the chapter we'll focus on Web Services that connect to a database and retrieve data.

For the most part, returning data from a Web Service is just as easy as doing so from a Web Form or a Windows Forms page. ADO.NET `DataSets` are ideal transport packages for Web Services, as they are one of the few objects that implement the `IXmlSerializable` interface. Implementing this interface makes them excellent candidates for transport over the wire via SOAP, as there's little work that we must do on them in order to encode them properly within a SOAP envelope. In fact, other than raw string or XML data, there's no better way to send data via Web Services in .NET.

In our next example, we'll take a look at a Web Service that returns `DataSets` to its client.

Stock Screener Web Service and Application

To help us better understand database use within Web Services, we'll build a Web Service along with a client application that consumes it. We are going to build a simple stock screener application that allows the user to filter stocks based on preset criteria. The application is going to use a Web Service that will service all its data needs.

Creating the Stock Screener Web Service

We'll start by creating the Web Service that is going to provide the client application with all the data. However, before doing so, we need to discuss the database requirements from which the data is going to be retrieved.

Preparing the Data

We are going to need to create two tables: one for the stock exchange (`tbl_stockExchange`) and another table to simply retain the data for the individual stocks (`tbl_stocks`). The tables are stored in a SQL Server database named **StockDB**. So, first of all, create a new database in SQL Server Enterprise Manager and call it **StockDB**.

If you are running this in MSDE, merely open Visual Studio's Server Explorer, select a table, double-click on it and the tab for the **SQL Pane** should appear, as shown in the screenshot below. Click on it and enter the following text:

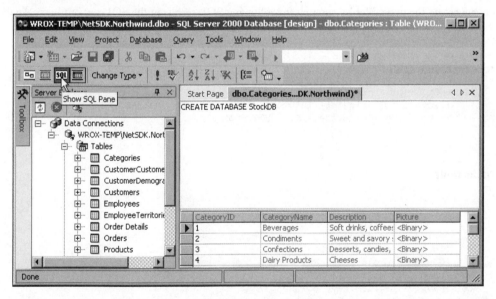

You can use the included SQL script to create the tables and constraints by entering the text into this pane, or you could use Enterprise Manager as we have below, depending on your installation.

tbl_stocks table

Field	Description
Symbol	The actual stock symbol
Price	Last price of the stock
Volume	Total traded volume of the stock in a trading session
Change	The price change of the stock

Table continued on following page

Field	Description
DayHi	The intraday high of the stock price
DayLow	The intraday low of the stock price
ExchangeID	The ID number of the stock exchange in which the stock trades

tbl_stockExchange table

Field	Description
ExchangeID	The actual stock symbol
ExchangeName	Last price of the stock

You can create the two tables by running the following SQL scripts in the SQL server Query Analyzer. A SQL file containing all of these scripts is available in the code download for this book, in FTrackADONET\Chapter08\StockScreener\stockscreener.sql.

tbl_stockExchange table

```
CREATE TABLE [dbo].[tbl_stockExchange] (
    [ExchangeID] [tinyint] IDENTITY (1, 1) NOT NULL PRIMARY KEY,
    [ExchangeName] [varchar] (10) NOT NULL
)
GO
```

tbl_stocks table

```
CREATE TABLE [dbo].[tbl_stocks] (
    [Symbol] [varchar] (4)  NOT NULL  PRIMARY KEY,
    [Price] [smallmoney] NOT NULL ,
    [Volume] [int] NOT NULL ,
    [Change] [smallmoney] NOT NULL ,
    [DayHi] [smallmoney] NOT NULL ,
    [DayLow] [smallmoney] NOT NULL ,
    [ExchangeID] [tinyint] NOT NULL
      FOREIGN KEY REFERENCES tbl_stockExchange(ExchangeID)
)
GO
```

The ExchangeID field in the tbl_stockExchange and the tbl_stocks tables have a Foreign Key-Primary Key relationship as shown in the following relationship diagram, which we have programmatically set above:

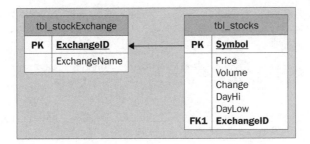

Now that we have created the tables, we are going to need to populate them with some data. For the tbl_stockExchange table, let's just input the two largest stock exchanges in the U.S., **NYSE** and **NASDAQ**. This population will have been performed by the SQL script, servicescreener.sql, (available with the code download), which we ran to create the tables. Because we have set the primary key, ExchangeID, as IDENTITY, it will be created automatically; we merely have to assign values to the ExchangeName column:

```
INSERT INTO tbl_stockExchange (ExchangeName)
VALUES ('NYSE')
GO

INSERT INTO tbl_stockExchange (ExchangeName)
VALUES ('NASDAQ')
GO
```

And here is the data for populating tbl_stocks:

```
INSERT INTO tbl_stocks (Symbol, Price, Volume, Change, DayHi, DayLow, ExchangeID)
VALUES ('AOL', 25.62, 18453453, 0.28, 26.12, 25.33, 1)
GO

INSERT INTO tbl_stocks (Symbol, Price, Volume, Change, DayHi, DayLow, ExchangeID)
VALUES ('CSCO', 18.74, 31234285, 0.07, 19.5, 18.66, 2)
GO

INSERT INTO tbl_stocks (Symbol, Price, Volume, Change, DayHi, DayLow, ExchangeID)
VALUES ('DELL', 24.27, 28347626, -0.44, 24.35, 23.98, 2)
GO

INSERT INTO tbl_stocks (Symbol, Price, Volume, Change, DayHi, DayLow, ExchangeID)
VALUES ('INTC', 32.65, 26532238, 0.51, 34.07, 32.29, 2)
GO

INSERT INTO tbl_stocks (Symbol, Price, Volume, Change, DayHi, DayLow, ExchangeID)
VALUES ('MSFT', 58.82, 15422872, -0.22, 59, 57.92, 2)
GO

INSERT INTO tbl_stocks (Symbol, Price, Volume, Change, DayHi, DayLow, ExchangeID)
VALUES ('ORCL', 16.34, 24887234, 0.16, 16.73, 16.22, 2)
GO
```

```
INSERT INTO tbl_stocks (Symbol, Price, Volume, Change, DayHi, DayLow, ExchangeID)
VALUES ('VRSN', 28.53, 13005832, 0.73, 30.12, 28.4, 2)
GO

INSERT INTO tbl_stocks (Symbol, Price, Volume, Change, DayHi, DayLow, ExchangeID)
VALUES ('PFE', 34.5, 8237492, 0.31, 34.8, 34.13, 1)
GO

INSERT INTO tbl_stocks (Symbol, Price, Volume, Change, DayHi, DayLow, ExchangeID)
VALUES ('IBM', 105.23, 10543389, 0.66, 106.27, 104.55, 1)
GO

INSERT INTO tbl_stocks (Symbol, Price, Volume, Change, DayHi, DayLow, ExchangeID)
VALUES ('C', 45.34, 6321239, -0.15, 45.9, 44.95, 1)
GO

INSERT INTO tbl_stocks (Symbol, Price, Volume, Change, DayHi, DayLow, ExchangeID)
VALUES ('NOK', 18.83, 29987234, 0.26, 19.22, 18.6, 1)
GO

INSERT INTO tbl_stocks (Symbol, Price, Volume, Change, DayHi, DayLow, ExchangeID)
VALUES ('T', 15.25, 127123432, -0.2, 15.5, 14.75, 1)
GO
```

To make sure that all is up and running, go into SQL Server Enterprise Manager and check that both tables are populated correctly:

Great! We now have the necessary database tables along with some useable data. Now we have to create five stored procedures on the database to accommodate the data needs of our Web Service:

Stored Procedure Name	Parameter	Description
sp_getMostActive	ExchangeID	Returns the top five most active stocks
sp_getPriceDiff	ExchangeID	Returns the top five stocks with the largest intraday price differential

258

Stored Procedure Name	Parameter	Description
sp_getlargestGain	ExchangeID	Returns the top five stocks with largest % price gains
sp_getlargestLoss	ExchangeID	Returns the top five stocks with largest % price losses
sp_getExchange		Returns the list of all the available stock exchanges

The implementation for these stored procedures is relatively straightforward. You can create the stored procedures in the SQL Server Query Analyzer or within Visual Studio .NET, though in our case we have created them programmatically with our SQL script. If you chose to do it through VS.NET you would have to open the Server Explorer pane and browse to the appropriate database within SQL Server where the stock tables are. You would then have to right-click the Stored Procedure item in the tree list and choose New Stored Procedure. In any case, all of the required stored procedures consist of very short queries.

sp_getMostActive

```
CREATE PROCEDURE dbo.sp_getMostActive
  (@exchangeID tinyint )
AS
  SELECT  TOP 5 Symbol, Price, Volume, Change, DayHi, DayLow FROM tbl_stocks
WHERE
  @exchangeID = ExchangeID ORDER BY Volume DESC
RETURN
```

sp_getPriceDiff

```
CREATE PROCEDURE dbo.sp_getPriceDiff
  (@exchangeID tinyint )
AS
  SELECT  TOP 5 Symbol, Price, Volume, Change, DayHi, DayLow FROM tbl_stocks
WHERE
  @exchangeID = ExchangeID ORDER BY (DayHi-DayLow) DESC
RETURN
```

sp_largestGain

```
CREATE PROCEDURE dbo.sp_getLargestGain
  (@exchangeID tinyint )
AS
  SELECT  TOP 5 Symbol, Price, Volume, Change, DayHi, DayLow FROM tbl_stocks WHERE
  @exchangeID = ExchangeID ORDER BY (Change/(price-Change)) DESC
RETURN
```

sp_getLargestLoss

```
CREATE PROCEDURE dbo.sp_getLargestLoss
  (@exchangeID tinyint )
```

```
AS
   SELECT  TOP 5 Symbol, Price, Volume, Change, DayHi, DayLow FROM tbl_stocks WHERE
   @exchangeID = ExchangeID ORDER BY (Change/(price-Change)) ASC
RETURN
```

sp_getExchange

```
CREATE PROCEDURE dbo.sp_getExchange
AS
   SELECT  ExchangeID, ExchangeName FROM tbl_stockExchange
RETURN
```

Building the Web Service

Now that we have all the stored procedures in place, we can start building the Web Service that will serve the client and return the requested data.

We are going to create a new **C# ASP.NET Web Service** project in Visual Studio .NET called **StockService**. The code for this project is available in the code download, in the folder `FTrackADONET\Chapter08\StockService`.

> *You can build this project yourself through the directions below, or run the code included. Remember that if you do the latter, you will have to create a virtual directory to it in IIS before it will open.*

This will assign the default location for the Web Service to http://localhost/StockService. Visual Studio .NET will create a default `.asmx` page called `Service1`, which we will rename to `StockService.asmx`.

```csharp
using System;
using System.Collections;
using System.ComponentModel;
using System.Data;
using System.Data.SqlClient;
using System.Diagnostics;
using System.Web;
using System.Web.Services;

namespace StockService
{
    /// <summary>
    /// Summary description for Service1.
    /// </summary>
    public class StockService : System.Web.Services.WebService
    {
        public StockService()
        {
            //CODEGEN: This call is required by the ASP.NET Web Services
            //Designer
            InitializeComponent();
        }

        private System.Data.SqlClient.SqlConnection sqlConnection1;
```

```
#region Component Designer generated code

//Required by the Web Services Designer
private IContainer components = null;

/// <summary>
/// Required method for Designer support - do not modify
/// the contents of this method with the code editor.
/// </summary>
private void InitializeComponent()
{
        this.sqlConnection1 = new System.Data.SqlClient.SqlConnection();
        //
        // sqlConnection1
        //
        this.sqlConnection1.ConnectionString =
            "initial catalog=StockDB;user ID=sa;pwd=;" + "workstation
            id=PARS;packet size=4096";


}

/// <summary>
/// Clean up any resources being used.
/// </summary>
protected override void Dispose( bool disposing )
{
        if(disposing && components != null)
        {
                components.Dispose();
        }
        base.Dispose(disposing);
}

#endregion
```

We are going to need four methods in this Web Service. Visual Studio .NET does not automatically rename the class and the public constructor, despite you renaming the corresponding file name, we will go ahead and change the name of the Web Service class from Service1 to StockService. We are going to need four public methods marked with the [WebMethod] attribute. However, we need only concern ourselves with two of those methods for now – the others we will be using later in a different project:

❑ GetExchangeInfo – This method will simply return all the stock exchanges that are available in the database. It returns a DataSet with two fields, the ExchangeID and the ExchangeName. This method does not have any parameters

❑ GetScreenerInfo – This method is going to return a DataSet filled with stocks that match the criteria of the screener. It has two parameters, one for the selected stock exchange and another for the selected criteria.

Let's start with getExchangeInfo. We define a regular function with the WebMethod attribute. We are also going to use the Description property of the WebMethod attribute to better document the functionality of our method:

```
[WebMethod (Description="Returns all the available stock exchanges.")]
public DataSet getExchangeInfo()
{
```

This method is relatively small as it simply calls the stored procedure we created earlier, sp_getExchange, and populates a blank DataSet with the resulting data. The only thing to keep in mind is that a Web Service runs on the Web Server much like an ASP.NET page, and so, by default, the security context falls within the ASP.NET worker process (also known as the ASP.NET account). You can create a custom SQL login account and give it appropriate permissions to access the required stored procedures or give execute permissions to the ASP.NET account on the stored procedures.

For this example, a VS.NET SqlConnection control was used at design time to establish a connection with the database:

```
SqlCommand sqlCmd  = new SqlCommand();
DataSet ds = new DataSet();
try
{
  sqlCmd.CommandType = CommandType.StoredProcedure ;
  sqlCmd.CommandText = "sp_getExchange";
  sqlCmd.Connection = sqlConnection1;
  SqlDataAdapter myAdapter = new SqlDataAdapter(sqlCmd);
  myAdapter.Fill(ds, "StockExchange");

}

catch( Exception ex)
{
  Debug.WriteLine(ex.ToString());
}
return ds;
}
```

Now we're ready to move on to our second and more important method, getScreenerInfo. We're going to need two parameters here: screenerIndex and exchangeIndex, both of which are of type int. Since the purpose of this method is to return the stocks that match a certain set of predetermined criteria, we need to know which stock exchange and what criteria the user has selected from the client application. We will take a closer look at this later when we build the client, but for now we have to match the integer value from the parameter, screenerIndex to a stored procedure that we created earlier (the stored procedure contains the necessary logic to fetch the data). We can easily accomplish this by using a switch statement:

```
[WebMethod (Description=
  "Returns the stocks that match the screener criteria")]
public DataSet getScreenerInfo(int screenerIndex, int exchangeIndex)
{
  SqlCommand sqlCmd  = new SqlCommand();
  DataSet ds = new DataSet();
  sqlCmd.CommandType = CommandType.StoredProcedure ;
  switch(screenerIndex)
  {
```

```
        case 0:
          sqlCmd.CommandText = "sp_getMostActive";
          break;
        case 1:
          sqlCmd.CommandText = "sp_getLargestGain";
          break;
        case 2:
          sqlCmd.CommandText = "sp_getLargestLoss";
          break;
        case 3:
          sqlCmd.CommandText = "sp_getPriceDiff";
          break;
      }

      try
      {
        SqlParameter myParam = new SqlParameter("@exchangeID",
            SqlDbType.TinyInt,1);
        myParam.Value= exchangeIndex;
        sqlCmd.Parameters.Add(myParam);
        sqlCmd.Connection = sqlConnection1;
        SqlDataAdapter myAdapter = new SqlDataAdapter(sqlCmd);

        myAdapter.Fill(ds, "ScreenerInfo");
      }
      catch
      {
      }
      return ds;
    }
    // Two other Web Methods here, which we will discuss later
    ...
  }
}
```

Since our stored procedures require a parameter, @exchangeID, we create a new Parameter object and pass it into our SqlCommand object. Upon executing the stored procedure using the DataAdapter, we populate a table called ScreenerInfo within the DataSet.

That's it for the Web Service! We can quickly test our Web Service by simply executing it in VS.NET (pressing *F5* to start).

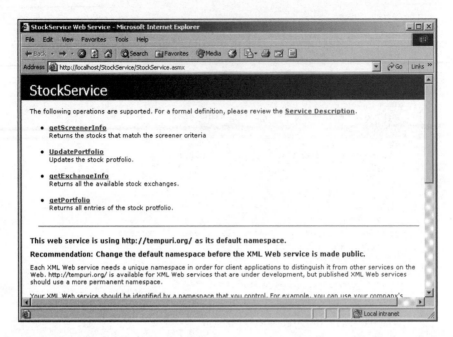

As you can see, the four public methods of our service are present along with the description that we entered using the Description property of the WebMethod attribute. As always you can view the WSDL contract of the Web Service by clicking on the **Service Description** link that appears on the top right corner of the page. Click the **getExchangeInfo** link to test the getExchangeInfo method of our Web Service and then click the **Invoke** button:

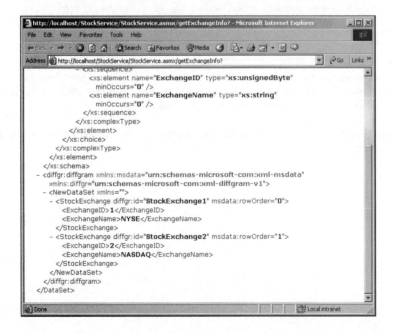

What you see here is essentially the `DataSet` that was returned from the `StockService` Web Service. Two entries for stock exchanges were returned, **NYSE** and **NASDAQ**. The top portion of the XML document is just schema and serialization info. As you know, `DataSets` are represented in XML format.

Now let's try to do the same with the other method of our Web Service, which requires parameters to be passed into it. Go back to the main page of **StockService** Web Service and this time click on the getScreenerInfo link:

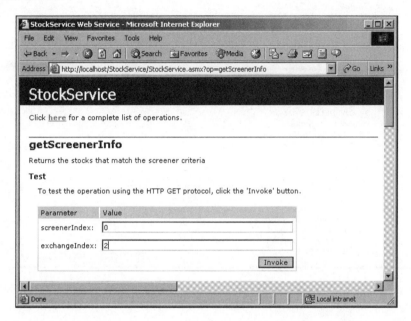

Two textboxes have been generated by the ASP.NET runtime in order to allow us to enter the required parameters and test our Web Service. Let's try the value 0 for the **screenerIndex** parameter that represents the "top five most active stocks" and 2 for the **exchangeIndex** that represents the NASDAQ stock exchange:

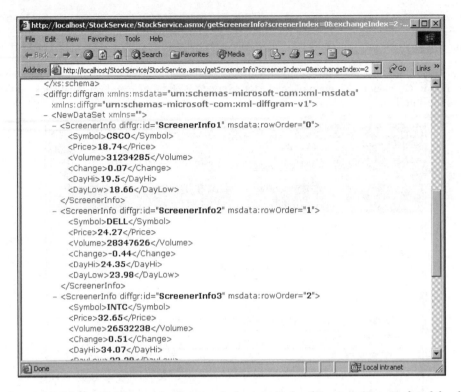

This shows the data for the five stocks that match the criteria for the most active stocks of the day. You should also notice the URL of the results page contains the parameters as value pair query strings:

http://localhost/StockService/StockService.asmx/getScreenerInfo?screenerIndex=
0&exchangeIndex=2

In case you are wondering, yes, you can access the result of that method directly by entering the parameters and their values in the URL following the path of the Web Service.

We're all done with our StockService Web Service; let's go on to develop the client application.

Building the Web Service Client

Creating the Web Service was a breeze and our client application is going to be just as easy to build. This code is already available in the folder FTrackADONET\Chapter08\StockScreener.

We just need a couple of combo boxes for the user to select the screening information, and a button to invoke the Web Service along with a DataGrid control to display the results:

❑ Open a new Visual C# Windows Application Project, and label the project file and corresponding form file (Form1.cs) as StockScreener.

❑ Place two ComboBox controls on the form. Label the first one cboStockExchange, and the second one cboScreener.

❑ Place the `ComboBox` controls next to each other, with the second one longer than the first one.

❑ To indicate what each of those combo boxes is for, create two label controls and place them above each combo box with appropriate labels, such as: **Stock Exchange** and **Stock Screener Type**.

Next we need a button and a `DataGrid` control:

❑ Place a button below the two combo boxes and name it `btnGetStocks`.

❑ Change the button's `Text` property to **Get Stocks**.

❑ Place a `DataGrid` control in the middle of the form and name it `stockGrid`.

❑ Set the `DataGrid`'s `Visible` property to `False`, so that it will not appear until there's some data.

At this point, your form should resemble the following screenshot:

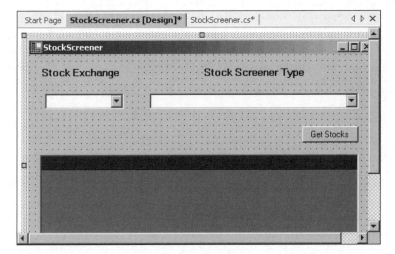

Now we have the UI elements in place, so let's switch to **Code** view. We also need to reference the `StockService` Web Service that we created earlier.

We need to bind the first combo box, `cboStockExchange` to the result of the `getExchangeInfo` method of our Web Service (which executes the `sp_getExchange` stored procedure for the data). Doing this will populate the combo box with all available stock exchanges as soon as the application is launched.

We simply create a new `DataSet` and assign it to the result of the `getExchangeInfo` method of our Web Service. We then bind the `DataSet` to the `cboStockExchange` combo box by using the `DataSource` property of the combo box. Next we use the `DisplayMember` and `ValueMember` methods to identify the field we want to appear in the combo box, as well as the field we want returned when an index is selected, similar to value pairs. All this data-binding logic needs to be placed within the `Form1_Load` method, so that it will take place as soon as the application launches:

```csharp
using System;
using System.Drawing;
using System.Collections;
using System.ComponentModel;
using System.Windows.Forms;
using System.Data;
using System.Data.SqlClient;

namespace StockScreener
{
  /// <summary>
  /// Summary description for Form1.
  /// </summary>
  public class Form1 : System.Windows.Forms.Form
  {
    private System.Windows.Forms.ComboBox cboStockExchange;
    private System.Windows.Forms.ComboBox cboScreener;
    private System.Windows.Forms.Button btnGetStocks;
    private System.Windows.Forms.DataGrid stockGrid;
    private System.Windows.Forms.Label label1;
    private System.Windows.Forms.Label label2;
    /// <summary>
    /// Required designer variable.
    /// </summary>
    private System.ComponentModel.Container components = null;

    public Form1()
    {
      //
      // Required for Windows Form Designer support
      //
      InitializeComponent();

      //
      // TODO: Add any constructor code after InitializeComponent call
      //
    }

    /// <summary>
    /// Clean up any resources being used.
    /// </summary>
    protected override void Dispose( bool disposing )
    {
      if( disposing )
      {
        if (components != null)
        {
          components.Dispose();
        }
      }
      base.Dispose( disposing );
    }
```

```csharp
#region Windows Form Designer generated code
/// <summary>
/// Required method for Designer support - do not modify
/// the contents of this method with the code editor.
/// </summary>
private void InitializeComponent()
{
  this.cboStockExchange = new System.Windows.Forms.ComboBox();
  this.cboScreener = new System.Windows.Forms.ComboBox();
  this.btnGetStocks = new System.Windows.Forms.Button();
  this.stockGrid = new System.Windows.Forms.DataGrid();
  this.label1 = new System.Windows.Forms.Label();
  this.label2 = new System.Windows.Forms.Label();
  ((System.ComponentModel.ISupportInitialize)(this.stockGrid))
      .BeginInit();
  this.SuspendLayout();
  //
  // cboStockExchange
  //
  this.cboStockExchange.Location = new System.Drawing.Point(22, 53);
  this.cboStockExchange.Name = "cboStockExchange";
  this.cboStockExchange.Size = new System.Drawing.Size(110, 21);
  this.cboStockExchange.TabIndex = 0;
  //
  // cboScreener
  //
  this.cboScreener.Items.AddRange(new object[] {
    "Top 5 Most Active ",
    "Top 5 Largest % Gain",
    "Top 5 Largest % Loss",
    "Top 5 Largest Intraday Price Differential"});
  this.cboScreener.Location = new System.Drawing.Point(168, 53);
  this.cboScreener.Name = "cboScreener";
  this.cboScreener.Size = new System.Drawing.Size(292, 21);
  this.cboScreener.TabIndex = 1;
  //
  // btnGetStocks
  //
  this.btnGetStocks.Location = new System.Drawing.Point(380, 98);
  this.btnGetStocks.Name = "btnGetStocks";
  this.btnGetStocks.Size = new System.Drawing.Size(80, 22);
  this.btnGetStocks.TabIndex = 2;
  this.btnGetStocks.Text = "Get Stocks";
  this.btnGetStocks.Click += new
      System.EventHandler(this.btnGetStocks_Click);
  //
  // stockGrid
  //
  this.stockGrid.DataMember = "";
  this.stockGrid.HeaderForeColor =
      System.Drawing.SystemColors.ControlText;
  this.stockGrid.Location = new System.Drawing.Point(15, 136);
  this.stockGrid.Name = "stockGrid";
  this.stockGrid.Size = new System.Drawing.Size(445, 175);
```

```
    this.stockGrid.TabIndex = 3;
    this.stockGrid.Visible = false;
    //
    // label1
    //
    this.label1.Font = new System.Drawing.Font("Microsoft Sans Serif",
        10.2F, System.Drawing.FontStyle.Bold,
        System.Drawing.GraphicsUnit.Point, ((System.Byte)(0)));
    this.label1.Location = new System.Drawing.Point(15, 15);
    this.label1.Name = "label1";
    this.label1.Size = new System.Drawing.Size(131, 22);
    this.label1.TabIndex = 4;
    this.label1.Text = "Stock Exchange";
    //
    // label2
    //
    this.label2.Font = new System.Drawing.Font("Microsoft Sans Serif",
        10.2F, System.Drawing.FontStyle.Bold,
        System.Drawing.GraphicsUnit.Point, ((System.Byte)(0)));
    this.label2.Location = new System.Drawing.Point(241, 15);
    this.label2.Name = "label2";
    this.label2.Size = new System.Drawing.Size(168, 22);
    this.label2.TabIndex = 5;
    this.label2.Text = "Stock Screener Type";
    //
    // Form1
    //
    this.AutoScaleBaseSize = new System.Drawing.Size(5, 13);
    this.ClientSize = new System.Drawing.Size(482, 321);
    this.Controls.AddRange(new System.Windows.Forms.Control[] {
      this.label2,
      this.label1,
      this.stockGrid,
      this.btnGetStocks,
      this.cboScreener,
      this.cboStockExchange});
    this.Name = "Form1";
    this.Text = "StockScreener";
    this.Load += new System.EventHandler(this.Form1_Load);
    ((System.ComponentModel.ISupportInitialize)(this.stockGrid))
        .EndInit();
    this.ResumeLayout(false);

}
#endregion

/// <summary>
/// The main entry point for the application.
/// </summary>
 [STAThread]
static void Main()
{
  Application.Run(new Form1());
}
```

```
    private void Form1_Load(object sender, System.EventArgs e)
    {
    localhost.StockService s1 = new localhost.StockService();
      DataSet ds = s1.getExchangeInfo();
      cboScreener.SelectedIndex = 0;

      cboStockExchange.DataSource = ds.Tables["StockExchange"];
      cboStockExchange.DisplayMember = "ExchangeName";
      cboStockExchange.ValueMember = "ExchangeID";
    //cboStockExchange.SelectedIndex = 0;


    }
```

Note that the cboScreener combo box needs to be populated with the various stock screening options. You can populate a combo box at design time by accessing its item collection in the properties window or at run time. Add the following entries in the item collection of the cboScreener control:

```
Top 5 Most Active
Top 5 Largest % Gain
Top 5 Largest % Loss
Top 5 Largest Intraday Price Differential
```

Notice that the order in which the screening choices are presented resembles the index numbers with which the stored procedures were executed in our StockService Web Service.

Now, all that's left to do is to invoke the Web Service and populate the DataGrid control when the user clicks the **Get Stocks** button:

```
    private void btnGetStocks_Click(object sender, System.EventArgs e)
    {
      localhost.StockService s1 = new localhost.StockService();
      DataSet ds = s1.getScreenerInfo(cboScreener.SelectedIndex,
          cboStockExchange.SelectedIndex +1);
      stockGrid.Visible = true;
      stockGrid.DataSource = ds.Tables["ScreenerInfo"];
      stockGrid.AllowSorting = true;
      stockGrid.AlternatingBackColor = Color.Beige;
    }
  }
}
```

There is nothing here that you haven't seen before. We just invoke the StockService Web Service, and call its getScreenerInfo method, which returns a DataSet with the stocks that match the criteria for the chosen stock screener. After this, we simply make the DataGrid control visible and set its DataSource property to the newly created DataSet. The only other noteworthy point here is that we're adding 1 to the SelectedIndex of the cboStockExchange control upon passing it into the getScreenerInfo method. The reason for this is that although in the UI the index starts at 0, in the database, where the ExchangeID is an identity column, its value starts at 1.

We're all done, so let's run the application:

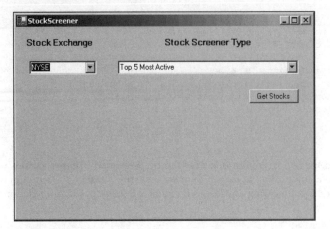

The `cboStockExchange` combo box has already been populated with the data returned from the `getExchangeInfo` method of our Web Service. We can just test with the default selection. Go ahead and click the **Get Stocks** button:

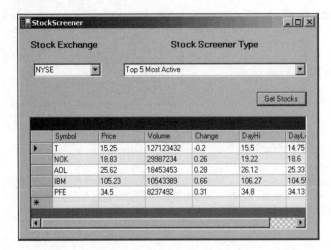

There you have it – the `DataGrid` control is filled with the data for the **Top 5 Most Active** stocks of the day on the **NYSE** stock exchange, just as we asked for.

As we've seen, application integration with Web Services within the .NET Framework is extremely easy, as most of the underpinning infrastructure work is being taken care of by the .NET Framework, so there's very little extra work that the developer needs to do in order to leverage a .NET Web Service.

As mentioned earlier, however, when you are trying to integrate your Web Services with those in a non-.NET platform, you do have to have a relatively good understanding of the Web Services technologies such as SOAP and WSDL, as you would probably have to make some manual modifications to the SOAP code.

`DataSets` are by far the most ideal mechanism for transporting data to and from Web Services within the .NET platform. The fact that a `DataSet` is nothing more than an XML document itself makes it a prime candidate for SOAP encoding. Of course, in this example, we only saw the very basics of what can be done with `DataSets`. As you have seen in previous chapters, `DataSets` offer an incredible array of functionality.

Updating DataSets via Web Services

So far, we've looked at a few simple Web Services that simply return some data using `DataSets`. In this section, we will use a `DataSet` not only as return value for a `WebMethod`, but also as a parameter. Using `DataSets` as function parameters in Web Services is just as easy as having them as return values. Of course, there are a few other things to take into consideration when dealing with database updates, which we'll get into later. For now, let's talk about the new application. Much like the previous example, we're going to have a tiny client application that will be served by a couple of methods in a Web Service. We'll call this application `StockPortfolio` and so, as the name suggests, it is a small stock portfolio management application. The client application will only be able to retrieve the content of the stock portfolio from the Web Service, and then update the changes to the portfolio by sending the data back to the Web Service, which will then go ahead and make the final update to the database. So, let's start by talking about the Web Service and the database table used by the Web Service to serve the `StockPortfolio` client application.

Creating the Web Service

In this case, since we only need two small `WebMethods`, we're going to simply add them to the Web Service we created earlier in this chapter, `StockService.asmx`. One method will send a `DataSet` to the client with all the data in the stock portfolio table, and the other method will accept a `DataSet` from the client containing changes made to the stock portfolio, which it will try to update. Let's look at the data needs for this application.

Preparing the Data

For the purposes of this application, we're going to need a small table with four basic fields that will hold some rudimentary information about a stock portfolio. For the sake of simplicity, we will not concern ourselves with multiple users or depth of information pertaining to the stock holdings in the portfolio; we only need the bare minimum of information. Let's create a table, `tbl_portfolio`, with four fields as shown below:

tbl_portfolio table

Field	Description
Shares	Number of shares of the stock held in the portfolio
Symbol	The actual stock symbol
Price	Last traded price of the stock
Purchase Date	The date when the stock was purchased and added to the portfolio

You can create the table by running the following SQL script in the SQL Server Query Analyzer. A SQL file containing all of these scripts is available in the code download for this book, in `FTrackADONET\Chapter08\StockPortfolio\stockportfoliodata.sql`.

tbl_portfolio table

```
CREATE TABLE [dbo].[tbl_portfolio] (
    [Shares] [smallint] NOT NULL ,
    [Symbol] [varchar] (4) NOT NULL ,
    [Price] [smallmoney] NOT NULL ,
    [Purchase Date] [smalldatetime] NULL
) ON [PRIMARY]
GO
```

Let's also populate the newly created table with some completely fictitious data:

```
INSERT INTO tbl_portfolio (Shares, Symbol, Price, [Purchase Date])
VALUES (50, 'ABC', 22.5, '3/10/2002')
GO

INSERT INTO tbl_portfolio (Shares, Symbol, Price, [Purchase Date])
VALUES (200, 'XYZ', 12.75, '4/10/2002')
GO

INSERT INTO tbl_portfolio (Shares, Symbol, Price, [Purchase Date])
VALUES (60, 'DDF', 33, '4/20/2002')
GO
```

With the database needs out of the way, let's move on to the new `WebMethods` for the `StockPortfolio` application. The first method is going to be called `getPortfolio`, which simply returns a `DataSet` containing the entire content of the `tbl_portfolio` table. This function will not have any parameters.

We will simply add this method to the existing Web Service that we created earlier, `StockService`. So, open the `StockService` project in Visual Studio.NET. We start by creating a new `SqlCommand` and `SqlDataAdapter` object to fetch the portfolio data and populate the `DataSet`. We will use these objects in conjunction with the `SqlConnection` object we created earlier:

```
[WebMethod (Description="Returns all entries of the stock portfolio.")]
public DataSet getPortfolio()
{
  DataSet ds = new DataSet();
  try
  {
    SqlCommand portCmd =
        new SqlCommand("select * from tbl_portfolio", sqlConnection1);
    SqlDataAdapter portDA = new SqlDataAdapter(portCmd);
    portDA.Fill(ds, "Portfolio");
  }

  catch (Exception ex)
  {
    Debug.WriteLine(ex.ToString());
  }
  return ds;
}
```

There's no need to discuss much about this function as, by now, we're familiar with simple data retrieval from a `WebMethod`. Let's move on to the second `WebMethod`, which is a bit longer and more involved than this one. The second method for use in the `StockPortfolio` application is going to as a parameter accept a `DataSet` that contains the changes that were made to the portfolio, and try to update those changes in the database. This method will also return a `DataSet` that reflects the latest updates that were reconciled with the data source. Updating `DataSets` using a `DataAdapter` object is easily done by using the `Update` method of the `DataAdapter` object. When the `Update` method is called, the `RowState` property of each row of the `DataSet` is examined and the appropriate `INSERT`, `UPDATE`, or `DELETE` statement is executed. The `DataAdapter` might need to execute two or statements per row depending on the nature of the change. Therefore, we need to manually add `SqlCommand` objects to our `DataAdapter` to handle the changes to the `DataSet` appropriately. Let's briefly look at the four main properties of the `SqlDataAdapter` object designed to facilitate data transfer:

Property	Description
SelectCommand	Contains T-SQL SELECT queries or stored procedures to retrieve data
UpdateCommand	Contains T-SQL SELECT queries or stored procedures to update data to the data in the data source
InsertCommand	Contains T-SQL SELECT queries or stored procedures to insert new data in the data source
DeleteCommand	Contains T-SQL SELECT queries or stored procedures to delete data from the data source

So, let's take a look at the `UpdatePortfolio` method in its entirety:

```
[WebMethod (Description="Updates the stock protfolio.")]
public DataSet UpdatePortfolio(DataSet ds)
{
  DataSet newDS;
  try
  {
    SqlDataAdapter portDA = new SqlDataAdapter();
    portDA.SelectCommand = new SqlCommand("select * from
        tbl_Portfolio",sqlConnection1);
```

Let's start by implementing the commands for SQL `SELECT` and `INSERT` operations:

```
    portDA.InsertCommand = new SqlCommand("INSERT INTO
tbl_portfolio (Shares, Symbol, Price, [Purchase Date]) " +
        "Values(@Shares, @Symbol, @Price, @PurchaseDate)", sqlConnection1);
    portDA.InsertCommand.Parameters.Add("@Shares",
        SqlDbType.SmallInt, 2, "Shares");
    portDA.InsertCommand.Parameters.Add("@Symbol",
        SqlDbType.VarChar, 4, "Symbol");
    portDA.InsertCommand.Parameters.Add("@Price", SqlDbType.SmallMoney , 4,
        "Price");
    portDA.InsertCommand.Parameters.Add("@PurchaseDate",
        SqlDbType.SmallDateTime , 4, "Purchase Date");
```

As you can see we created a new `SqlCommand` object with a query to return all the fields of the `tbl_portfolio` table and set it to the `SelectCommand` property of our `SqlDataAdapter` object, `portDA`. In much the same manner, we assign a new `SqlCommand` object to the `InsertCommand` property of the `portDA` object, but in this case we also have to add a few parameters to accommodate the fields of the data that is going to be inserted into the datasource, `tbl_portfolio` table. Therefore, we create four `SqlParameter` objects and add them to the `Parameters` collection of `InsertCommand`. Each `SqlParameter` object contains the parameter name, type, size, and the actual field in the data source where it's going to insert that field. Now that you've seen how `InsertCommands` are populated, let's move on to populating the `UpdateCommand` property. Let's look at the code first:

```
portDA.UpdateCommand = new SqlCommand("UPDATE tbl_portfolio Set Shares =
    @Shares, " + "Price = @Price, [Purchase Date] = @PurchaseDate WHERE
    Symbol = @Symbol", sqlConnection1);
SqlParameter shareParam = portDA.UpdateCommand.Parameters.Add("@Shares",
    SqlDbType.SmallInt, 2, "Shares");
shareParam.SourceVersion = DataRowVersion.Current;
SqlParameter symbolParam =
    portDA.UpdateCommand.Parameters.Add("@Symbol", SqlDbType.VarChar ,
    4, "Symbol");
symbolParam.SourceVersion = DataRowVersion.Original;

SqlParameter priceParam = portDA.UpdateCommand.Parameters.Add("@Price",
    SqlDbType.SmallMoney , 4, "Price");
priceParam.SourceVersion = DataRowVersion.Current;

SqlParameter purchaseDateParam =
    portDA.UpdateCommand.Parameters.Add("@PurchaseDate",
    SqlDbType.SmallDateTime , 4, "Purchase Date");
purchaseDateParam.SourceVersion = DataRowVersion.Current;
```

As you can see, populating the `UpdateCommand` property is very similar to the `InsertCommand`, except that we explicitly created `SqlParameter` objects and also set the `SourceVersion` property of the parameters. The reason for doing so is because the `DataSet` contains two versions of the changed data, `Current` and `Original`. We want to update the data source with the current version, so we set `SourceVersion` to `DataRowVersion.Current`. Lastly, we need to populate the `DeleteCommand` property of the `portDA` to handle data deletion to the data source:

```
portDA.DeleteCommand = new SqlCommand("DELETE FROM tbl_portfolio WHERE
    Symbol = @Symbol", sqlConnection1);
SqlParameter myParm = portDA.DeleteCommand.Parameters.Add("@Symbol",
    SqlDbType.VarChar, 4, "Symbol");
myParm.SourceVersion = DataRowVersion.Original;
```

We delete rows from the table by the `Symbol` field, using a simple Transact SQL `DELETE` statement. Upon setting all the required properties of the `DataAdapter` object, we can simply call the `Update` method and pass in the `DataSet` as shown below:

```
portDA.Update(ds, "Portfolio");
```

After updating, we just have to iterate through the rows in the table and reconcile any erroneous rows using the `AcceptChanges()` and `RejectChanges()` methods of the `DataRow` object:

```
foreach (DataRow myRow in ds.Tables["Portfolio"].Rows)
{
  if (!myRow.HasErrors)
    myRow.AcceptChanges();
  else
    myRow.RejectChanges();
}
```

OK, so the data is now updated. At this point we need to send a `DataSet` back to the client application reflecting all the changes that were made to the data. We also need a new `DataSet` that doesn't contain the `Rowstate` information of the previous `DataSet` to which modifications had been made, and the best way to do that is to get a brand-new `DataSet` from the data source:

```
newDS = new DataSet();
portDA.Fill(newDS, "Portfolio");
```

We had already defined the newDS variable to be of type `DataSet` back the very beginning of the function so that it would be available throughout the entire function and not just in the `try` block. If there's any error during the update, a blank `DataSet` will be created and sent back to the client.

```
  }
  catch (Exception ex)
  {
    newDS = new DataSet();
    Debug.WriteLine(ex.ToString());
  }
  return newDS;
}
```

As you can see, there can be a lot of code involved when manually assigning commands to the `DataAdapter` object. It's not at all difficult but it can fast get very long, especially when `DataRows` have a large number of columns. The only other choice is to use the `CommandBuilder` object, which also automatically generates all the required commands for the `DataAdapter`. The `CommandBuilder` object works by generating the necessary commands right when the `RowUpdating` event is fired. Also, we're not doing much about error handling in case there are erroneous rows in the `DataSet` that cannot be successfully updated. For our purposes, we will leave the validation of the data to the client application.

Creating the Client Application

The `StockPortfolio` client application consists of a `DataGrid` control and two buttons to get and update the portfolio information. To create the UI, follow the steps below:

- ❑ Open a new Visual C# Windows Application Project, and label the project file and corresponding form file (`Form1.cs`) as `StockPortfolio`.

- ❑ Place a `Button` control on the top right of the form. Label it **Get Portfolio** with its `Name` property set to `btnGetPortfolio`.

- ❑ Place the `DataGrid` controls under the `btnGetPortfolio` button and change its `Name` property to `grdPortfolio`.

- ❑ Place another `Button` control on the lower right portion of the form. Label it **Update Changes** with its `Name` property set to `btnGetPortfolio`. Also change the `Enabled` property of this control to `False`, as we will manually enable it later.

- ❑ Import the `SqlClient` namespace at the beginning of the project.

At this point your form should closely resemble the figure below:

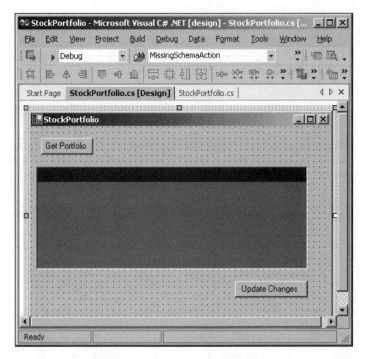

Lastly, don't forget to add a Web Reference to the `StockService.asmx` to enable us to invoke that Web Service later. In the application, we're going to need a class-level member variable of type `DataSet` to hold the data we get back from the Web Service. The reason we don't have to use a method-level variable as we did before is because we need to access it from the other method, as well as when trying to update the changes made to the `DataSet` in the `DataGrid`. So add the following declaration to where the member variables of the class are defined:

```
using System;
using System.Drawing;
using System.Collections;
using System.ComponentModel;
using System.Windows.Forms;
using System.Diagnostics;
using System.Data;
```

```
namespace StockPortfolio
{
  /// <summary>
  /// Summary description for Form1.
  /// </summary>
  public class StockPortfolio : System.Windows.Forms.Form
  {
    private System.Windows.Forms.Button btnGetPortfolio;
    private System.Windows.Forms.Button btnUpdate;
    /// <summary>
    /// Required designer variable.
    /// </summary>
    private System.ComponentModel.Container components = null;
    private System.Windows.Forms.DataGrid grdPortfolio;
    private DataSet ds;

    public StockPortfolio()
    {
      //
      // Required for Windows Form Designer support
      //
      InitializeComponent();


      //
      // TODO: Add any constructor code after InitializeComponent call
      //
    }

    /// <summary>
    /// Clean up any resources being used.
    /// </summary>
    protected override void Dispose( bool disposing )
    {
      if( disposing )
      {
        if (components != null)
        {
          components.Dispose();
        }
      }
      base.Dispose( disposing );
    }
    #region Windows Form Designer generated code
    ...
    #endregion
```

After that, double-click the `btnGetPortfolio` button to enter functionality to populate the `DataGrid` with the contents of the portfolio from the `StockService` Web Service. Of course the very first step is to instantiate the Web Service and call the `getPortfolio` method. We have gone through that process numerous times, so let's just look at the code:

```
    /// <summary>
    /// The main entry point for the application.
    /// </summary>
```

```
    [STAThread]
  static void Main()
  {
    Application.Run(new StockPortfolio());
  }

  private void btnGetPortfolio_Click(object sender, System.EventArgs e)
  {
    try
    {
      localhost.StockService s1 = new localhost.StockService();
      ds = s1.getPortfolio();
      grdPortfolio.Visible = true;
      grdPortfolio.DataSource = ds.Tables["Portfolio"];

      grdPortfolio.AllowSorting = true;
      grdPortfolio.AlternatingBackColor = Color.Beige;
    }
    catch (Exception ex)
    {
    Debug.WriteLine(ex.ToString());
    }
    btnUpdate.Enabled = true;
  }
```

There you have it. Nothing we haven't seen before. Upon obtaining the `DataSet`, we enable the `btnUpdate` button, so that updates can be made. Let's move on to the second main method of the client application, which we can get to by double-clicking the `btnUpdate` button. The very first thing we have to do is check to see whether or not any changes have actually taken place in the `DataSet`. As you have seen in the previous chapters, we can do that by using the `HasChanges` method of a `DataSet`, which will simply return `true` if there have been any changes made to the `DataSet` and `false` otherwise. Obviously if we determine that no changes were made to the `DataSet`, there's no reason to continue with the update operations.

If the individual row contains any errors, we will reject the changes from the `DataSet` and they won't be updated to the database. Keep in mind, however, that since this is not a strongly typed `DataSet`, we can't really do sophisticated validation without a lot of code. Also the `DataGrid` control tries to maintain some level of data integrity when data is added or modified in it. For example, if you try to input a character in a field that contains integer data, the `DataGrid` will simply reject the data.

After a brief check of the data, we're ready to invoke the Web Service and send the data changes to be updated. The `UpdatePortfolio` method returns a `DataSet` containing the new data including the changes that were passed into it. We create a new `DataSet` to contain the result of the Web Service and set the `DataSource` property of the `DataGrid` control to the new database. Keep in mind that we first have to reassign the new `DataSet` to our `ds` variable, which is the class-level variable we had created to contain the data for the `DataGrid`. Let's look at the entire function now:

```
  private void btnUpdate_Click(object sender, System.EventArgs e)
  {
    if (ds.HasChanges())
    {
      localhost.StockService s1 = new localhost.StockService();
```

```
        DataSet newDS = new DataSet();
        newDS = s1.UpdatePortfolio(ds.GetChanges());
        ds = newDS;
        grdPortfolio.DataSource = ds.Tables["Portfolio"];
        grdPortfolio.Refresh();
    }
}

private void StockPortfolio_Load(object sender, System.EventArgs e)
{

}
    }
}
```

That's it for the code. Let's run the client application and the Web Service. You can have them both open in a single Visual Studio.NET solution, as long as you have set the client application as the **StartUp Project**. When the client application is loaded, click the **Get Portfolio** button and, after an initial pause, you will see the `DataGrid` below it populated with the data we entered for the `tbl_portfolio` table:

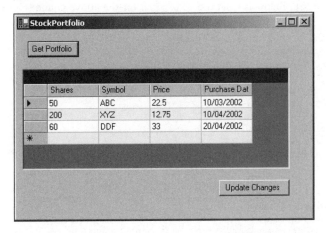

Since the `DataGrid` control allows us to easily make any changes to the data, go ahead and change some of the data and/or add new rows of data. Notice that the `DataGrid` tries to enforce some data integrity by not allowing characters for the `Shares` or the `Price` field. The figure overleaf shows the `DataGrid` control with some changed data:

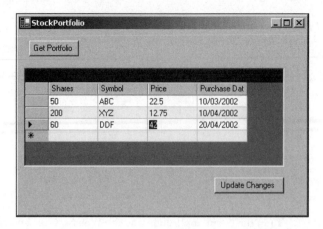

Upon clicking the **Update Changes** button you can check the contents of the `tbl_portfolio` table and will see that the new data has been entered. That's pretty much it for this application, but before we leave the sample entirely, let's look at one more thing, the `DiffGram`. As you know, the `DataSet` keeps track of the changes in `DiffGrams`. You can see the `Diffgram` for a `DataSet` by using the `WriteXml` method of the `DataSet`. Below is what the `Diffgram` for the above changes looks like:

```xml
<?xml version="1.0" standalone="yes"?>
<diffgr:diffgram xmlns:msdata="urn:schemas-microsoft-com:xml-msdata"
    xmlns:diffgr="urn:schemas-microsoft-com:xml-diffgram-v1">
  <NewDataSet>
    <Portfolio diffgr:id="Portfolio1" msdata:rowOrder="0"
        diffgr:hasChanges="modified">
      <Shares>150</Shares>
      <Symbol>ABC</Symbol>
      <Price>32.5</Price>
      <PurchaseDate>2002-03-10T00:00:00.0000000-08:00</PurchaseDate>
    </Portfolio>
    <Portfolio diffgr:id="Portfolio2" msdata:rowOrder="1">
      <Shares>60</Shares>
      <Symbol>DDF</Symbol>
      <Price>33</Price>
      <PurchaseDate>2002-04-20T00:00:00.0000000-07:00</PurchaseDate>
    </Portfolio>
    <Portfolio diffgr:id="Portfolio3" msdata:rowOrder="2">
      <Shares>200</Shares>
      <Symbol>XYZ</Symbol>
      <Price>12.75</Price>
      <PurchaseDate>2002-04-10T00:00:00.0000000-07:00</PurchaseDate>
    </Portfolio>
    <Portfolio diffgr:id="Portfolio4" msdata:rowOrder="3"
        diffgr:hasChanges="inserted">
      <Shares>500</Shares>
      <Symbol>TUV</Symbol>
      <Price>42</Price>
      <PurchaseDate>2001-02-12T00:00:00.0000000-08:00</PurchaseDate>
    </Portfolio>
  </NewDataSet>
```

```
    <diffgr:before>
      <Portfolio diffgr:id="Portfolio1" msdata:rowOrder="0">
        <Shares>50</Shares>
        <Symbol>ABC</Symbol>
        <Price>22.5</Price>
        <PurchaseDate>2002-03-10T00:00:00.0000000-08:00</PurchaseDate>
      </Portfolio>
    </diffgr:before>
  </diffgr:diffgram>
```

Notice the `diffgr:hasChanges="inserted"` and `diffgr:hasChanges="modified"` annotations. This way the `DataSet` keeps track of the changes and keeps the original and current versions of the data.

Caching Data-Driven .NET Web Services

Much like any other web application, a Web Service requires consideration of scalability at design time in order to produce robust and available Web Services. Caching Web Services alleviates some of the load from the Web Server and allows the cached files to be served in more efficiently. This is particularly important in the case of data-driven Web Services, where the Services are quite often much more resource-intensive.

There are a number of ways you can implement caching for your Web Service. You can write the logic into your code to manually handle certain resources based on a certain set of criteria. For instance, in the case of our `StockService` Web Service, we could have generated XML files with the output results of the various stock screeners that we had programmed, and just simply cached the static XML pages on the server ready to be served to the user. Of course, it will take a concerted effort and planning to access and understand the nature of the data the audience. If the stock data were to change once a day or once every few hours, that caching strategy would work quite well. As a matter of fact, SQL Server 7.0 and above were shipped with a stored procedure called `sp_makewebtask`, which allows you to populate data to a template file that can easily be formatted in XML. This task could then be scheduled to run every so often to update the static XML file. As good as that sounds, there are a handful of new caching technologies that are available for use with ASP.NET and .NET Web Services that are quite dynamic and customizable, not to mention the fact that they all are very easy to implement.

We will briefly examine various caching features of Web Services in .NET (which are almost exactly the same as those in ASP.NET) and possible situations in which their use would be appropriate. We'll first start by talking about output caching and continue the discussion by talking about various Data/Application caching techniques.

Output Caching

Output caching allows ASP.NET Web Services to be stored or cached in a special location on the server and served directly to the client using very few resources. Output caching keeps the targeted page in cache and enables the developer to specify the duration desired for a `WebMethod` to remain cached. This is ideal for situations in which the data of the Web Service is not going to be subject to much change within a specified time range.

In the case of our `StockService` Web Service – a scenario in which the stock information is not going to change for a specified amount of time – it makes little sense for the Web Service to constantly hit the database for every client request, when we already know that the data has not changed. Let's take that scenario one step further and imagine a situation where due to a sudden spike in buy or sell interest in the stock market, the trading volumes increase significantly, and people would want to view the latest market statistics using our Web Service, which then results in a huge spike in client requests. Our Web Service would still be hitting the database every time to get the data, even though our database has not been updated. In such a situation, the use of output caching would be absolutely ideal. With output caching enabled, the performance of our Web Service would improve significantly, as the methods of our Web Service would just be serving static data without all the internal work of fetching new data.

Let's see output caching in action for the `getExchangeInfo` method of our `StockService` Web Service. It only takes one property of the `WebMethod` attribute, `CacheDuration`, to enable output caching:

```
[WebMethod (CacheDuration=600,
    Description="Returns all the available stock exchanges.")]
public DataSet getExchangeInfo()
{}
```

The values for the `CacheDuration` property are set in seconds, and so the above example would cache the `getExchangeInfo` method for an entire 10 minutes, during which data would be served to the client in a static manner without the use of too much of our resources. That's all there is to output caching, it's that simple! Let's move on to talking about data caching, which is a bit more sophisticated.

Data Caching

Caching can also be used in ASP.NET Web Services to share objects and/or data among several Services on the same server by storing key-value pairs. Data caching using the `Cache` object in ASP.NET Web Services is quite rich in functionality, such as automatic expiration, and support for dependencies, as well as callbacks. In ASP.NET Web Services you can access the `Cache` class by using the `HttpContext` class or by simply using the `Context` property. You can quite easily add or remove keys at run time using the `Cache` class. Let's look at a quick example:

```
if (HttpContext.Current.Cache["myKey"] == null)
  Context.Cache.Add("myKey","myValue");
```

In the above code snippet, we're checking to see if there exists a key in the `Cache` object by the name of `myKey`; if not then we simply add a new key, "myKey" with its value set to "myValue". You can just as easily remove an entry from the cache:

```
Context.Cache.Remove("myKey");
```

You can also set dependencies, which allow for cached objects to also store a "dependency" for that object or piece of data. When the dependency target undergoes any change, the cached data will then be removed completely from memory. The dependency is typically a file, other cached keys, or a specific point in time. Automatic expiration simply removes the cached object from memory if the object has no dependencies on it. You can do all this and more using the parameters of the `Add` method of the `Cache` class:

```
public object Add(
    string key,
    object value,
    CacheDependency dependencies,
    DateTime absoluteExpiration,
    TimeSpan slidingExpiration,
    CacheItemPriority priority,
    CacheItemRemovedCallback onRemoveCallback
);
```

The following table provides more information about the parameters of the Add method:

Parameter	Description
key	The cache key used to reference the item.
value	The item to be added to the cache.
dependencies	The object dependencies for the item. When any dependency changes, the object becomes invalid and is removed from the cache.
absoluteExpiration	The actual time when the added object expires and is removed from the cache.
slidingExpiration	The amount of time between the time the added object was last accessed and when that object expires.
priority	The relative cost of the object, as expressed by the CacheItemPriority enumeration. The cache uses this value when it removes objects; objects with a lower cost are removed from the cache before objects with a higher cost.
onRemoveCallback	A call-back delegate that, if enabled, is called when an object is removed from the cache. You can use this to notify applications when their objects are deleted from the cache.

One last note about caching strategies in ASP.NET Web Services, don't forget about the good old Application object. You can use it almost exactly the same as you do in ASP.NET. It is ideal for situations in which there is a very small amount of data that is going to be used for the entire duration that an ASP.NET Web Service is available. Keep in mind that Application objects reside in memory until they're manually removed or the IIS process in which they reside is stopped. You can access them in a similar way to how you would in ASP.NET:

```
Application["myKey"] = myValue;
```

The Global.asax file contains a number of events in which you can add, remove, or code other logic pertaining to the Application object, such as the Application_Start method, which enables you to add data to the Application object upon the initial launch of your ASP.NET Web Service:

```
protected void Application_Start(Object sender, EventArgs e)
{
}
```

Regardless of what caching strategy you choose for your ASP.NET Web Service, it is always a good idea to put it to test using any one of the countless Web Application stress tools available on the market. You can obtain the free Web Stress tool from Microsoft at: http://webtool.rte.microsoft.com/download.asp. If you have Visual Studio .NET Enterprise edition, you can use the Application Center Test tool, which is a lightweight version of Application Center 2000 server.

Web Services Security

It goes without saying that one of the most critical aspects of any type of Web Application is security. This is especially the case when you're dealing with data-intensive applications that are going to be handling sensitive data. Security has also taken center stage in the enterprise these days in the wake of increasing security lapses. Fortunately, the .NET Framework is packed with a plethora of comprehensive security offerings that can be used in ASP.NET Web Services. In addition to the security offerings for Web Services by Microsoft, there have been a number of new technologies and specifications that have been submitted to the standards body in an effort to gain industry-wide support. In this section, we're only going to touch on a few of the concepts, since the topic of Web Services security could easily be the single topic of a whole book. We'll start by covering some of the very basics of ASP.NET security, which apply very well to Web Services.

ASP.NET and .NET Web Services Security

Keep in mind that Web Services operate on IIS as well as the HTTP protocol and thus adhere to all the limitations and restrictions of these technologies. We'll start this section by talking about the various techniques of providing authentication as provided by ASP.NET.

Authentication

Authentication is basically the process of verifying a user through various credentials, such as user ID and password, by validating those credentials against some authority. ASP.NET and ASP.NET Web Services can take advantage of seven types of authentication. The table below lists the various authentication types available for Web Services and ASP.NET applications:

Authentication Type	Description
Anonymous Authentication	As the name implies, Anonymous Authentication is the lack of authentication. No authentication takes place under this mode.
Basic Authentication	The user ID and password and/or other credentials are transferred from the client to the server in clear text. The user information must correspond to a valid Windows account. This type of authentication will suffice only if the possibility of intrusion with malicious intent is not a concern, since the user information is not encrypted over the wire. At times SSL (Secure Socket Layer) is used along with Basic Authentication to provide a greater level of security.

Authentication Type	Description
Certificate-based Authentication	This is a key-based authentication scheme using PKI technologies in which the client is required to obtain a certificate that corresponds to a user credential. This is an asymmetric key encryption technique in which key pairs are used (public and private keys).
Digest Authentication	In many ways this is very similar to Basic Authentication. The main difference is that user credentials are not transferred in clear text and instead are encrypted using a hashing algorithm. The only problem is that it is not as widely supported as Basic Authentication. Only IE 5 and above browsers have support for it.
Forms-based Authentication	Although not a standard, Forms Authentication is quite popular since it's quite customizable. Unauthenticated user requests are redirected to an HTML/ASP.NET form in which user credentials are requested, and upon verification, the user gets redirected to the requested page. All subsequent requests by the same client in a single session are automatically authenticated.
Passport Authentication	An authentication service offered by Microsoft in which users can get authenticated through a single logon for a number of sites and services that support the .NET Passport services. As of the writing of this book, .NET Web Services do not support Passport authentication in part due to the technology's reliance on cookies. However that is rumored to be changing soon.
Integrated Windows Authentication	The login information of a valid Windows account for the current user is used for authentication purposes. Although this not really practicable for use on the Internet unless VPNs are used, it is ideal for intranet use.

You can set the authentication type of your Web Service by setting a value to the mode attribute of the <authentication> tag in the Web.Config file of your Web Service project. The line below will set the authentication mechanism for your Web Service to Windows Authentication:

```
<authentication mode="Windows" />
```

All the above techniques of authentication work over at the HTTP level in conjunction with IIS and not SOAP. IBM has submitted a proposal to the World Wide Web Consortium (W3C) specifying a SOAP extension mechanism in which authentication information is encoded in the SOAP header.

Authorization

Authorization is basically a mechanism through which a user is granted access to the requested resources. There are a number of ways effective authorization can be implemented in .NET and Web Services. At the basic level, the `authorization` tag within the `Web.Config` file is a very quick and easy approach for configuring authorization for your Web Service. You can allow or deny a particular user, group of users, or roles access to your Web Service as shown below:

```
<authorization>
  <allow users="[one or more users]"
      roles="[one or more roles]"
  <deny users="[one or more users]"
      roles="[one or more roles]"/>
</authorization>
```

The `authorization` tag has two different subtags that it supports. These subtags are `allow` and `deny`. The `allow` tag allows you to explicitly identify a comma separated list of `users` and `roles` that can access the requested URL. The `allow` tag supports `users`, `roles`, `anonymous`, and `all` access. The `deny` tag specifies a comma separated list of `users` and/or `roles` that are denied access to the requested resource. For example, you can easily allow a user by the name of `Daniel` to access your Web Service and deny everyone else access to your site by using the following code:

```
<authorization>
  <allow users="Daniel" />
  <deny users="*" />
</authorization>
```

There is certainly a lot more to what can be done with the `authorization` tag than we have mentioned here, but you get the basic idea. You can also do custom authorization by creating custom `Permission` objects and assign rights to them with a fine level of granularity. Lastly, you can access the `User` member of the `Context` object to get information about the current user, such as the particular `role` object to which they belong.

Secure Sockets Layer (SSL)

If you have had any experience with web applications, you have bound to have worked with SSL. SSL is by far the most prominent and prevalent security protocol used on the Web, mainly due to wide acceptance by browsers and other Internet-centric software and services. Secure Sockets Layer is implemented via RSA encryption, a public key encryption system operating at the session layer of the OSI model. You can use SSL in a number of ways to augment the security of your Web Service. In its simplest form, however, you can simply reference the Web Service with the HTTPS protocol, and, as long as port 443 is available and proper certificates are installed, things should be up and running. This would provide a basic level of encryption for all communication between the Web Service and its clients.

As you have seen, in many ways, ASP.NET Web Services share a great deal in common with regular ASP.NET pages when it comes to security. But there are more advanced features that are based on modifications to the very SOAP headers that carry the Web Service payload, which can be accessed using the `System.Web.Services` namespace, including custom encryption and authentication. Furthermore, new initiatives such as WS-Security, as suggested by the Global XML Web Services Architecture (GXA) from Microsoft, are striving to bring wider vendor-neutral support for Web Services security.

Best Practices for Data-Centric Web Services

By this point in the chapter, you should have a good understanding of the basis of .NET Web Services with the use of ADO.NET to facilitate the transfer of data in a distributed environment. In this section of the chapter, we'll go over a few points to keep in mind while designing your data-centric Web Service:

❑ **Do you really need a Web Service?**

Before starting to implement a piece of functionality as a Web Service, take a moment to review the requirements and determine if Web Services would provide an advantage over alternative solutions. Web Services are absolutely great for what they do, but they're not the ideal technology to use in every case. For instance, if you're planning on running your Web Service from the same machine in which the clients reside, you're probably better off using a component instead. Web Services have some overhead, which, although well worth it for the value they offer, could certainly be done without in a situation where better alternatives exist. Web Services are ideal in a distributed environment, especially when security boundaries prevent RPC ports from functioning.

❑ **Avoid Chatty Paradigms**

As is the case with any client-server application, one of the main design goals for your Web Service should always be to try to minimize the number of communication round-trips between the client and the server. All data communication between a Web Service and its clients is marshaled and encoded with the XML-based SOAP protocol and thus carries some overhead in addition to the overhead imposed by the HTTP protocol itself. It also goes without saying that the amount of data to be transferred should also be minimized.

❑ **Performance Considerations**

As mentioned numerous times throughout this chapter, Web Services are essentially web applications and are therefore subject to many of the issues and concerns surrounding web applications, such as bandwidth and availability. Always design your Web Service with the client in mind and implement extensive stress testing to get a good understanding of the number of clients your Web Service can successfully handle. This goes hand in hand with all the rest of the points for consideration mentioned in this section.

❑ **Asynchronous Access**

Data-centric Web Services can be very resource intensive and at times take a little while before returning the results to the client. In such a case, consider asynchronous access for Web Service invocation in the client application. Asynchronous access could be quite easily implemented by the use of callback delegates in .NET. This way, the client application will not be stalled while waiting for results to return from the Web Service.

❑ **Alternatives to DataSets**

Datasets are a fantastic mechanism for transferring data effectively over the wire via Web Services in .NET. The fact that they're virtually nothing more than XML documents makes them absolutely ideal for SOAP encoding, and although they come very close, they're not a "one size fits all" solution. If you're just sending very small pieces of information, you can always use some of the basic types available such as int or string. For instance, even if you have a few pieces of data that need to be sent to the client, you can always send them as a comma-delimited list in a string, which can then be read into an array by the client using the Split method. This would alleviate the need of the client to import the System.Data.SqlClient namespace and the extra overhead of using the DataSet. You can even use custom data types such as Structures when there are small pieces of data that require some level of encapsulation. All structures and arrays are easily serialized in XML by the .NET Framework, and can at times provide a powerful alternative to DataSets.

Summary

Throughout this chapter you have seen how easy it is to develop Web Services within the .NET platform using Visual Studio .NET. More importantly you saw how little effort was involved in making a Web Service access return data. We also learned that ADO.NET Datasets are the best standard way to package and send data over the wire via Web Services, since DataSets are essentially nothing but XML documents. You can also take advantage of the caching features of ASP.NET Web Services to further augment the availability of your Web Services.

XML Web Services, although rapidly gaining maturity as a technology, is still at its infancy stages and will continue to evolve and strive to finally make heterogeneous interoperability in the world of distributed computing in the enterprise a reality. The Microsoft .NET platform has already taken a huge step in making the creation and integration of XML Web Services with Windows-based applications incredibly seamless.

FAST TRACK

ADO.NET

Index

More important entries have **bold** page numbers.

ASP Today

p2p.wrox.com
The programmer's resource centre

A unique free service from Wrox Press
With the aim of helping programmers to help each other

Wrox Press aims to provide timely and practical information to today's programmer. P2P is a list server offering a host of targeted mailing lists where you can share knowledge with four fellow programmers and find solutions to your problems. Whatever the level of your programming knowledge, and whatever technology you use P2P can provide you with the information you need.

ASP
Support for beginners and professionals, including a resource page with hundreds of links, and a popular ASP.NET mailing list.

DATABASES
For database programmers, offering support on SQL Server, mySQL, and Oracle.

MOBILE
Software development for the mobile market is growing rapidly. We provide lists for the several current standards, including WAP, Windows CE, and Symbian.

JAVA
A complete set of Java lists, covering beginners, professionals, and server-side programmers (including JSP, servlets and EJBs)

.NET
Microsoft's new OS platform, covering topics such as ASP.NET, C#, and general .NET discussion.

VISUAL BASIC
Covers all aspects of VB programming, from programming Office macros to creating components for the .NET platform.

WEB DESIGN
As web page requirements become more complex, programmer's are taking a more important role in creating web sites. For these programmers, we offer lists covering technologies such as Flash, Coldfusion, and JavaScript.

XML
Covering all aspects of XML, including XSLT and schemas.

OPEN SOURCE
Many Open Source topics covered including PHP, Apache, Perl, Linux, Python and more.

FOREIGN LANGUAGE
Several lists dedicated to Spanish and German speaking programmers, categories include. NET, Java, XML, PHP and XML

How to subscribe:
Simply visit the P2P site, at http://p2p.wrox.com/

Register your book on Wrox.com!

When you download this book's code from
wrox.com, you will have the option to register.

What are the benefits of registering?

- You will receive updates about your book
- You will be informed of new editions, and
  will be able to benefit from special offers
- You became a member of the "Wrox Developer Community", giving
  you exclusive access to free documents from Wrox Press
- You can select from various newsletters you may want to receive

**Registration is easy and only needs to be done once.
After that, when you download code books after logging
in, you will be registered automatically.**

Just go to www.wrox.com

wrox

Programmer to Programmer™

Registration Code: 760457916566LI01

Wrox writes books for you. Any suggestions, or ideas about how you want
information given in your ideal book will be studied by our team.
Your comments are always valued at Wrox.

Free phone in USA 800-USE-WROX
Fax (312) 893 8001

UK Tel.: (0121) 687 4100   Fax: (0121) 687 4101

Fast Track ADO.NET – Registration Card

Name _____

Address _____

_____

_____

City _____ State/Region _____

Country _____ Postcode/Zip_____

E-Mail _____

Occupation _____

How did you hear about this book?

☐ Book review (name) _____

☐ Advertisement (name) _____

☐ Recommendation _____

☐ Catalog _____

☐ Other _____

Where did you buy this book?

☐ Bookstore (name) _____ City_____

☐ Computer store (name) _____

☐ Mail order_____

☐ Other _____

What influenced you in the purchase of this book?

☐ Cover Design ☐ Contents ☐ Other (please specify):

_____

How did you rate the overall content of this book?

☐ Excellent ☐ Good ☐ Average ☐ Poor

What did you find most useful about this book? _____

_____

What did you find least useful about this book? _____

_____

Please add any additional comments. _____

_____

_____

What other subjects will you buy a computer book on soon?

_____

What is the best computer book you have used this year?

_____

> **Note:** This information will only be used to keep you updated
> about new Wrox Press titles and will not be used for
> any other purpose or passed to any other third party.

wrox

Programmer to Programmer™

Note: If you post the bounce back card below in the UK, please send it to:

Wrox Press Limited, Arden House, 1102 Warwick Road,
Acocks Green, Birmingham B27 6HB. UK.

Computer Book Publishers